MONTY'S
IRON SIDES

FROM THE NORMANDY BEACHES TO BREMEN WITH THE 3RD DIVISION

MONTY'S IRON SIDES

FROM THE NORMANDY BEACHES TO BREMEN WITH THE 3RD DIVISION

PATRICK DELAFORCE

CHANCELLOR PRESS

First published in 1995 by Alan Sutton Publishing Ltd, an imprint of
Sutton Publishing Limited
Phoenix Mill • Thrupp • Stroud • Gloucestershire

This 1999 edition published by Chancellor Press,
an imprint of Bounty Books, a division of the
Octopus Publishing Group Ltd., 2–4 Heron Quays, London, E14 4JP

British Library Cataloguing in Publication Data
A catalogue record for this book is available from the British Library.

ISBN 0 75370 263 0

Typeset in 9/11 Plantin Light
Typesetting and origination by
Sutton Publishing Limited.
Printed in Great Britain by
Redwood Books Limited,
Trowbridge, Wiltshire.

CONTENTS

Acknowledgements   vii

Introduction   ix

1   Monty's Division   1

2   Forming Up – 'Four Years and Not a Shot Fired in Anger'   6

3   The Crossing – 'The Excitement of the Unknown'   16

4   'The Game's Afoot, Follow Your Spirit'   23

5   Queen Red Beach – 'Scene of Utter Destruction'   27

6   Sword Queen White Beach – The Taking of Cod, Morris and Hillman   33

7   185 Brigade's Plan – 'A Bold Dash for Caen'   40

8   Expanding the Bridgehead – 'Don't Shoot, Jock, We're the Paddies'   50

9   Stalemate – War of Attrition   58

10   The Terrible Operation Mitten – 8 Brigade Front   62

11   The 'Battle-Bruised Landscape' of 185 Brigade   67

12   The Taking of Caen – 'The Heavy Reek of Death'   72

13   Operation Goodwood – 'Troarn, Our Deepest Tribulation'   78

14   The Breakout from the Bridgehead – August   90

15   Operations Walter and Wallop – 'Just Like Africa Days'   98

16   In Limbo – Waiting for the War to Start Again   104

17	The General – 'Good Baptism of Fire'	108
18	Operation Market Garden – September	110
19	Operation Aintree – October	116
20	Autumn on the River Maas – 'Uncomfortable, Dangerous and Boring'	134
21	Winter Patrolling on the River Maas – 'Wacht am Maas'	142
22	New Year's Resolutions – 'Spitting Distance of the Boche'	150
23	Operations Veritable, Ventilate and Heather – February	156
24	Operation Plunder – 'Cracking About in Northern Germany'	168
25	On the Way to Bremen – The Final Swan	183
26	The Suburbs of Bremen – 'The Enemy Broke in Complete Disorder'	189
27	The Attack on Bremen – The 'Schwim-Panzers'	196
	Bibliography	207
	Appendix A The Commanders	208
	Appendix B Divisional Casualties	210
	Index	211

Acknowledgements

Practically every regiment in the 3rd British Division has produced interesting and well-written unit histories, usually published shortly after the end of hostilities. These are all acknowledged in the Bibliography, as indeed are a number of most helpful unpublished journals made available to me. I would also like to thank the fifty or so individual members of Monty's Iron Sides who sent me their recollections. A special 'thank you' to Maj. Humphrey Wilson MC, Royal Norfolks, who not only allowed me to use extracts from his regimental history, but also permitted use of many of the photographs within it; to Mrs Renison for allowing me to include extracts from the journal of her husband, Lt.-Col. Bill Renison DSO of the 2nd Battalion East Yorkshire Regiment, and to Revd W.I.G. Wilson for extracts from his history of 1 KOSB.

I would like to express my appreciation to the following: Bob Basshan, Maj. Ken Baxter MC, George Bennett, P.W. Bowes, Peter Brown, Maj. Raymond Burt, Victor Campbell, Alan Candler, A.J. Catt, John St John Cooper, Roland Curtiss, Bernard Cuttiford, Maj. W.J. Derbyshire, John Eales, Eric Edwards, Frank Faulkner MM, John Foster, Ernie Frobisher, Joe Garner, Ernie Goozee, Fred Hartle, S.J. Hooper, Harold Isherwood, Lt.-Col. E. Jones MBE, MA, Maj. H. Jones MC, David Knight, A.J. Lane, R.J. Lincoln MC, Lt.-Col Eric Lummis, Les Markland, Jim Nelson, C.E. Packer MM, Ray Paine, Lt.-Col. W.J. Parsons MBE, Albert Pattison, Clifford Payne, Lt.-Col. M.A. Philp, Harold Pickersgill MBE, Jack Prior, Maj. Mike Quarmby, Jim Reid, Maj. A.J. Rennie, Lionel A. Roebuck, James Smith, Lt.-Col. C.G. Stonor OBE, MC, Perring Thomas, Bill Wellings, George Wilson, Fred Wiltshire, Revd Jim Wisewell.

Introduction

This is the story of one year in action – 1944–5 – of one of Britain's most famous infantry divisions, perhaps the most illustrious of all.

In 1809 it was known as the 3rd Division, then in the First World War as the 3rd (Iron) Division. In the Second World War it was called the 3rd (British) Division to distinguish it from the Canadian 3rd Division, and more recently it has become the 3rd Armoured Division.

This book covers a brief, glorious and very dangerous year in battle, from the bloody assault on the Normandy beaches on D-Day, through the attritional fighting around Caen, Operations Goodwood, Bluecoat and Market Garden, the brutal battles to take Overloon and Venraij (Operation Aintree), winter on the river Maas, Operation Veritable in the Rhineland, the Rhine crossing and finally to the capture of Bremen.

This was Monty's Division – christened the 'Iron Sides' – which, as part of the British Expeditionary Forces, he commanded with much distinction in 1940. It was fitting that his division, which had suffered the humiliation of Dunkirk, was in the van of the final British Liberation Army in 1944. Norman Scarfe, author of *Assault Division* (1947), made the point that the name Iron Sides for the 3rd Division might refer back to the Cromwellian recruitment of his famous doughty soldiers from East Anglia (Lincolns, Suffolks and Norfolks). So *Monty's Iron Sides* seems to be an appropriate title for this book.

Two officers from the author's 11th Armoured Division (the Black Bull), Jack Churcher and Cyril Blacker, later went on to command the 3rd British Division. This was entirely appropriate as both divisions fought side by side during Operation Bluecoat in August 1944 when 3rd Division earned its first Second World War Victoria Cross (Cpl. Sidney Bates) at Sourdevalle. Again in the fighting around Venraij and Overloon, 11th Armoured was in action a few miles away and the author, a young RHA FOO, supported units in both divisions and was blown up comprehensively at Oploo.

In October 1943 the 3rd Division was fortunate enough to have a new GOC in Maj.-Gen. Tom Rennie, who had previously commanded 51st Highland Division and won a DSO at El Alamein. Unfortunately it was to be a short tenure of some eleven months before wounds received in Normandy invalided him back to the UK. His charismatic successor, Maj.-Gen. 'Bolo' Whistler, a famous Desert Rat, then took command and steered the Iron Division through the next traumatic ten months of fighting in France, Belgium, Holland and the Fatherland.

This is the story of Monty's Iron Sides told by the soldiers – privates, NCOs and junior officers – from *every* one of the fighting battalions. So this book is dedicated to the 2,600 or so young Iron Sides who were killed in action in that brutal final campaign to free north-west Europe from the Nazi hordes.

If there are errors of name, rank, dates and places, they are mine alone.

CHAPTER ONE

Monty's Division

In 1937 a certain Bernard Montgomery had been promoted from commanding the 1st Royal Warwicks, to become brigadier of 9 Infantry Brigade at Portsmouth, together with 7 and 8 Brigades of 3rd British Division. In his memoirs he wrote: 'I made the 9th Infantry Brigade as good as any in England and *none other could compete with us in battle on the training area.* We were selected to carry out the special exercises and trials needed by the War Office in 1937 and 1938 and generally were in the public eye a good deal.' During the winter of 1938/9 Montgomery was informed that he had been selected to command the 3rd Division in England – a regular division with HQ on Salisbury Plain. He was then in northern Palestine quelling an Arab rebellion. 'I was delighted. The 3rd Division was part of the British Expeditionary Force to go to Continental Europe in the event of war,' he wrote. 'The war clouds were banking up and it looked as if it might begin to rain . . . . I was to take command of the 3rd Division in August 1939!' Montgomery became ill in Haifa and was invalided back to England. Although by now a major-general, he lost command of the 8th Division in Palestine *and* the promise of his future command of 3rd Division was cancelled because of the Army mobilisation. This decreed that all future appointments lapsed automatically and those commanders actually in the jobs remained there. 'Britain was mobilising for war and I was in a pool of Major-Generals waiting for employment. This did not suit me at all . . . . I pestered the War Office.'

Alan Moorehead wrote that Monty said, 'There is one man fit to take the Third into battle. That is myself. *I must have the 3rd Division. I am the only man fitted to command it.'*

He assumed command of his Iron Division on 28 August 1939 and told an East Yorkshire officer, 'I knew it in the last war – it was known as the "Iron Division" then and it is going to be known as the "Iron Division" in this war. Good luck!'

But on arrival on the Franco-Belgian frontier in October he was unimpressed and wrote a strong personal memorandum on 'Discipline' to all his senior officers:

CONFIDENTIAL PERSONAL MEMORANDUM – DISCIPLINE

1. I am not at all satisfied with the general standard of discipline, turn-

out, smartness, soldierly bearing, and so on that I notice in the Division.

2. I see men lounging about in the streets with their tunics open, hats on the back of their head, cigarettes behind their ears.

Today in Seclin I saw some parties of soldiers being marched through the streets in all sorts of kit; in the same party some men wore steel helmets, some soft caps, some no headgear at all with hair disgracefully long.

NCOs are very slack about calling men to attention when a senior officer appears.

At night there is a certain amount of cafe life, resulting in a good deal of drunkenness and a great deal of shouting and singing in the streets. We have got to keep the men in hand and I consider the following rules should be in force in unit areas:

(a) All men to be out of the cafes by 2100 hrs. and in their billets by 2130 hrs.

(b) No man to be outside his unit area when off duty unless in possession of a special pass. In this connection it should be noted that LILLE is out-of-bounds to all other ranks at all times, and to all officers after 2130 hrs.

(c) Any cafe selling spirits to other ranks will be at once placed out-of-bounds to troops.

As an aid to discipline I consider that as long as the soldier has brass buttons and titles he should polish them; the present conditions permit of this being done; when battle is joined we can think again.

The cars of commanders flying flags are not saluted. It is quite simple for a soldier to understand that a military car flying a flag *must* contain an officer of the rank of Brigadier or upwards; the colour of the flag is immaterial.

3. These things have got to cease, and at once. In the life we are leading, scattered in billets, it is very easy for the men to get slack and for discipline to get out of hand. Officers, NCOs and unit police have got to see that our standard of discipline, smartness, and turn-out is kept at a high level.

4. I know there are many difficulties; we have many men who have been soldiers only a few weeks, and we have large numbers of reservists who may tend to pull our standard down unless we are careful. But I will not allow any let-up in this matter, whatever the difficulties, and all officers to whom this memorandum is addressed will give this subject their immediate attention.

13 Oct 39.B.L. Montgomery
Major-General,
KFB. Comdr. 3rd Division.
<u>Distribution: on reverse.</u>

As part of Monty's deliberate campaign to instil pride among his troops he devised a new divisional sign of three black triangles surrounding an inverted red triangle. This signified the 3rd Division with its three infantry brigades, each with its three battalions – Monty's 'combination of threes'. He referred to 9 Brigade as the 'International Brigade' with its English (Lincolns), Scottish (King's Own Scottish Borderers) and Irish (2nd Royal Ulster Rifles) units. After Dunkirk it was commanded by Brig. B.G. Horrocks, who was destined to become one of the Second World War's finest Corps commanders.

⌐Monty was still not happy with the composition of his division and on 11 April 1940 he wrote to Lt.-Gen. A.F. Brooke, commander of 2 Corps. 'I consider that in a front line fighting Division it is necessary to have commanders who have that character and personality that will inspire confidence in others. They must be mentally robust and be possessed of initiative, energy and "drive". They must possess enthusiasm and be able to impart that enthusiasm to those under them.' Of Lt.-Col. S. he wrote, 'He has no fire, lacks character . . . is not able to "binge up" the show and keep it on its toes.' Lt.-Col. C. was 'a mouselike creature, seems very nervous.' Lt.-Col. H. was 'charming, gentle and pleasant, lacks energy and drive, doesn't "smack it about".' Maj. G. 'looks dismal and depressed'. The famous Monty purges had started!

He made himself known to every man in the division and made it very clear that he was their leader. Cpl. Clifford Arthur Payne with the 2nd Battalion East Yorkshires recalls:

Well one fine day we had a very important visitor and he was no other than the great Field Marshal himself – General Montgomery as he was then. In fact he commanded the 3rd British Infantry Division in those days. Of course you know all his patter about putting all the troops in the picture as it were. Well we all paraded in the camp and up he came in his jeep and out he jumped on to the bonnet with a loud hailer in his hand. Then he started his routine of shouting 'Come closer, boys, I'm not going to bite you'. He told us he was leaving us to take up another position.

Training both by day and night went on continuously in the 'Phoney War' with emphasis on fighting patrols, siting of weapons, digging in, sniping and weapon training. This all paid off handsomely when the German panzer blitzkrieg tore through the French, Belgian and British armies in May 1940. Brilliant defensive actions were fought by 3rd British at Louvain and the Dyle river, the Escaut canal, the counter-attack at Wattrelos, the defence of the Yser canal, and finally at the Dunkirk perimeter.

'My 3rd Division moved into its position on the left of the Dunkirk bridgehead on the 29th–30th May. We held the line of the canal between Furnes and Nieuport,' Monty wrote in his memoirs. When Brooke was ordered back to England, Monty was promoted to command 2 Corps, but 'I asked [after the evacuation from the beaches] to be allowed and was permitted to go back to my 3rd Division to reform it and get it ready for what lay ahead.' What transport and weapons were available in the UK now were all allotted to 3rd Division. 'So we moved to the south coast like an avalanche to defend it against the Germans.' In July 1940 Monty was promoted to command 5 Corps.

Colin Stonor was 2 i/c 'C' Company 1 KOSB and has three Monty stories:

When the 1 KOSB were reforming after Dunkirk 3 Div went to the beaches at Brighton. Slit trenches at the top of the beach with one strand of Dannert wire! The GOC (Monty) visited my platoon position and we had an amusing discussion about the siting of a Bren gun. And the section commander won the argument. Much of our training was in convoy disciplines, minimum lights at night and proper spacing by day with an exercise at the end of it. I remember Monty being very cross with 7th Guards Bde for switching on too much light to find their positions – this at a 3 Div 'wash up' *after* the exercise! [Later] We were billeted in the West country. Monty again came to visit us in the village. A wet day but we paraded in the village street. Monty ordered 'All hats off so that I can see you', but he seemed in good form, as he finished the inspection by

Monty talks to 'Bolo' Whistler at a Brigade HQ near Bremen, May 1945. (IWM, BU 3986)

saying 'Well I suppose they all have their feet under the table now, or is it their heads on the pillow?' The human touch.

For the next four years 3rd British trained and trained and did not fire a shot in anger, while 51st Highland, 50th Tyne and Tees and the 7th Armoured (Desert Rats) earned immortal fame in the North African campaigns. But Maj.-Gen. W.H.C. Ramsden persuaded the CIGS, Gen. Alan Brooke, that 3rd Division should lead the assault on the French shores – and thus avenge the defeat of Dunkirk.

CHAPTER TWO

Forming Up

'Four Years and Not a Shot Fired in Anger'

From the beaches of Dunkirk in May 1940 another four years of waiting and training, and more waiting and more training, were to elapse before the Iron Division was to see action again. Many divisions – those that did not get to North Africa or Sicily – claimed the possibly doubtful honour of being the most highly trained division in the British Army. There is no doubt that the 3rd British Division took full advantage of those four years to build up its expertise in combined operations and beach assault tactics.

When the division landed in France it was probably the most 'British' of all the famous divisions fighting in north-west Europe. It included the King's Own Scottish Borderers, a Highland gunner regiment, the Royal Ulster Rifles, the two roses of East Yorkshire and South Lancashire, the East Anglians (Suffolk, Norfolk, Lincolns) and the Midlands (Warwick and Shropshire), besides cockneys from the Middlesex Regiment and the Recce Regiment from Northumberland. They were all 'senior' battalions, mostly regular 1st and 2nd battalions of a regiment but, as Norman Scarfe pointed out, 'no more than an average of one in three were regular soldiers. But it was nevertheless a Regular Division.'

What actually happened during those four years from 1940 to 1944? During 1940 and 1941 the division was variously in the West Country, on the south coast between Brighton and Littlehampton, in Gloucestershire, then Buckinghamshire, and in early 1943 it went to the Scottish Lowlands.

These are some of the stories relating to that curious twilight period.

Iain Wilson, the 1 KOSB chaplain, wrote:

The four long years [were] marked by unspeakable frustration, by hard and sometimes bitter training, often by boredom and gloom and suspense. But in those four years, almost unknown to ourselves we had learned so much – physical toughness and agility, fighting skill and confidence and most precious jewel of all, we had learned to know and trust one another: we had learned comradeship . . . humorous and a little cynical, based on a rich tolerant appreciation of the individual, savoury with grousing and flavoured with bad language. In moments of real trial and crisis it would suddenly become earnest, warm, steadfast and even tender as a woman.

Padre Iain Wilson, 1 KOSB.

1 KOSB on the march during exercises near Salisbury Plain. Members include Pipe Major John Slattern (top picture, right) and Capt. Ronnie Will (top picture, second from the left). (Lt.-Col. Colin Stonor)

'From July 1943 to March 1944 2 KSLI [The King's Light Infantry of 85th Regiment of Foot] was constantly on the move', wrote Guy Radcliffe, their adjutant, 'from one training area in Scotland to another. Indeed we moved seven times in that period – a tedious and exhausting business – but one which was good training for the daily moves of the early campaign. Our CO, Lt.-Col. R.J. Maurice [was] of infinite patience and the greatest personal charm that I have ever known.'

Roly Curtiss, aged eighteen, was posted to 33rd Field Regiment RA at Muir of Ord in late 1943.

We were billeted in bell tents which were camouflaged with a thick layer of snow. We practised wet landings and manoeuvres. Our small group of signallers were definitely 'Rookies', many of the others were regular soldiers who had been evacuated from Dunkirk. Our equipment comprised Sherman tanks for the O.Ps and 105 mm guns mounted on Sherman chassis (Priests) for the gun positions. The tanks were all named after racehorses – 'Eclipse', 'Epinard' etc. After combined op. training we went into Dingwall where there was a fish and chip shop and a small cinema.

Sgt. Frank Faulkner had served with the Sappers since 1 September 1939. 'For the next three months we built concrete pill-boxes on the French–Belgian border. 3 Div in Dec '39 moved up to the Maginot Line, being the first British troops to serve there. When we landed in Normandy 3 Div Engineers consisted of three Field Coys, 17, 246 and 253, 15 Field Park Coy (Stores) and 40 CRE.'

The 92 (Loyals) LAA Regiment RA trained for the assault landings in Scotland, as Jack Prior, their IO, relates: 'The dual role performed by the batteries in their training ensured that they understood what was required of them by the infantry brigades to which they were attached.' Their 40-mm mobile self-propelled Bofors and troops of 20-mm guns were used either as a close anti-aircraft support or in an infantry/gunner role, firing at ground targets. 'Our CO, Peter Henderson, was very much a leader from the front – clear of the action to be taken and concise in his orders to get it done. A "bon mot" of his was that "any fool can be uncomfortable".'

Lt. Perring Thomas, then a troop commander in 20th A/Tank Regiment RA, remembers:

The troop converted from 4 towed to 4 SP guns in winter 1942/3 at Lockerbie after a limited number of US-made M10 Tank destroyers arrived. Their weight was 30 tons, range 120 miles, fired a 12 lb shell, and 42 rounds of AP shot and 14 rounds of HE were carried. They looked like tanks, behaved like tanks and a major difficulty in action was to dissuade infantry commanders, short of armoured support, from attempting to use them to lead attacks.

John Eales:

I was conscripted aged 18 in 1943 [into the 2nd Bn Royal Ulster Rifles], April 1st to be exact, a right April fool. In the mountains of Ayrshire we did mock battles with real ammo. We learned how to dig trenches, these was 6-ft long and about 3-ft wide and 4½-ft deep, this trench digging all the time did seem a waste of time. . . . Apart from that we had 10-mile route marches in full Pack, that is march ½ mile, ran ½ mile and so on.

Harry Jones commanded 10 Platoon, 'X' Company and joined 2 KSLI in Berwick-on-Tweed on 18 May 1943.

That winter of '43 the weather was atrocious, but in all conditions we continued with our arduous training in 'combined operations' with the Royal Navy and RAF. We sailed in Landing Craft Assault (LCA's), flat-bottomed boats, their sides only chest-high and with no overhead cover. Waves crashed over us, soaking us to the skin. We then carried out assault landings in the Moray and Cromarty Firths, attacking mock defences and strongpoints. During some of these exercises we were subjected to live ammunition fired just above our heads, accompanied by live shells fired from the supporting RN ships. Then the dismal, wet return across the lochs to our base.

Once, based on the shores of Loch Sunart: 'By day I would watch golden eagles slowly appearing above the skyline and then soaring gracefully up into a clear blue sky.' On one exercise Harry 'deployed my platoon known as a close-bridge garrison to protect a [vital] bridge, laid dummy minefields on the approaches and sited a road block to prevent tanks breaking through. . . . We had been on the bridge for several days when suddenly a cavalcade of military staff cars drew up unannounced and out stepped the General [not Rennie], the Brigadier, my Battalion Commander and Company Commander.' The General then criticised the siting of the road block. Harry replied that the decision was his, 'if I had made the wrong decision it would be myself who would probably be killed. The General stormed off into his staff car, smoke rising from his hat. A few weeks later the General was sacked by General Montgomery!'

In December 1943 the division moved north from Inveraray in Argyll to Inverness on the Moray Firth to work on combined operations exercises with Force S (for Sword) of the naval task force under Rear-Adm. A.G. Talbot, who were to be their naval partners for the D-Day assault now being planned. New 'big' friends appeared – the Assault Regiment RE's and 13/18th Hussars' Sherman tanks fitted with amphibious Duplex-Drive (DD) able in theory to 'swim' several miles in the sea before blasting a way through the beach defences.

Long-lasting partnerships were being formed. The three Field Regiments

RA were integrated in practical terms for close support. 76th (Highland) Field Regiment supported 8 Brigade's 1st Suffolk, 2nd Battalion East Yorkshires and 1st Battalion South Lancashires. 33rd Field Regiment linked with 9 Brigade's 2nd Battalion Lincolns, 1st Battalion King's Own Scottish Borderers and 2nd Battalion Royal Ulster Rifles. 7th Field Regiment integrated with 185 Brigade's 2nd Battalion Warwicks, 1st Battalion Norfolk and 2nd Battalion King's Own Shropshire Light Infantry.

Moreover, individual batteries within each Field Regiment usually supported 'their' infantry battalion.

In October 1943 Maj.-Gen. T.G. Rennie DSO, MBE had become the new GOC, having commanded 51st Highland Division previously. In the next four months no less than seven full-scale exercises were held in the Moray Firth, with Burger 1 and Burger 2 involving the town of Burghead, followed by Grab, Smash, Crown and Anchor, Leapyear in March, and finally Baron in the lead up to Overlord.

Despite missing the invasion of Sicily and the débâcle at Dieppe, intense training continued to take place in Galloway around the Solway Firth. Moffat was the HQ of the divisional Battle School commanded by Lt.-Col. Carse, East Lancashire Regiment. In the damp misty hills of Dumfriesshire the division practised assaults against fixed defences with live DF programmes fired by the three 25-pounder gunner regiments. Sappers built and then destroyed concrete strongpoints (17, 246 and 253 Field Companies RE). Maj. H.S. Gillies, CO 'C' Company 1 KOSB, wrote: 'Jan '44. LCT in Moray Firth at Burghead Bay – led my Coy ashore. Men were fit and trained to the minute – most important we had all learned to trust and rely on each other. Three days of exercise. My clothes froze on me, high state of physical fitness, did not even get a cold.' Lt.-Col. Christopher Welby-Everard, CO 2nd Battalion the Lincolns: 'By 1944 the unit had been thoroughly trained in combined operations and had experienced many a wetshod landing in Scotland. We felt that we were well trained, particularly for an assault role and that we were ready for anything. . . . Where was all this training leading us to? Here we were in the fourth year of the war and yet most of us had not yet seen a shot fired in anger.'

The training was realistic. Lionel Roebuck, East Yorkshires, recalls that actual German Teller plate mines were used to practise lifting and disarming. The 1st Suffolk spent much time and energy planning the breaking open of two strongpoints, Morris and Hillman. 'D' Company was split up to provide specially trained breaching platoons for the three other rifle companies. A detachment from 246th Field Coy RE (a mine clearance team of one officer and 26 ORs) worked closely with 1st Suffolk for nearly a year. The plan was for 'B' Company to breach Morris and 'A' Company Hillman.

Jack Harrod, IO of 2nd Lincolns, remembers: 'Obstacles of every kind now guarded the beaches of Loch Fyne and strongpoints had been constructed in the guardian hills. Exercises were carried out to the din of real artillery support, the boom of the bangalore torpedo, and the staccato chatter of the Vickers MG and the Bn returned to camp day after day tired and mudstained but in high spirits.'

The islands of Eigg and Rhum were vigorously assaulted by the Lincolns in the face of machine gun fire:

> Who in the Bn will forget Exercise Kilbride where we waded 200 yards to get ashore or Exercise Millhouse where we saw the full weight of our artillery support and the accuracy of our anti-tank guns; or Exercise Blindman where the Churchills worked so close to the infantry that their BESA fire appeared to be cutting the leading section in half? And who will forget the shocking living conditions in that tented camp on the windy side of the hill and the everlasting rain?

Exercise Euclid in January 1944 was a gigantic TEWT and planning exercise. 'Brigadier J.C. Cunningham MC controlled the discussions with consummate skill and considerable humour,' continued Jack Harrod.

Lt.-Col. M.A. Philp wrote in his journal, 'Worm's Eye View', as OC Royal Signals 185 Brigade:

> We were commanded by a short fierce little man [K.P. Smith] who suffered from the inability of his liver to get into his stride before 1100. No one went near him until then. He was very much a 'fighting' soldier in that his thoughts were constantly with his battalions, gunners and sappers. At 'O' groups he always forgot about locating BA HQ. The BM and I usually decided where HQ was to be sited. Auldearn House, a magnificent Scottish country house outside Craigelachie was our HQ to plan the Normandy assault. When the Brigadier stepped off the LCT into the loch by mistake, up to his neck, none of us dared laugh. Major General Rennie sat at conferences puffing his pipe, saying little. In an intractible situation he would take his pipe out, scratch his head and with a few sentences of clarity untie the Gordian knot.

Lt. Geoffrey Forrest from 2nd Royal Warwicks:

> I was sent there to sort out 185 Brigade's show with the Brigadier, BM, Staff Captain, G III and Signals Officer and a very interesting 3 weeks I had. Because I had been 'in' on the planning my Brigadier sent me to 9 Canadian Infantry Brigade of 3rd Canadian Infantry Division [who were to assault the beaches on D-Day] with the idea of listening in on our Bde net and keeping the Canadian brigade informed of what was happening on our front.

The last of the huge exercises carried out in the north was Leapyear, a realistic sea-borne operation with Force S on 27/8 March from Chanonry to sail north-east up the Firth to Lybster and Wick. Despite very rough weather, the delayed attack on Burghead was successful as the flotillas of LCTs landed under gunfire and RAF Sunderlands' 'bombing' cover. Humphrey Wilson recalls: 'High ranking spectators were able to watch this full dress rehearsal of what was to be the greatest invasion ever staged.'

The LSIs (Landing Ships Infantry) were newly built American ships of about 7,000 tons, each carrying eighteen LCAs (Landing Craft Assault). As each LCA held about a platoon strength up to thirty-five men, a whole battalion would fit into an LSI. These were prefabricated, but with luxuries such as excellent messes, with drinking water fountains and peacetime food (white bread, any amount of tea, sugar, butter, etc.) Canteens offered the luxuries of cigarettes, tobacco, chocolate, sweets, soap – no rationing of any kind!

The waterproofing of all vehicles, from jeeps and carriers to motorcycles and tanks, was a formidable and very messy job. The REME Light Aid detachments of ten had to work twenty-four hours a day in shifts. Norman Scarfe made the observation: 'There was no point in being <u>nearly</u> waterproof – you either drowned your vehicle or drove it ashore.' Roly Curtiss, 33rd Field Regiment: 'The Reg moved to Selkirk – a large country estate called The Hainings with a large lake. Our tanks, SPs and other vehicles were waterproofed and attempts made to float a Brengun carrier across the lake. Large "Mae West" type bags were fastened around the sides but only partially successful.'

The divisional planning staff arrived from London on 26 February 1944 to finalise Exercise Baron in Aberlour House on the river Spey near Rothes.

21st Army Group Operations order for the D-Day landings (then of course a top secret) was 'Task for 3 Brit. Inf Div to secure the high ground North of Caen, and if possible, Caen itself; to relieve 6 Airborne Div on the bridges over the Canal de Caen and the R. Orne at Bénouville and Ranville.' Brig. E.E.E. Cass's 8 Brigade had the honour of leading the attack with 185 Brigade to land next, form up at Hermanville and then thrust towards Caen on the Beuville–Biéville–Lebisey axis. Finally 9 Brigade would hold the right flank between 185 Brigade and 3rd Canadian Division on the line Mathieu–Cambes and St Contest.

Codenames were a vital part of the secret nature of this vast and dangerous undertaking. Caen was 'Poland', the two 6th Airborne bridges inland were 'Rugger' and 'Cricket'. The Caen canal was 'Portugal', and the forming-up area in the Channel was 'Piccadilly Circus'. 3rd Division's objective was to land on 'Sword' beach. West of Ouistreham to the mouth of the river Orne at Lion-sur-Mer, were the beach segments known as 'Queen Red' and 'Queen White'. Key enemy strongpoints were named 'Rover', 'Morris' and 'Hillman'. Other key codenames were 'Japan', 'Brazil', 'Mexico', 'Dublin' and 'Belfast'.

The 3rd Reconnaissance Regiment (once the 8th Battalion North-umberland Fusiliers), commanded by Lt.-Col. Hugh Merriman, was equipped with Humber armoured cars. Later in the campaign it was re-equipped with Daimlers in lieu. In January 1944 it was stationed at Langholm and Inchyetle near Inverness, then in the Banff–Dufftown area before moving south in April to Blenheim barracks in Aldershot. Although the main regiment was due to land at D+12 as Divisional Reserve for the assault landing, it had two key roles. Firstly, as one of the key Beach Groups under Maj. Gill, Capt. Stevens and Lts. Brough, Farnworth and Brogan; secondly, as 'contact detachments' under Maj. Gaskell, to provide twelve communications networks between all battalions and the three brigade HQs.

In April 1944 the division moved south during Exercise Handsup and settled in closed camps mainly around Portsmouth and Haywards Heath. KOSB was at Denmead near Portsmouth and the officers packed their tartan trousers and sent them home. 2nd Battalion Lincolns was in a tented camp in Creech Wall Wood, 4 miles north-east of Portsmouth, the South Lancs at Cowplain near Portsmouth and the Norfolks at Borde Hill, Sussex.

Guy Radcliffe wrote:

. . . after our arrival at Haywards Heath the companies trained hard – a difficult task to keep the men really fit and occupied – but not overtired. Everyone who could be spared was allowed to go away on weekends. . . . The whole of April a month of brilliant sunshine and the most seemingly peaceful spring passed in this way. Most of the admin of the camp was done by a squadron of the Northamptonshire Hussars. Looking back at this time I remember it was a happy time.

Jack Prior relates how 'an officer from 317 Bty, 92 LAA was sent out to a nearby American unit to borrow their film on VD which was reportedly so horrific as to make big brawny soldiers faint all over the place.'

Harry Jones, 2 KSLI, wrote:

One of the brighter moments for me was a visit to the local pub where I met Polish Spitfire fighter pilots with whom we had many a happy sing-song accompanied by one of the pilots on his accordian. These pilots were on daily fighter 'sweeps' across the Channel and unfortunately quite a few did not return including my friend with the accordian. [After Fabius] we were annoyed to hear that our new General [Rennie] had requested that we march past him at the light infantry pace – 140 paces to the minute – still wet from the landing and carrying our full equipment. We did it.

Operation Fabius in May 1944 was a full-scale combined services operation. 2 RUR started from Droxford near Portsmouth and sailed out into the English Channel with a powerful naval escort, and disembarked near Littlehampton. The Downs above Goodwood was the objective, a preview of the D-Day beach organisation, and a grey, blustery sea drenched everyone to the skin. On 19 May Monty visited the Ulster Rifles: 'I know this battalion very well indeed, in 1938 I was Brigadier in command of this Brigade. I always say that this Brigade has had very good Brigadiers! I had made two prophecies (1) that the war would come in 1940 instead of 1939 and (2) that Portsmouth would win the [FA] Cup. I was wrong and right!' Three days later HM King George VI inspected 9 Infantry Brigade at Waterlooville. Lt.-Col. M.A. Philp in 'Worm's Eye View' wrote: 'Monty inspected the brigade stood on bonnet of jeep. "Gather round, I want to talk to you" technique. The men broke ranks, sat on the grass. Troops loved it, the officers thought <u>too</u> much showmanship about it all. Later HM KGVI asked 1 Bn Norfolks about various families around Sandringham. He smoked incessantly, but absence of stutter which afflicted him on formal occasions.'

Lionel Roebuck recalls:

On the last pay day before leaving camp each man was given 200 French Francs mostly in 5 Franc notes. These were blue-green in colour, square and had a picture of the French Flag on the reverse side. In addition we all had a tin of Taverner & Rutledge quality boiled sweets and two FLs [condoms]. The latter were used to protect rifle barrels from the sand and seawater during the landing and by some as waterproof containers for watches and other valuables. Although the game of Housey-Housey run by the NCOs who were on to a good thing, was the only officially allowed gambling game, additional gambling schools on the results of card games, using a mixture of the new issue money and English money were soon started. Pitch and Toss using any flat secluded area to toss up two half pennies, became a popular way to gamble, betting on two heads or two tails, one of each resulting in a new throw. Lectures were given on the correct behaviour and attitude towards the French civilians and unofficially the problems of taking too many prisoners!

Eventually, for security reasons, all the camps were turned into 'concentration' laagers. John Eales, 2 RUR: 'They gave us all an Airborne type bike, very light and easy to carry. The camp was sealed with a barbed wire fence patrolled by Military Police with red caps. To the squaddy that was to stop anyone getting in. I think it was also to stop us getting out!' 'After leave at Rowlands Castle near Havant we [Roly Curtiss, 33rd Field Regt. RA] were issued with BAFVs [French francs] and billeted in woodland completely surrounded by high chainlink type fencing. I needed 24/- for a rail fare home on a 24 hour pass, but I only had 3/-. A pitch and toss school was set up and I succeeded in winning enough to travel to Grimsby and spend three hours there.' Cinemas, NAAFI canteens and ENSA shows helped enliven the boredom of waiting. But war is all about waiting.

Cpl. Payne, 2nd Battalion East Yorkshires, recalls:

I was to meet the General [Montgomery] later on, when he took charge of 21st Army Group. In his little talk [to the Bn] he said that he and the War Office were willing to sacrifice the Third Division providing we made a breach in part of the defence, so that he could keep pouring troops in after us. Of course the Division at battle strength would be anything like twelve thousand men. It was going to be a dear do, wasn't it? I thought there and then what a nice gentleman the General was. But as I say, he left us to go and torment someone else.

Iain Wilson was the chaplain to 1 KOSB and wrote an excellent history of the regiment:

It is difficult to resist the temptation to dwell upon the years between 1940 and 1944 when we trained and journeyed together, leading a curiously self-contained life from the Sussex Downs to the Moray Firth. The winter snows on Salisbury Plain, the gentle Devonshire valleys, the woods and gardens of Buckinghamshire, the cliffs above Dover, the wild lands and seas of Moidart and Morar, the ancient peace and simplicity of our Borderland – in these settings we lived, worked and played together, sharing all things that men can share, from our very uniform and food, to our worship of God. It had greatly changed us from the exhausted men who had staggered off destroyers and minesweepers and countless 'little ships' in June 1940.

After the issue of a special assault jerkin, a Mae West, a light gas respirator, a new steel helmet, a brand new battledress, two 24-hour ration packs, BAFVs, a French phrase book, spare underwear and boots, plus a vomit bag, each infantryman carried a load of about 65 lb weight. Bren-gunners and the mortar platoons carried rather more. The entrenching tool/spade also was a vital 'accessory'. So, heavily laden, the Iron Division went to war again, with extra artillery, a tank brigade, assault engineers, 'Funnies' and commandos – almost 40,000 men at arms.

CHAPTER THREE

The Crossing

'The Excitement of the Unknown'

Guy Radcliffe, Adjutant 2 KSLI, recalls their journey towards Newhaven:

We all wondered whether the people who watched us go by, they never cheered, they sometimes waved, would recognise by the heavily loaded vehicles . . . that this was the real thing. . . . Everyone was rather quiet filled with an inner sadness, but also with excitement, the excitement of the unknown. [Later] As a craft was about to leave the quay [at Newhaven] a WRNS driver left her vehicle and walked over to the side of the craft and said to a commando driver 'Goodbye – Good luck'. In that simple phrase we all felt that she had said goodbye for everyone of those that each one of us loved. May 30th was sweltering and the 1st June cloudy and overcast and by the 3rd all the assault troops were aboard 'S' Force in Portsmouth harbour waiting for the 'off'.

Maj. W.R. Birt commanded a squadron of flail tanks of 22nd Dragoons who were to lead the beach attack in front of 3rd Division:

0215 hrs June 2. The wait has prolonged itself. We are eight hours behind programme. Heavy with rum laced tea we doze in the back of the car. Under the green balconies a group of soldiers have been singing for hours to the tinkle of an RAF man's ukelele. A strong tenor leads a drowsy bee-contented hum. They sing over and over again, 'Roll me over, love'. Then the mood changes. With notes long-drawn they turn to 'Home, Sweet Home' and 'Love's Old Sweet Song'. From the balconies close above us in the darkness, girls' voices join in sweetly, strongly. There is a sudden move ahead of us. The ukelele and the tenor voice tumble into a truck and above the growl of the lorries we hear the lilt of 'Goodbye, ladies'. We jerk forward and are on the loading dock. There under the arc-lamps is the great gaping mouth of our landing ship, its monstrous belly lamp-lit and up whose throat there crawls a procession of tiny men in tiny vehicles.

'On the morning of 4th June 1944, my Platoon consisting of myself and

36 infantry soldiers, climbed into lorries and began the long-awaited journey to the South Coast,' recalls Harry Jones, 10 Platoon commander, 'X' Company 2 KSLI. 'It was a warm sunny day and I was amazed at the sight of hundreds of tanks, guns, ammunition stacks and stores, lining the roads nose-to-tail. The whole countryside appeared to be one massive depot.' Harry sailed from Newhaven in a LSI. After the famous 24-hour delay caused by adverse weather 'Ike' bravely unleashed his Anglo-Saxon armies.

Jack Harrod, IO of 2nd Battalion Lincolns, wrote:

It was on the morning of June 5th – after a false start the previous day – that the main body left its sub-marshalling area and after experiencing every possible aspect of officialdom in the short journey to the embarkation hard, finally found itself aboard LCIs alongside Southsea pier. Landing craft of every type filled the Solent making an impressive sight. We of Bn HQ felt that our own LCI painted newly white with the Divisional sign on either side of the bridge and the Regimental crest on the wall of the wardroom, was a pretty ship in which to embark on this crusade . . . she remains for ever 'our' ship. And we imagine wherever she now is she still carries proudly the sign of the Iron Division.

Anti-seasick tablets were issued by Lt.-Col. G.E. Wood of 9th Field Ambulance. The divisional HQ ship was HMS *Largs*, with Adm. Talbot and Maj.-Gen. Rennie aboard, and Infantry Landing Ships included *Dacres*, *Glenearn*, *Cutlass*, *Battleaxe*, *Broadsword*, *Astrid*, *Maid of Orleans*, *Goathland* and *Locust*.

The CO of 2nd Battalion East Yorks travelled across on the LSI, HMS *Glenearn*, with whose captain and crew he had worked in several practice landings. Lt.-Col. C.F. Hutchinson presented the naval captain with a silver bugle inscribed with the regimental crest, and in return received a ceremonial pike bearing the regimental badge of the Royal Marines. As they passed at sea the destroyer *Undaunted*, her commander Angus Mackenzie wearing a Highlander's bonnet, played the bagpipes from his bridge. A bugler of the East Yorks sounded the General Salute as his LSI passed the Command Ship HMS *Largs*.

Maj. Robert Moberley's history of the 2nd Battalion Middlesex, whose medium machine guns and 4.2-in mortars were to render so much vital support in the days to come, wrote:

For the assault landing 'A' MG Coy would come under command of the 8 Brigade infantry battalions. 1 Platoon with the South Lancs, 3 Platoon with the East Yorks and 2 Platoon with the Suffolks. 185 Brigade would follow up with 'C' MG Coy with 2 platoons of D, the Mortar company at H+240 and H+270. The troops were issued with 200 French francs, small booklet of French phrases, blurb about France and the French, Mae West lifebelts, chewing gum, tommy cookers, META fuel, water sterilising tablets, tins of 20 cigs, biscuits, chocolate, bullybeef, two 24 hr packs, three bags 'vomit', small bottles of anti seasick pills, compo packs, watercans, self heating soups and cocoa. Some lucky men who went in US built LSIs had a luxury voyage watching Mickey Rooney and Judy Garland film in the cafeteria.

'And when the vast invasion fleets moved out silently into the windy English Channel, it was as if a million trumpets began to blow again, a great heartfelt chorus of sanity and freedom, heavy with menace for the Nazis, thrilling with hope for those whom they had enslaved,' wrote Iain Wilson, 1 KOSB. Captain Hugh Gunning, a professional journalist, but now official observer with 3rd Division, was at sea for five days on LST 382 with the KOSB together with M. Pierre Jeannerat, a French newspaper correspondent who would 'cover' the news of the beach landings.

Harry Jones, 2 KSLI:

The night crossing was choppy . . . the Channel was filled with ships of all descriptions – battleships, cruisers, destroyers, minesweepers and hundreds of all types of landing craft many of them flying barrage balloons. Overhead were hundreds of aircraft all heading for the French coast – American Flying Fortress bombers, Lightning and Typhoon fighters. Below decks I opened a sealed envelope and took out the map of the coastal area in Northern France upon which we were to land. The beach in Normandy was codenamed Sword, the most easterly of all the landing beaches. Our sector was Queen beach with French town of Hermanville a mile or two inland. Our division's objectives ran from the coast to Caen.

Cpl. Clifford Arthur Payne, 2nd East Yorks:

A Padre gave us a sermon on board ship and at the finish we sang the hymn 'For those in peril on the sea'. After that we began to move again and overhead there was a terrible noise of plane engines. Of course it was dark about one or two o'clock. We learned later that it was the Airborne boys going over. I tried to sleep but it just wouldn't come to me. Anyway I was seasick and I didn't care if the first shell hit us, I was so bad.

Guy Radcliffe, adjutant 2 KSLI, wrote:

Landing craft are not the ideal ships in which to make a rough Channel crossing. Their blunt bows sent cascades of spume over the ship, the quarters on LCIs are cramped and in LCTs non-existent. Most men felt none too well and on the LCTs especially it was difficult to keep dry. But the cheerfulness was amazing!

Two hundred troops of 1 KOSB set sail from Portsmouth in a LSI, via

Spithead to the lee of the Isle of Wight for the fleet RV at 'Piccadilly
Circus', as Hugh Gunning wrote:

1st KOSB had a wretched time in their crossing of the Channel. LSTs
roll like a porpoise but they have plenty of weight in a rolling sea. The
LCI is a cockleshell, pitching, tossing, throbbing its way through the sea.
It is a trim little vessel functional in its design with its two ramps at the
bow and every modern facility for pouring men off a ship on to a beach.

Maj. H.S. Gillies was CO of 'C' Company:

The sea was very high – great green troughs of waves, other craft
plunging and rolling as they made their way onwards. Ahead lay the
coast of France, then quiet and expressionless, puffs of smoke here and
there. The skies were full of aircraft circling over the fleet for its
protection. Above the wind could be heard the dull thudding from the
heavy guns of the battleships and cruisers [*Warspite*, *Ramillies*, *Roberts*,
Dragon, *Frobisher* and *Danae* had guns deployed on to Sword beach
defences]. One of the most heartening sights was a tank landing craft
from which the artillery were firing salvo after salvo of rockets onto the
enemy defences.

The Forward Observation Officers (FOOs) of 17/43rd Battery of 7th
Field Regiment RA under Maj. I.H.H. Rae were the KSLI gunner support.
Each assault battalion had unusually specific naval vessel support. For
instance 1 Suffolk had HMS *Dragon*, a 6-in gun cruiser, and HMS *Kelvin*, a
destroyer, at their beck and call, provided the Forward Observation
Bombardment (FOB) was alive and well and in the right place!
Captain H.C. Illing, OC 'A' Company Royal Warwicks, recalls:

Dawn came – few had had much sleep – even fewer managed to eat
breakfast – some looked very ill in spite of sea-sick pills, boiled sweets and
cups of tea. Land was just in sight and the rumble of the naval guns rolled
back to us across the water as we steered in line ahead through the narrow
lanes swept by the minesweepers towards the shore. Soon it was time to
assemble as the craft fanned out into line abreast. Kits were put on – guns
checked over – all was ready and the men moved forward to their stations.
Occasionally a whining sound would swish over the ship – our first
experience of an angry missile.

Humphrey Wilson, Royal Norfolks, wrote:

Overhead there was a never-ending stream of aircraft. I don't think
anyone saw an enemy machine on D-Day. We were certainly never
bothered by them. How right Field Marshal Montgomery was when he

said 'Win the air battle first'. Without this overwhelming air superiority we should probably still be fighting in France.

Lt.-Col. M.A. Philp, 185 Infantry Brigade HQ Signals:

We passed the two battleships Warspite and Ramilles, couple of miles on our port side, shelling enemy batteries near Le Havre. A slow leisurely great tongue of flame licking from the barrel, huge mushroom of smoke formed at the leading end of the flame, sound of heavy dull boom reaching us some seconds later. To the west suddenly a landing craft exploded in one enormous flash of flame. When it cleared away there was nothing to see – quite terrifying – one moment a ship on the sea, the next it had gone.

At dawn, after a marvellously good breakfast was served, Sapper A.J. Lane, 263 Field Company, aged twenty-two from Llanelly, saw the huge outline of the escort destroyer close on the starboard side.

Her great hulk loomed large in great silhouette against the faint skyline. My sickness and misery was suddenly added to by shock and dismay because I was aware of an explosion that seemed to lift the destroyer out of the water and smash somewhere around her midship area. I watched giddy and disbelieving as her middle went down, leaving her two ends upturned and floating visibly. She had struck a mine just as I had, for those few sad precise moments, watched her. . . . I remember my horror at seeing some of the wreckage and human figures disappearing directly under our ship – also my furious astonishment that nothing was being done to save the poor devils in the sea. They were obviously doomed to die. . . . It was my first sight and experience of what war and battle were all about.

'It was the worst 48 hours in my life on that landing craft,' recalls Albert Pattison, then platoon sergeant of the 6-pounder A/Tank guns with 1 Suffolk. 'Worse than swimming 2 miles off the Dunkirk beaches in 1940, aged seventeen. Isn't it marvellous what fear can make you do!'

Pte. Stanley Gardner, 1 Suffolk, kept a journal: 'On board the "Battleaxe", a converted American freighter, the boys were playing cards, gambling away their last English money and starting on their new French money. At 8.45 the decks were crowded with troops – hundreds of sun-burned fit young men in khaki with their safety belts on and everyone with a black triangle on their arms.' Stanley was twenty and destined to be taken prisoner in three weeks' time. Later:

dawn was just breaking and as we looked out over the rough sea we could see a huge red glow on the horizon. This must be France. A destroyer speeding by about 8 miles from us struck a mine and blew up scattering wreckage in all directions. At 3.30 we queued up with our trays for breakfast of porridge, two hard boiled eggs, four rounds of white bread and butter and jam and a mug of tea. We gave our rifles the once-over, filled the magazines and made sure our ammunition and grenades were ready for use. At 4.45 the word came over the loudspeaker for us to get dressed [for battle]. At 4.50 the captain told us he could see the French coast – a blazing inferno with the Navy shelling it and the RAF bombing it. Then came the order 'Marines of ALC 23 lower away'. Slowly the winches began to turn and we slid down the ship's side and bumped into the stormy sea. We were then 7 miles from shore. We made ourselves as comfortable as possible, some sitting, some standing but all singing. New songs and old – sentimental – patriotic and ballads but we all sang.

Brig. G.G. Mears was Commander Royal Artillery of 3rd Division. The three Field Regiments were a vital supporting factor in the landings on Sword beach.

Air photographs both vertical and oblique were studied by all ranks and everything possible was done to make them familiar with the bit of France on which they were to land. The embarkation began and units broke up into their shiploads. Guns were in their LCTs. COs were with their Brigadiers, and BCs and FOOs were with their Bns. 2 i/cs and their recce parties were in their allocated craft. Wireless sets after most careful netting were sealed, not to be opened until the battle was on. Packets of orders and crates of maps were on board all craft to be distributed when at sea. Everything that imagination, forethought and care could do, had been done. Now it all depended on the weather. The sea was rough. Some LCTs carrying the assault guns of the Royal Marines were swamped. The bombardment increased in intensity as the three Field Regiments of each division [50 Tyne Tees and 3 Canadian] opened fire from their LCTs on the run in. . . . Not one had been fired at by any enemy weapon.

Lt. S. Rosenbaum was a young officer with 113/114 Field Battery, 33 Field Regiment RA:

Major Wise's (the FOO) launch was sunk by the rough seas and transferred to that used by the FOO of 7th Field Reg. RA. 76 Field Reg's launch was also sunk and its FOO killed. At 0655 we opened fire at 11,000 yards – the rounds falling between the beach and 400 yards inland. The rate of fire was 3 rounds per minute for each of the Div's 72 guns (4 tons of HE every minute on our immediate front). Also HE filled rockets were being fired from LCTs. A fearsome sight as they launched their missiles simultaneously. John Humphries having given the first orders to fire then handed over to me. The range dropping by 200 yards a time every minute or so. The houses on the foreshore looked like the English seaside.

John Foster was a bombardier gun fitter in 'B' Troop 101 Battery 33rd Field Regiment RA:

I had a grandstand view. We were in the assault group with our 105 mm SP guns to assist the infantry when we got trapped on the beach and had to wait on the engineers making a new way off the beach for us. The gun compartment sat quite a bit up off the ground. I could see all around me dead and dying and men getting shot sitting in their trucks, especially the wireless trucks. The Germans were shooting from the reinforced cellars under the houses. Our landing craft AA gun received a direct hit. One minute it was firing away. The next minute a gaping hole and the handrail hanging over the ship. Of the 18 LCTs which put our three artillery regiments ashore, 14 became total wrecks – 5 from obstacles, 3 from mines and 6 from enemy fire.

CHAPTER FOUR

'The Game's Afoot, Follow Your Spirit'

Sword beach from west to east consisted of four 'sub' beaches, Oboe, Peter, Queen and Roger, and was known to be defended by 716 Coast Defences Infantry Division. The probability was that 21 Panzer Division was close to Caen, perhaps near the south-west suburbs. Queen beach had two small resort villages to contend with, Riva-Bella and La Brèche to the left (east) and the rather larger Lion-sur-Mer on the right (west), 2 miles apart. All the houses had been turned into fortresses and the flat countryside behind heavily mined. The open beaches were mined, with many underwater obstacles, including 'hedgehogs' in overlapping rows, only exposed at low tide, backed by pillboxes and concrete emplacements whose guns commanded the beaches. Inland there were several strongpoints with codenames of cars: Hillman, Morris, Rover, and fish: Cod, Sole, Trout. Rommel had had plenty of time to strengthen his Atlantic Wall defences. It was hoped that the naval big guns and RAF bombers would have destroyed them in the preliminary huge supporting barrages.

The enemy defending Queen beach was the 736th Regiment. In their pillboxes and fortified villas they covered the beach defences with machine guns, 75-mm guns and mortars. They had been drenched with fire from the Royal Navy, RAF and seaborne artillery. The beaches had been well marked by the Royal Naval midget submarine crews of X20 and X23. Brig. Lord Lovat's Commando Brigade was in support of 8 Infantry Brigade. 4 Commando was to take Ouistreham and 41 Marine Commando was to advance westwards to Lion-sur-Mer and link up with the Canadian 3rd Division. The rest of Lord Lovat's command would link up with the airborne troops who had dropped 6 miles inland at Bénouville.

The landing plan called for four LCTs each carrying four DD tanks apiece to be put 'ashore' at H-5 minutes, followed at H-Hour by another four LCTs carrying Hobart's unique 'Funnies', flail tanks of 22nd Dragoons, flame-throwing Crocodiles, and Petards throwing drum-bombs. RE assault groups would begin work clearing the deadly beach obstacles. At H+7 came eight assault landing craft bearing the two leading infantry companies, and at H+20 another eight LCAs with two more infantry companies. At H+25 followed two LCAs with more Beach Group backup teams. At H+35 more backup 'Funny' tank support and bulldozers; at

H+60 nine LCTs with SP guns; at H+90 ten LCTs with more tanks. The tenth wave was twenty-one DUKWs loaded with ammunition, stores and more gunner support. Cossac, the Army Group planners, had forecast losses of ten per cent of the landing craft sunk and a further twenty per cent damaged.

The beach obstacles consisted of a ramp of balks of timber about 15–16 ft long, height about 8 ft, with the lower end facing seaward. Also vertical posts about 6–8 ft high and finally 'hedgehogs' of three strong metal girders lashed together at the centre and splayed out. In most cases Teller mines or other explosives were fastened to the top of each of the obstacles, which were half covered at half tide and fully exposed at low tide.

The immediate task of the Beach Group was to get the beach marker signs up: red and green banners to guide the follow-up waves of craft through lanes cleared of mines and obstacles. Their second task was to make the beach a working, functional area, clear remaining mines and barbed wire, mark beach exits through the dunes and seafront houses, develop lateral roads running along the beach head, recover 'drowned' vehicles and – vitally – keep everybody moving. The beachmasters were kings of the beaches and quite rightly brooked no arguments from anyone, including senior officers!

H-Hour was 0725 hrs.

On the right – Queen White beach – 'A' squadron of 22nd Dragoons Flails with AVREs of 77 squadron 5 ARE provided four breaching teams directed on the holiday villas of the small seaside resort of Lion-sur-Mer. On the left – Queen Red beach – 'C' squadron 22nd Dragoons Flails with AVREs of 79 squadron 5 ARE were to breach on the more open beach of La Brèche. The casino at Riva-Bella was a particularly difficult strongpoint. The Queen sector guarded the entrance to the Caen canal, which was heavily fortified and was within range of the long-range guns from the promontory of Le Havre to the east.

Raymond Birt, 22nd Dragoons, wrote:

Queen Red beach was tougher still. Stretches of 'Fortress Europe' on 2nd British Army's front were held on the coastal perimeter by garrison troops with little stomach for fighting: renegades, some of them, from Russian POW camps or mean-spirited men of 'punishment' battalions stiffened with a sprinkling of tough Nazi officers and NCOs. But on Queen beach the defence was grim and fanatical. The Germans fought the irresistible wave of tanks and men that was flung upon them until it was seen to be engulfing them. Then firing their useless rifles and shouting perhaps their final salute to the Fuehrer who had willed their deaths, they ran out into the fire of the tank guns – men thirsty for the privilege of destruction in battle.

There was fierce shooting at close range: like so much of the fighting on Queen beaches, tanks ran for the gun emplacements in a grim race to put their shells almost point blank through the mouths of the concrete 'boxes' before they themselves were put out of action. The team was thus able to complete its breach and shoot in the assault infantry before moving up to sweep [with flail tanks] its lateral communications. In spite of this intense opposition on the beaches all eight lanes on the beaches themselves were through before 0800 and infantry of the East Yorks and South Lancs were passing through to the first lateral under very heavy mortar and small arms fire.

Spr. A.J. Lane, an assault engineer with 263 Field Company RE, carried besides his 'normal' kit a Bren gun with two heavy boxes of magazines, some of them being 100-round mags:

When I dropped off the ramp, my Brengun etc took me down like a stone leaving me with several feet of water above my head. By underwater walking towards shore I saved myself from a watery end. I could see some people were either drowned or drowning already, some I could see were screaming and waving their arms while going backwards and seawards. Many were wounded whilst in the water and were unable to move in the advancing tide. The whole area was under fire with casualties already high and rising.

Lane had been trained to remove or destroy beach obstacles to make the necessary gaps in the coastal defences – such as hedgehogs, tetrahedrons, Element 'C' barriers, poles, mined ramps, ground mines and barbed-wire entanglements. Some of the RE teams were to use AVRE (armoured vehicles RE) and flail tanks (Crabs), some of which carried fascines (bridges for crossing ditches or sea walls), bobbins and Sommerfield Track (for covering mud and sand), and petards (for breaching concrete obstacles and pillboxes). Lane's CO described the situation:

The scene on the beach was indescribable – an absolute inferno, burning tanks, broken-down vehicles and very many dead and wounded lying about in a narrow strip between the sea and the barbed wire at the back of the beach. There were shells, mortars and the occasional bomb falling and a considerable amount of small arms fire. For a few moments I thought none of the things we had planned had come to pass. We were late and the tide was almost high. We were all on one beach instead of spread along the whole divisional front. Our task of clearing beach obstacles was obviously hopeless so I organised four sections into parties for clearing beach exits and laying track to clear some of the congestion.

On D-Day the assault engineers of 5 ARE suffered 117 casualties including their CO, Lt.-Col. Cocks, who was killed, and 22nd Dragoons had 42 casualties. Fifteen of their twenty-six Sherman flails were knocked

Troops and carriers clearing their way off Queen Beach. (IWM, B 5104)

out or damaged that day. Tpr. Bernard Cuttiford had joined the Staffordshire Yeomanry, part of 27th Armoured Brigade commanded by Brig. Prior Palmer. The other two Sherman tank regiments were 13/18th Hussars (QMO) and the East Riding Yeomanry. Cuttiford wrote: 'First ashore on the White Area of Sword Beach were the 13/18th with their DD tanks, who were dropped off at about 800 yards [in fact further out], and then swam ashore under their own steam. We were next with our ordinary land Shermans with wading equipment.' Twenty-four tanks of A and B squadrons 13/18th Hussars 'swam' for shore. En route two were rammed by the AVRE 'fleet' and sank immediately, four were disabled by enemy fire on the beach and five more were swamped by breakers. So only five were effective on White beach and eight on Red beach, but they were soon joined by five unable to launch at sea.

CHAPTER FIVE

Queen Red Beach

'Scene of Utter Destruction'

The East Yorks (and South Lancs) manned assault craft were lowered overside of the *Empire Battleaxe* and HMS *Glenearn* between 0430 and 0600 hrs 7 miles out from shore. In the crossfire from mortars, artillery and snipers the MO was hit on disembarking, so the wounded were only 'patched up', and Maj. Barber was killed when a mortar bomb landed in 'D' Company HQ. But, by 0830 hrs, when the first reinforcements landed, the forward companies were out of sight of the beach.

Lionel Roebuck's excellent journal 'Five Yorkshire Tykes' describes the plan of attack:

> 2nd Bn East Yorks had to attack on the extreme left section of Sword beach called 'Queen Red'. Our 'A' and 'B' Coys supported by swimming DD tanks were to break through the beach obstacles. 'A' Coy with 'C' Coy of 1st Bn South Lancs would land on our right, attack and eliminate the strongpoint Cod, a defence feature covering a wide area along the beach frontage. Simultaneously 'B' Coy would move across open ground, attack the first inland strongpoint Sole, with support of 'C' Coy following close behind them, and eliminate it. The next task was to move further inland to strongpoint Daimler, a massive complex of defence works with strong obstacles, a most formidable objective, attack it, put it out of action so as to stop the four 75 mm guns positioned there from shelling the beach. This task was the main responsibility of 'C' Coy.

One of the dramatic stories of D-Day was Shakespearian drama at its best. Using a loud hailer as his LCA approached the beach Maj. C.K. 'Banger' King, OC 'A' Company 2 East Yorks, encouraged his sleepy seasick troops with Shakespeare's *Henry V*:

> He that outlives this day and comes safe home
> Will stand a tip-toe when this day is named
> And gentlemen in England, now a-bed
> Shall think themselves accurs'd, they were not here.

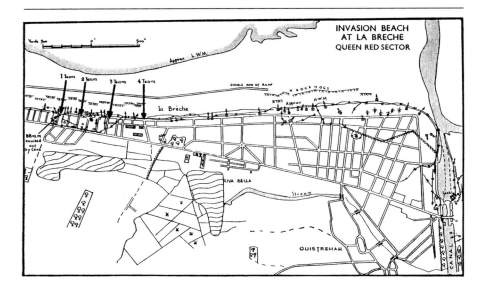

Lionel Roebuck, who was in 13 Platoon 'C' Company, recalls 'Banger', who earned two DSOs, as a smart, military type with an Airborne Regiment flash on his shoulder: 'a real soldier's soldier if ever there was one'. Two of 'Banger' King's three platoon commanders were Canloan officers (Lts. Neily and Stirling Reid). 'C' Company under Maj. D. Barrow also had two Canloan platoon commanders (Capt. James McGregor and Lt. Leonard Robertson). The latter has given a vivid account of the landing, supported by DD tanks to break through the beach obstacles:

The East Yorkshires were in. As C Coy moved in to land behind A Coy and to the right, we discovered that all the wire entanglements and beach obstacles which were to be cleared by the sappers hadn't been. Maj Barrow spotted an opening and made for it with 13 and 14 Platoons following in their LCAs. Not for me it wasn't. I figured that one or two might get through and not be spotted by the Jerries but certainly not four craft. Gave the order for full speed ahead . . . as I wanted to hit the wire hard and crash the entanglement with the mines without them going off. It was a chance to take but we didn't have all day to figure it out. The Marine corporal in charge of the LCA hesitated, and I really didn't blame him, but when I went to take the wheel he gave her the gun. Heads down! Here we go! The first wire parted like a string. The second wire jarred us and really gave us a scare as we just missed hitting an iron rail with a tellermine on top. Shells were falling all around us; a craft on our left received a direct hit and started to settle but on we went. . . . On the third wire we stuck and stayed. The corporal of the Marines thought we had hit the beach so he dropped the ramp and away I went with two of my men right behind me before we realized we were hooked on the wire. The three of us had gone right over our heads in water but we bobbed right up. I gave a yell to pull up the ramp and gun her while we got out of the way. The LCA broke loose and followed us and touched down and my men poured out. Bullets, shrapnel and what have you was flying around like a swarm of angry bees. Pte Woodhead was the first hit in our pl, stopping one in the arm. He was the one who the night before had said, 'If you will lead I will follow you anywhere.' Blood was flowing and bodies of other Pls from A and B Companies were floating face down in the water here and there. Things were moving so fast that one had hardly time to think or be scared. Our main thought was to get the hell off the beach. While the rest of the Pl made for dry land I grabbed Woodhead and his PIAT bombs and literally dragged him ashore. While doing so he was hit for the second time. Private Herbert simply disappeared – we never saw him again. . . . We were on the beach and soon organized and on the move. 15 Platoon was the first in the Coy to get moving as a unit and with the least casualties . . . two killed and two wounded, the lightest in the battalion, I believe. We felt very lucky indeed. My men were just grand all the way, even finding time to joke now and then.

Lionel Roebuck:

All around was a scene of utter destruction, wrecked boats lay broadside on, dead comrades floated face down in the tide, others lay in grotesque positions on the beach. Exploding shells fell as we raced on towards a gap in the defences. It was being made wider by brave stalwart REs who swept the sands with their mine detectors, then laid out white tapes to mark a safe track. The sand dragged on our feet and slowed down on our progress. The gap was to the left of the beach strongpoint Cod in process of being put out of action by 'A' Coy E. Yorks and 'C' Coy S. Lancs. On the sloping grassy bank which covered the huge bunker were three dead Germans. They were immaculate in their grey overcoats and smart uniforms, caught as they had run away, they lay, two of them face down in a neat line. The track led away from the beach going towards the lateral road.

Cpl. Clifford Payne's carrier was carrying

all the ammo for the lads and also a big NAAFI pack with cigs and chocolate. . . . I was nosing down the ramp and just as the water was lapping over the top of the waterproofing I touched the bottom and levelled out in bottom gear going flat out, virtually under water. All I could see through my visor was dirty murky water. I had gone through some German beach defences we called 'dragons teeth'. They were railway lines set in concrete with a large mine on the top and bottom. Having flat bottomed boats we floated over most of their defences.

Pte. Harold Isherwood was the 2-in mortar man (who also carried a case of bombs and a Sten gun) in 'B' Company, who spent much of the voyage over in the *Glenearn* playing cards with the new issue of French currency. He saw 'one of our ships take a direct hit and fold up like a penknife and vanish into the sea'. On the beach pinned down by small arms fire he put down a smoke screen with his mortar, but later a shell blast blew 'a small pebble into my arm which I still have to this day. The shell landed amongst some officers and I saw torsos and limbs blown high into the air.'

The East Yorks battled their way inland in the wake of the DD tanks of 13/18th Royal Hussars and the AVREs of 5 ARE and attacked Sole. Lionel Roebuck: '[By 1000 hrs] Sole had been over-run, put out of action with help from the beach area by the guns of 76th Field Reg, a troop of SP guns of 20th A/Tk Regiment, plus tanks of 13/18 Hussars.' Captain Featherstone, 76th Field Regiment, FOO with 'C' Company, was establishing his OP nearby and was 'slightly embarassed by the appearance of 80 Germans surrendering from a dug-out'. Lionel Roebuck again: 'The prisoners were filing out readily to be taken back under escort to the beach. One escort, "Tabby" Barker, soon returned looking disturbed. A group of French commandoes had relieved him of his catch and sent him back. He was apprehensive about their fate.'

The Queen Red beaches had their first two exits blocked by damaged tanks and the gapping teams had suffered crippling losses. But within two hours three exits had been cleared. There were few mines on the beach, but fields of mines were found behind the dunes and along the lateral road. Almost half of the AVREs, flail tanks and bulldozers were soon out of action and 629 Field Squadron and 5 ARE suffered heavy casualties. A beachmaster, Lt.-Cdr. Edward Gueritz, recalls: 'There were bodies lying about scattered all the way from the water's edge. Tanks and a couple of RE vehicles were trying to get up to the sea wall. There were wounded men trying to crawl to safety – but at that stage – we couldn't stop and help them much.'

Jim Nelson was a member of the 2nd East Yorkshire Regiment 3-in mortar detachment. It was his 21st birthday:

The skipper of our LCT got to hear about this, sent for me and asked why with a name like mine I was in the Army. He gave me a good tot of Navy rum, wished me Many Happy Returns and said he would try to give us a dry landing. [Later] We hit the beach at a good speed, went down the ramp and could see many bodies floating past at the edge of the beach. This was our first taste of the real war after three or four years of training for this very invasion. [Half an hour later when the engineers had bulldozed a way] We looked back and saw a German shell hit the bridge of the LCT we had just landed from. We heard the howl of mortars or shells heading towards us. Something hit me in the back just below the shoulder blade. I remember gasping as the breath was knocked out of me, in the best Hollywood tradition, to my mate 'They've got me, Eddy'.

A week later Jim changed his blouse, shirt and vest and discovered a hole in all of them and in his back. He attended the ADS for several weeks afterwards.

Still on the beach: 'A German bomber released a stick of bombs, about five of us dived into the same empty slit trench only dug for one. Comical to see the five of us all on top of each other, the last three about three feet above ground.' Later French Canadian commandos eliminated the German mortar positions inland which were bombarding the Yorkshires' tracked mortar carriers crammed full of HE bombs.

Lionel Roebuck again:

Arthur Littlewood and Winterbottom, a thin pale-looking soldier, climbed a wall to join us, warned of a sniper from a high building to the right. Cliff Milnes the boxer, had been badly wounded – hit when trying to cross over open ground. His legs were shattered and he died. Sgt Arthur Thompson who had led those left out of his beleaguered and decimated D Coy off the beach had found him. Cliff, a non-smoker, said 'Give us a cig, Tommy' and lit him one to smoke. More wounded came by along the track with flesh wounds mainly from mortar bomb or shell splinters on their way to the beach FDS. [Later] We found in a big farmhouse with a huge gable, no windows in the yellow stonework, our depleted C Coy gathered in shelter by the farmhouse wall. Col C.F. Hutchinson DSO, the CO, and Major D. de Symons Barrow MC, the C Coy CO, were planning to attack Daimler strongpoint from the rear, making use of a path through the woodland.

The CO was caught by mortar fire in a sunken lane, wounded and had to be evacuated. Lt. Leonard Robertson describes the attack on the gun position at Daimler, which was taken by 'A' and 'C' Companies:

In the afternoon, after working our way inland, our Coy came upon an unknown enemy position and 15 Platoon got the job of clearing it up. Later on, 14 (McGregor) and 15 Platoons took on the Coy's main objective. All went well at first. Mac with 14 Platoon was on the left while we in 15 advanced on the right. Mac struck first and flushed five prisoners, which kind of cheered us up. We pushed on to cleared ground until we came in sight of the Coy's second main objective where we halted, then decided to turn to the left and help Mac and 14 Platoon. They had hit the enemy stronghold square on. It was a very large pill box, well concealed and well fortified. Mac had gone up to the entrance and called on them to surrender. They didn't give him a chance, but cut him down with a burst of gun fire hitting him in the chest and stomach. When we arrived his sergeant was in charge of the Platoon with Mac lying out in front of the pill box. The sergeant couldn't get near him nor blast the entrance with their PIAT for fear of hitting Mac. I took over this Platoon along with my own and surrounded the position. Later on I got close to

Mac but couldn't get him away. Left a rear guard and reported back to Coy Headquarters. There I found that 13 Platoon with some Coy HQ had joined D Coy for the next objective and orders had been left for us to give covering fire from where I had left the rear guard. Promptly returned and again surrounded the pill box and covered the next objective at the same time. Went to see Mac again to see what I could do. Mac was dead.

Robertson covered him with his gas cape and, thrusting McGregor's bayoneted rifle into the ground, hung his helmet on the butt to mark the spot where the first Canloan officer had been killed in action.

In the captured dugouts were liberal supplies of wine and champagne. Nevertheless the East Yorks continued to St Aubin d'Arquenay – empty and in ruins. Relieved by 1 KOSB, the East Yorks spent the night west of Hermanville.

By the end of D-Day the East Yorks had lost 5 officers and 60 men killed and 4 officers and 137 men wounded.

CHAPTER SIX

Sword Queen White Beach

The Taking of Cod, Morris and Hillman

Two key units were seconded to No 5 Beach Group to co-ordinate the opening of exits through the defences and the subsequent traffic control off the beach [wrote Lt. Ken Baxter of 2nd Battalion Middlesex Regiment]. The group consisted of Major Max Langley, Lts Comben, Rowson, Webber and myself and our task was to organise four principal exits on Queen White Beach whilst a similar group from 3rd Reconnaissance Reg under Major Neville Gill was to provide the same on Queen Red. [On the way in] we suddenly came upon the midget submarine X-23, a complete surprise to us – as it should have been. . . . The first setback was a returning LCT with her ramp jammed in the half-lowered position. These craft, four to each beach, carried the specially equipped AVRE tanks that were to work in groups of threes. The centre tank was armed with a 'snake', a sixty foot-long heavy tube of explosive to be pushed through the beach defences and detonated. [Later] Steadily the flotilla of LCAs pressed onwards towards the beach. Four hundred yards from the shoreline, the Royal Marine Commando frogmen slipped over the side to start the job of clearing underwater obstacles.

Ken and his group landed opposite strongpoint 0880, codenamed Cod, at H+20.

The 1st Battalion South Lancashires (Prince of Wales Volunteers) claims in its regimental history (by Col. B.R. Mullaly) that it was the first British unit to brew tea on French soil! In the first of two waves, 'A' and 'C' Companies under Maj. J.F. Harwood and E.F. Johnson touched down from their LSIs at 0720 hrs on a strip of sandy beach with dunes, in front of the village of Coleville-sur-Orne. Despite heavy MG and mortar fire they made good progress and the second wave – Battalion HQ, HQ Companies 'B' and 'D' – landed twenty-five minutes later and at once took casualties from small arms, mortars and 88-mm gun fire. This wave landed opposite Cod, which was jointly attacked by 'C' Company. The CO, Lt.-Col. R.P.H. Burbery, was killed by a sniper. Three regimental flags with the roman numeral XL in silver (40th Regiment of Foot) were used as markers. One held by the battalion landing officer was easily spotted by incoming craft and another

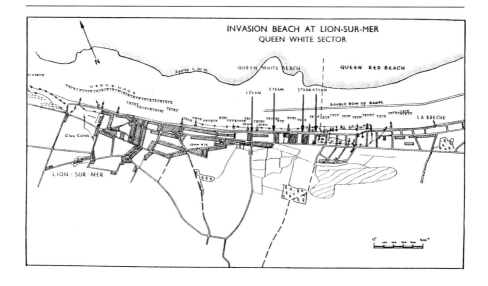

was held by the CO. The 2 i/c Maj. Jack Stone took over while 'B' helped deal with Cod. Their CO, Maj. R.H. Harrison, and his immediate successor, Lt. Bob Bell-Walker, were killed in action, but by 0830 hrs the opposition was overcome.

Harassed by machine gun fire and German stick grenades from the concrete fortifications, Ken Baxter related that:

> further action was promptly eclipsed by the arrival of Lt Tony Milne with his Vickers MG platoon in Brengun carriers of 2nd Bn Middlesex who were the first infantry fighting vehicles to land. Without a moment's hesitation, water-proofing shields were ripped away, gun clamps freed and the leading carrier drove straight at the trench line above our heads with a long swinging traverse from the Vickers depressing into the trench as they closed. A brief pause – silence – then at the end of the trench system some 15 survivors appeared in hasty surrender. COD was taken.

Bill Wellings was with 'A' Company South Lancs.

> At 0725 hrs our assault craft dumped us on the landing beach Sword Queen White. We were in a bad state, cold, wet, sick, glad to get off that bloody LCA. Our first holdup after landing was the wire. It must have been 8' high and 12' deep so our Bangalore team went into action. The first 6' length was slid under, then the second length was locked in and pushed under and the 3rd length was connected. The third man ran back and I think he forgot to light the fuse for it didn't go off. Our OC Major Spook Harwood told us to keep our heads down while he went off to

investigate. On his way he caught a burst of Spandau fire. He crawled forward and managed to light the fuse. He must have been in acute agony. As I ran through the gap in the wire he looked at me with a half smile on his face and I heard him say 'Carry on Wellings, I'll catch up later'. He died of his wounds about 0315 hrs on 7th June. We managed to get to the safety of the seaside villas. To my left CSM Murphy stood beckoning the next wave to come forward, the Coy runner Dickie Dallow by his side. Suddenly there was a fierce explosion and they both were killed instantly.

George Wilson, a platoon commander, South Lancs: 'We stepped off the landing barge into waist high deep water. We had a comparatively untroubled trip across the strip of sand – some 75 yards. I lost only one man killed and two with minor wounds and left them in the shelter of the seawall at the top of the beach and then walked through a large gap in the barbed wire belt.' Well briefed by the large-scale, accurate models of the beaches studied in England, George made his way to the first RV:

I found that the Coy CO and senior subaltern had been killed on the beach and the handful of men I found at the RV were remnants of the Company plus of course my almost intact platoon. As the senior survivor I took over the remnants of the Company and headed for our next RV – a group of buildings on the west side of the village of Hermanville. There I met Capt. Arthur Rouse, the Adjutant, and another party of South Lancs.

Later George was ordered to make a right flank recce:

We very soon came under small arms fire and were being picked off one at a time. We managed to get a Bren gun into position but the corporal and Bren gunner were both hit. My runner was hit and I received a small wound in my left arm. At this stage the enemy came through the cornfield in very purposeful fashion. I got a burst off at them from my Sten. [Later] My own CO, 2 i/c Capt. Murison (LOB) arrived, saw I had been hit and ordered me back to the beach for evacuation.

Lt. Eddie Jones, who commanded 8 Platoon 'A' Company, remembers:

Lion-sur-Mer looked astonishingly like Blackpool, instead of the promenade was a low sea wall, gently shelving golden sands, a line of boarding houses, though the sands were covered with tripods with mines on top. My own platoon, 8, in the centre of the Coy and Bob Pearce with 7 Pl. on my right pretty well on target but 9 Pl. Bill Allen with Coy HQ had been swept too far left and landed directly opposite COD, the enemy strongpoint. Both Bill Allen and Spook Harwood, my Coy Co were shot and killed or mortally wounded attempting to breach the wire entanglements with wire cutters. An AVRE Churchill tank came waddling up the beach, ploughed through most of the wire, then lost a track on a mine.

The surviving tanks of 'A' squadron 13/18th Hussars gave support, as Tpr. Bernard Cuttiford recalls:

There was very heavy congestion on the White Area and very limited exits. There was some shelling and sniping, making it a bit uncomfortable as it took nearly an hour to clear from the beach. The Colonel bypassed the assembly area and formed us south of Hermanville. 'C' Sqn (mine) pushed on and seized the high ground above Periers-sur-le-Dan overlooking Beuville which was reached after a fast advance and the ridge was found to be clear.

'B' and 'D' Companies of the South Lancs occupied Hermanville-sur-Mer with little opposition and Battalion HQ was sited near the church. Meanwhile 'A' Company was involved in street fighting in Lion-sur-Mer. Capt. A.R. Rouse wrote: 'A good deal of confused fighting followed with platoons and sections taking on their own targets. There were many acts of individual heroism. The confused fighting on the beaches lasted for a considerable time.' The South Lancs received a warm (French) welcome in Hermanville, where the battalion consolidated, with smiles, roses and Normandy cider. During the day they had 5 officers, including Col. Burbury and Maj. Harrison, and 13 ORs KIA, with another 6 officers and 83 ORs wounded, and a further 19 ORs missing – 126 altogether.

The Taking of Morris and Hillman

Lt.-Col. Dick Goodwin wrote:

The task given to my battalion 1 Suffolk was to land as reserve Bn in the Assault Brigade at H hour plus 60 mins, assemble inland, marry up with my tank squadron from 13/18th Hussars and capture in succession a four-gun battery, the village of Colleville-sur-Mer and a RHQ strongpoint which lay just south of Colleville. Both the battery (MORRIS) and the HQ strongpoint (HILLMAN) were surrounded by two belts of wire with a forty to fifty yard minefield between the two belts. This was a fairly comprehensive task for a Bn, the HQ strongpoint itself being some five hundred yards by two hundred and fifty yards. I gave to each of three rifle companies one of the three tanks and a breaching platoon from my fourth rifle Coy to whom was attached engineer and assault pioneer detachments to breach the two belts of wire and the minefield in each case.

In fact Hillman contained at least two 105-mm and two 75-mm guns, and numerous MG positions linked by trenches and pillboxes. The battalion had landed in one flight from twenty-five LCAs and by 0930 hrs had assembled near Hermanville and were advancing left into Colleville. Pte. Stanley Gardner with 'B' Company wrote in his journal: 'We had our first view of the German gun positions on the rise ahead. We stayed by the roadside for a while observing their position. It consisted of six pillboxes, some finished, some under construction, each one containing a heavy gun which fired down the beach.'

Col. Goodwin:

A shell had killed Capt Llewellyn, the FOB [Forward Officer Bombardment] and his entire party on the LCA next to mine. They controlled the fire of my naval support for the day – a 6-in cruiser and a destroyer – so for that day's operations I was without that support. . . . We moved quickly off towards Colleville and had little difficulty dealing with the battery and the village. As the Bangalore Torpedoes were being placed for the blowing of the outer wire, the garrison of sixty five surrendered.

Pte. Stanley Gardner: 'To my surprise white flags began to appear. Out they came, by ones and twos [mostly Poles], a woebegone, bomb happy crowd. We spent the rest of the day there.'

The RAF and the 6-in guns of the cruiser HMS *Dragon* had softened up Morris, which surrendered at 1300 hrs. But Hillman, half a mile away, was a far tougher nut to crack, defended by the Headquarters Company and infantry of 736th Grenadier Regiment. 246 Field Company RE was to clear the mines and barbed wire to allow 'A' Company 1st Suffolk (under Capt. Ryley) through. Lt. Arthur Head was the sapper officer who then crawled forward to place charges under the wire defences. Eric Lummis wrote in his '1 Suffolk in Normandy': 'Not a single bomb was dropped on Hillman because of heavy cloud and inadequate equipment for bombing blind. Six B 17s were allotted to drop a total of 228 one hundred pound bombs on Hillman. . . . No flails were allocated to 1 Suffolk to deal with the minefield', and as the CO pointed out, there was no available naval gun support. By now 76th Field and 33rd Field Regiments were ashore and their 25-pounders were in action on the beaches. Norman Scarfe's regiment, the 76th Field, in action on Queen Red beach, complained that there weren't enough calls for fire! Smoke targets (GRAB) were now fired on Hillman but the first attack that went in at 1310 hrs was swept away. The CO wrote:

the enemy were underground, fired their weapons from a steel cupola projecting 2 or 3 feet above ground level. The outer wire was breached about 50 yards apart . . . the pioneers were covered by small arms fire and smoke . . . casualties began to mount. Nothing we could do in the way of close supporting fire reduced the enemy's fire. The CO Coy was killed leading a charge. I found his body later on. He was right in the middle of the strong point. The leading platoon CO and his section commander were found dead over 200 yards inside the position . . . the steel cupolas were impervious to tank fire.

The GOC, Gen. Rennie, who had come ashore at 1030 hrs, visited Hermanville and 1 Suffolk. He told Lt.-Col. Goodwin: 'you must capture the strongpoint before dark and be dug in before the expected enemy armour counterattack is due in.'

'A' Squadron of the Staffordshire Yeomanry now arrived to join 'C' Squadron 13/18th Hussars with, in support, a two-battery 25-pounder fire plan. A combined attack through laboriously cleared minefields was more successful. Cpl. Rayson of 9 Platoon took part in the attack. 'A flail tank then appeared from somewhere and made a large track through the minefield, then up came three Sherman tanks and in we went again. . . . We put several grenades down the ventilation shafts plus a few smoke ones.' Fifty prisoners were taken and the success signal was given at about 2000 hrs that evening, after savage fighting in the deep shelters and galleries. By dawn another seventy prisoners had been taken, including a full colonel. During the day 1 Suffolk lost 2 officers and 5 ORs KIA and 25 ORs wounded. By nightfall the battalion was firmly dug in on the slopes of Perier ridge.

The Middlesex had a hand in the attacks on Morris and Hillman. Pte. Fred Wiltshire in 'A' Company: 'At the strongpoint 097785 MORRIS one of our carriers was hit by an antitank gun but our officer in charge fired a burst from his Vickers MG and killed the antitank gun crew. Soon after we came under mortar fire going through Colleville to attack Codename HILLMAN. A young French girl and a chap said they would look after one of our wounded comrades. He was my mate. He is now in Hermanville cemetery.'

The 2nd Battalion Middlesex Regiment mortars and MMGs were integrated throughout the division, with 'A' MG Company with the three assault infantry battalions: 1 Platoon with South Lancs, 3 Platoon with East Yorks and 2 Platoon with 1 Suffolk. L/Sgt. Watson was with 'A' Company HQ:

Our little party was in an LCI, five of us, two officers, three ORs and a 'Syd Walker's Barrow', a hand-cart carrying the 22 set which we were supposed to set up on landing. On arriving near the beaches we were faced with the worst sight possible. Tanks, carriers, bulldozers were all blazing away, men were running here and there. All around us landing craft were beaching and troops were going ashore under heavy shellfire. There was a direct hit on our stern as we were pulling into land. Several men were wounded, lying on deck, unable to move, blood everywhere! What a war! Why was I picked for D-Day?

L/Sgt. Watson and his 'ginger haired pal and the survivors were transferred to a Yankee Liberty boat. The skipper was first class, stood up on the bridge and shouted "Now for a song" and started to sing "There'll always be an England" – everyone was singing . . . our pull-in was first class.'

The MG carriers of 1 and 3 Platoons were ashore from LCTs by H+45.

CHAPTER SEVEN

185 Brigade's Plan

'A Bold Dash for Caen'

The immediate bridgehead on Sword beach would be secured by H+120 and Brig. K.P. Smith's 185 Brigade with Staffordshire Yeomanry tanks would advance from Hermanville to Lebisey and thence to Caen with 2 KSLI up, 2 Royal Warwicks on the right and 1 Royal Norfolks on the left flank. The rifle companies of all three battalions would land in one wave of LCIs with a small Battalion HQ on foot. Their vehicles would land at H+240. Between the beach and their objectives was open, rolling cultivated land similar to East Anglia, with a built-up area of rococo villas along the coast. Three main ridges lay between the sea and Caen, which itself lay in a valley, due south. Half a mile south of Hermanville (the assembly area) was the first ridge; 2 miles further south lay the second ridge with the village of Biéville on its summit. The third ridge was a further 1½ miles further south (and 3 miles north of Caen) crowned by thick woods and the village of Lebisey.

The ambitious plan for 1 Corps included orders for the Intermediate Brigade, i.e. 185 Brigade Group, to capture Caen and a bridgehead south of the river Orne at Caen. It seems surprising that Gen. Montgomery had ordered Gen. Dempsey, and then down the line via Gen. Crocker and Gen. Rennie to Brig. K.P. Smith, to capture the large well-defended city of Caen with one infantry brigade.

Back on the Beaches

Because of the high tide and a heavy swell, obstacle-clearing teams found it impossible to deal with tetrahedra and stakes . . . as the water rose, the narrow strip of beach became crowded with a nightmare jumble of men and machines forming up for their inland objectives. Exits were continually being blocked [wrote Maj. Raymond Birt, 22nd Dragoons] either by vehicles caught in soft sand or by those that foundered on mines. 629 Squadron RE had lost so many men and machines that they could no longer carry out beach clearance. [The 22nd Dragoon flail tanks] remaining on the beach forced their way out of the mass of men and equipment and began to beat out gaps to relieve the pressure on existing lanes. Every tank commander had to use his own initiative to keep traffic moving inland at all costs to clear out snipers, to sweep out lorry parks and to open the mine-infested roads. Sgt Turner, Corporal Aird and Trooper Hogg were all killed by mortar or small arms fire. By about 1000 [hrs] the worst was over and Captain Wheway was able to rally his remaining tanks just above the beach between two villas whose gardens were thickly dug with weapon slits and trenches, deep and secure beneath the foundations of the houses themselves.

The CRA Brig. G.G. Mears recalls:

By H+20 (0745 hrs) the first FOOs were ashore with the reserve companies. The leading Field Regiments would not be landing before H+60. Later the congestion on the beaches became a very serious problem. For the AA defence of the beaches, each division had under its command one Heavy and one Light AA Regiment. The LAA batteries landed first and by dusk a proportion of the HAA batteries and searchlights was in action and had a busy night. Four subalterns from 3rd British Div. volunteered for duty as airborne FOOs and dropped by parachute on the night D–1/D-Day and two were made prisoner.

With blackened faces, 2 KSLI under Lt.-Col. F.J. Maurice landed from their LCIs at 1010 hrs in 4 or 5 ft of water under shellfire.

We passed through the village of La Brèche and after a mile came to Hermanville. As we marched in single file with a gap of five yards between each man, French people came out of doors to welcome us, some shouting 'Vive les Anglais' to which I [Lt. Harry Jones, aged twenty-one, 10 Platoon 'X' Coy] replied in my best Churchillian French 'C'est la liberation'. The town's chief fireman in full regalia wearing his large bright-brass helmet rushed down the road to give me a great big hug . . . the plan was that we should ride on the tanks of the Staffordshire Yeomanry and attempt to capture Caen on D-Day. Unfortunately the tanks had great difficulty getting off the very congested beaches and some were knocked out by German 88 mm anti-tank guns firing from Periers Ridge about 800 yards south of us.

At 1230 hrs, without tank support, the KSLI set off on foot. Harry Jones had a series of adventures. He captured a German soldier armed with an automatic pistol. Harry had fired two revolver shots at him and missed! They lay in a ditch together to escape bullets flying overhead. He found one of his young corporals shot in the head. 'He died instantly. I valued him as someone I could lean on for advice, loyalty and friendship.' Then he opened fire with a Bren gun on lorries crammed with fleeing Boche 500 yds away. He discovered a bunker that had recently been occupied by the enemy – it had a very strong acrid smell of German tobacco. In Beuville he rescued his company commander who was 'holed up' by snipers who had shot two soldiers from the village church belfry, one on his right and one on his left. He asked a friendly M-10 of 20 A/Tank Regiment for help, and 'a shell smashed into the belfry and the bells suddenly rang out like the sounds of the bells in "Hunchback of Notre Dame"'.

Earlier that afternoon 'W' Company advanced on Periers-sur-le-Dan against considerable opposition. The enemy gun battery had not been knocked out by RAF or shore bombardment and fired on open sights at 2 KSLI. Maj. Wheelock with 'Z' Company was ordered to attack the battery but unfortunately the FOOs of 17/43rd Battery, 7th Field Regiment, were with 'X' and 'W' Companies, so fire could not be brought down. The battle was bitter, as the battery was surrounded by wire and the gunners well dug in. A Polish deserter showed the KSLI a way through the wire behind the battery. A brave sapper officer then 'spiked' the enemy guns, but thirty casualties had been taken including Lt. Percival, KIA, and Capt. Heatley, wounded. 'W' Company later mopped up around the Chateau de Biéville. On the western outskirts of Biéville a German shell landed a few feet away from Harry Jones' CO and two other platoon commanders during an 'O' group: 'advancing round the corner of a wood about 500 yards away were five or six German tanks! We hurriedly dispersed and I returned to my platoon. Despite all the UK training here we were closely grouped together, presenting an easy target!'

The war diary of the Staffordshire Yeomanry for D-Day mentioned: 'A terrible jam on the beach where no organisation appeared to be operating and no marked exits were to be seen. The majority of our tanks remained stationary for approx. 1 hour . . . and even after leaving the beach, vehicles remained head to tail for long periods on the only available routes.' By noon less than two squadrons of Yeomanry had managed to form up off the beaches and these were confined to the road network directly across the planned route of advance. Brig. K. Pearce Smith and the 2 KSLI CO, Lt.-Col. F.J. Maurice, both riding bicycles, met outside Hermanville to discuss the problem – whether the infantry should advance without tank support towards Caen – or not? They did advance, on foot! From the vicinity of Biéville the KSLI, with one squadron of tanks, made a bold dash for Caen. They were stopped by ferocious fire from Lebisey Wood, a mile to the south, and both leading company commanders were killed.

Tpr. Bernard Cuttiford, 2 Troop 'C' Squadron Staffordshire Yeomanry:

German guns and transport were engaged from Periers ridge but accurate shelling forced us to take cover. German 88mms knocked out five of our tanks and the MO's half track before they were silenced. Next we were ordered to clear Beuville and Biéville. Supported by the 2nd KSLI we crossed open country under murderous fire from a battery of 122 mm field guns at close range (talk about cowboys and Indians) however no losses were sustained [by SY] and after some confused and heavy fighting both villages were cleared.

Lt. Perring Thomas was troop commander, 'B' Troop 41 A/Tank Battery, 20 A/Tank Regiment, with M-10 tank destroyers: 'As soon as we left Hermanville about 2 pm, we came upon 5 Sherman tanks on fire and a very unhealthy look about the whole area. Walking wounded came back. The infantry were "over the hill" and progress was pretty difficult.' Biéville was barely 3½ miles short of Caen. 22nd Panzer Regiment under Col. von Oppeln had no less than twenty-four Mark IV tanks with 75 mm long-barrelled guns in front of Periers and Biéville. A spirited counter-attack now thrust for the coast. Lt. Perring Thomas: 'Late afternoon gunfire was heard on the far side of Biéville. Shortly afterwards two Mk IV Panzer tanks came out of cover about 2,000 yards away in the direction of Periers-sur-le-Dan. [The ideal fighting range was 800 yds or less.] Other tanks must have been working their way forward in dead ground and two more tanks suddenly appeared in hulldown position about half a mile away.' Perring Thomas' No. 1 M-10 gun was knocked out early on in the fight that followed, but the rest of his troop engaged: 'hits began to be observed and very rapidly both Panzers were stopped and on fire'.

Tpr. Cuttiford reported:

The CO ordered the release of 'A' Sqn [Staffordshire Yeo] to take up battle positions west of Biéville. The enemy [tanks] advanced fast and were engaged as soon as they reached the western end of the anti-tank obstacle. Two were knocked out, the others moved west into wooded country in the direction of Le Landel. Two troops of 'A' Sqn caught these tanks as they emerged at a range of about 600 yards and Sgt Joyce's gunner destroyed three of them before they reached cover. Another group of enemy tanks moved fast for the high ground above Periers-sur-le-Dan where 'B' Sqn destroyed three and drove the rest off.

In a short space of time no less than thirteen Mark IVs had been knocked out and the counter-attack halted. The indomitable 2 KSLI pushed ahead. 'Y' Company, under Maj. Steel, reached the northern outskirts of Lebisey at 1730 hrs, but were held up by heavy MG fire. 'They were driven back with heavy losses including the death of their CO', recalled Harry Jones.

Capt. R.R. Rylands, 2 i/c 'W' Company, wrote:

It was now evening. 'X' Coy were roughly level with us to the east. 'Z' were capturing the battery at Periers-sur-le-Dan and 'Y' had gone down the axis on to the dominating feature ahead – Lebisey. This place was reputedly weakly held but in fact was strongly held by Panzer Grenadiers, and 'Y' had a difficult tussle in which the Coy CO was killed. We consolidated in the orchard reached by 7 Pl. 'X' Coy moved in to our rear. Capt Dickie Tooth, our South African FOO from 7 Field Reg RA – our guardian angels – came forward to arrange rough treatment for the dead ground in front of us – and 'D' Day was over.

Lt.-Col. Tapp, CO 7th Field Regiment:

Although the KSLI got two companies into Lebisey wood they were in a very exposed position – no protection on the right or left flanks and nothing coming up behind. There were sounds of German tanks milling about on the ground between Lebisey and Caen. Furthermore the Lebisey ridge is very flat and the corn was high so visibility was poor. The Bn CO decided to consolidate his position round Biéville and Beuville. During the night the Germans heavily reinforced Lebisey with elements of 21 Panzer and 12 (SS) Panzer – it was to be six weeks before they were ejected.

At 1800 hrs Lt.-Col. Maurice realised further progress was hopeless and ordered the leading company to withdraw after dark to Biéville – which it did by 2315 hrs. Brig. K.P. Smith: 'Lebisey was a long straggly village with narrow heavily wooded lanes and commanding views of the whole area. . . . It was a formidable obstacle not revealed in the air photographs.'

Capt. Mike Quarmby of the 4th Dorsets landed in 4 ft of water from a (small) LCI at 1700 hrs on D-Day with some eighty Dorset ORs, many of whom were destined to join 3rd Division as reinforcements:

On the evening of 7th June we [Mike and twenty ORs] joined 2 KSLI at Biéville under full observation and continuous shelling so there could be no movement in daylight. Just as we reached the area in total darkness a terrific 'stonk' of shells came over and I leapt into the nearest slit trench – on top of the RSM! I was posted as 2 i/c to 'Y' Coy then commanded by Dick Dane, Major Steel had been killed on D-Day. Dick did not survive more than a month as he was later killed at Eureville. Guy Radcliffe the Adjutant was wounded by a mortar bomb. As I had served a period as Adjutant with 4 Dorsets in UK, Colonel Jack Maurice was greatly relieved to find someone to stand in for Guy. But for this good fortune I might well have met my end before we even got into Caen.

During D-Day 2 KSLI suffered 107 casualties and the CO, Lt.-Col. Maurice, earned the DSO.

On the right flank 1 Royal Norfolk, under Lt.-Col. R.H. Bellamy, touched down at about 1100 hrs, discarded their overtrousers and some of their bicycles and assembled near Colleville. Their orders were to reach strongpoint Rover between Beuville and the river Orne bridge by last light. It was clear that Hillman was giving 1 Suffolk a good deal of trouble, so two companies, 'A' under Capt. A.M. Kelly and 'B' under Maj. E.A. Cooper-Key, were sent off under Maj. Humphrey Wilson to detour round Hillman. For 2½ hours a firefight ensued, as Pte. W. Evans, 12 Platoon 'B' Company, recalls: 'We had covered two or three miles and were doing well until we came to a cornfield. Then Jerry machine guns in a small [*sic*] Pill Box opened up. The lads were soon being cut to pieces as the machineguns with their tremendous rate of fire scythed through the three foot high golden corn. That was the day I first saw the red poppies of France in the cornfield . . . .My nose was stuck right amongst them.' Later both companies disengaged and by last light the battalion was dug in round Rover at Bellevue, a mile further south, but still 4 miles north of Caen. A probable enemy counter-attack with tanks from 21 Panzer – who had reached Biéville – was now expected. In the firefight with Hillman, 'A' and 'B' Companies suffered about 50 casualties (including 6 KIA) and on D-Day 20 Norfolks were killed in action.

The landmark on the beach for Capt. H.C. Illing, OC 'A' Company 2nd Royal Warwicks, was a gable-ended house observed through binoculars. Their three LCIs beached at 0955 hrs: 'We could see the spouts of water shoot up as enemy bombs and shells fell into the sea and small clouds of black and white smoke rise up as the enemy fire came down on the beaches. The naval guns had lifted to targets behind as our planes swept overhead.' One LCI was hit offshore three times by shellfire, both its ramps shot away by mortar fire, and another hit a mine as it grounded. Dazed, by 1130 hrs all four rifle companies and Battalion HQ were half a mile inland at the assembly area. Marcus Cunliffe, the adjutant and author of the regimental history, wrote: 'Much of the battle was unpredictable. At one moment the scene was deceptively peaceful, at the next there came the "ping" of the sniper's bullet fired from some unseen cranny, the whine and crash of an approaching shell, the sudden murderous crump of mortar fire or the soft rapid deadly understatement of the Spandau MG. All these and many other sounds, the Royal Warwicks was soon to recognise as part of its new Lexicon.' And Capt. Illing: 'the war still did not seem really quite what we expected'.

The battalion was directed south-east through Colleville to Bénouville and Blainville on the river road to Caen, following the west bank of the river Orne. The commandos who had seized the canal bridges were now being counter-attacked by tanks and infantry of 21 Panzer. The Royal Warwicks were to link up and relieve the commando units. With the help of the glider fleet of 6 Airborne Division's follow-up, which descended literally on top of 'B' Company (killing two signallers by mistake), the village of Bénouville was taken. It was left in flames and guarded by 'D' Company while the remainder of the battalion, supported by tanks, pushed on and took Blainville 1½ miles south-east, and by midnight were dug in there. D-Day had cost the Warwicks 4 killed and 35 wounded.

Revd Jim Wisewell, 223 Field Ambulance RAMC, recalls:

Gordon Buffard, studious bachelor in 1944 – landed with others of us at about 10.15 a.m. on D-Day at Lion-sur-Mer. Remembering the bitter cold of a wet landing in the Moray Firth in January, he decided not to get

Bofors Gun on its Crusader chassis of 92 LAA Regt moving in from the beach on D-Day.

Lion-sur-Mer on D-Day – rococo villas.

his feet wet and climbed on one of the tanks with which we had shared the LCT. There were still snipers in some of the houses on the promenade and he would have been a sitting duck. But he landed unscathed – and dry! Perhaps they saw the Red Cross armlet and held their fire, observing the Geneva Convention. Our CO, Lt. Col. J.A.D. Johnson, MC, freely admits that, though we were often sandwiched between gun batteries, the German artillery respected our Red Cross. True, we did lose some ambulances and stretcher-carrying jeeps, but only once was the firing intentional.

Jack Hepworth from Cleckheaton, now living near Bradford, was at one end of a rolled-up stretcher when we landed, and I was at the other. Shelling and mortaring made the beach at Lion-sur-Mer unhealthy and the Beach-master roared at us to get off inland! Small arms fire and mortars were pretty constant as we pushed through the tumbled bricks and twisted telegraph wires littering the streets. At one point we took cover in a shallow gutter, waiting for a lull. Before it came, the door opened in a house across the way and a young nurse came out, mounted her bicycle and rode calmly away. Shamefaced we got up and did not stop again until we got to Hermanville. I meet her every year on June 6th. She is Jacqueline Thornton who married a soldier of the 3rd Division.

The support brigade landed at 1300 hrs and the brigadier, John Cunningham, was amazed to meet not only the GOC, Maj.-Gen. Rennie, in Hermanville, but also the Corps commander, Lt.-Gen. John Crocker – both of them of course wearing their red hats! New orders were issued for 9 Brigade, to relieve the Airborne troops at 'Rugger', shortly to be called 'Pegasus' bridge, instead of pushing south-west for Carpiquet aerodrome and Caen via Cazelle, Cambes and St Contest.

It was clear at this early stage that the ambitious plans to reach Caen by the end of D-Day had been abandoned.

'I got as far as my armoured car,' wrote Brig. John Cunningham at Brigade HQ, 'and my anti-tank gunner Arthur Onions and others converged on me. We received a stick of six mortar bombs. It killed six including three inside the armoured vehicle, and wounded six more. I was unable to transmit my new orders. Dennis Orr [Cunningham's 2 i/c] had already gone to Pegasus Bridge, so could not take over from me and some delay occurred.' Cunningham had both arms smashed and was invalided out of the army in 1947. Col. Orr was promoted to brigadier of 9 Brigade.

John St John Cooper, 2 RUR, crossed the Channel in LCI 973: 'in the tiny wardrooms the company commanders "Digger" Tighe-Wood, John Aldworth, Stewart de Longueuil and John Hyde, studied their maps. Below men lay in their bunks, heads resting on haversacks, each one feeling alone – alone as never before – thinking of home – Derry, Belfast, Dublin,

Ballymena. Some prayed, some were sick, to others came the peace of sleep.'
The 2nd Battalion RUR landed from LCIs at 1000 hrs, west of Ouistreham.
They landed in 4–5 ft of water in a heavy surf. CSM Walsh of 'A' Company
and Rifleman Ryan MM of 'B' Company took a lifeline ashore to help
beaching, as many of the riflemen were small in stature and were carrying
heavy kit and a bicycle. At their assemby area, Lion-sur-Mer, half a mile
inland, they were met by guides and dug in for the night at Point 61 north-
east of Periers-sur-le-Dan. Seven snipers and a further ten POWs were
captured.

Maj. Alastair Rennie, OC 'C' Company 1 KOSB, recalls:

We landed at 1030 wet with the rising tide. Engineers and 'Funnies'
casualties strewing the shoreline. Lord Lovat prominent, still directing the
Commandos. Rapid exit through minefield clearance. Gas capes covering
dead; forlorn German prisoners. Apprehensive French appear, expecting
German counterattack. Advance to Hermanville. Increasing enemy
reaction. Dig first foxholes, indispensable for survival as 21 Panzers begin
their co-ordinated defence. Abandon bicycles due to carry us to Caen
that evening.

Maj. H.S. Gillies, OC 'C' Company:

Our first rude awakening, news was received – our Brigade HQ had been
decimated by a mortar concentration. Time wore on. Afternoon well
advanced, ordered by route march to St Aubin d'Arquenay to protect the
landing zone of Air Landing brigade, 6th Airborne later that evening –
paramount importance. Towards sunset, unforgettably moving,
impressive spectacle glider-borne Bd. came in low from the sea, landed in
open country immediately to our front. Supply parachutes in all colours
came drifting down from the escorting planes as the gliders cast off and
swooped into the corn.

Sgt. Fred Hartle, 16 Platoon 'D' Company, heard the company pipers
playing 'Blue Bonnets' as they left the beaches. Skirting a minefield on the
way to St Aubin he then heard the 'phut, phut' of German mortars for the
first time. In an orchard he came across a sniper's hideout in the branches of
a tree, a smock with a wallet inside hanging on the platform. The infantry
companies of 1 KOSB managed to get a brew of tea and dug in towards the
end of D-Day. On their way, near Lion-sur-Mer, their padre Iain Wilson
saw 'a few French civilians pressing cider and wine on the men and cheering
feebly. Old old woman waved a Union Jack and Tricouleur'.

Jack Harrod, IO of 2nd Battalion Lincolnshires, wrote in his *Bn History
Tenth Foot*: 'We cleared the beach immediately without a single casualty – a
remarkable record in such an operation. A tribute to the efforts of the Navy,
the RAF and the assaulting brigades. On the beaches we made our first

contact with the enemy but every one had his hands up and was being shepherded into the PO cage with energetic lunges from British bayonets.' But while the battalion was digging in around Cresserons, 'D' Company suffered thirteen casualties, guarding the division's right flank.

Frank Faulkner was the Recce Sergeant with 2 Platoon 17 Field Squadron RE, commanded by Lt. Ted Crush. The troop sergeant Jim Graham was Frank's closest friend.

On D-Day our task was to get 185 Brigade off the beach through the minefields and obstacles. In our spare time we acted as infantry. We advanced as far as Lebisey wood where we came under very heavy mortar and MG fire and tank attack. We were forced to withdraw to the Chateau de Beauville area. Our OC Major D. Willison was wounded and evacuated with two other officers and our 2 i/c Capt. Watson killed. This left us very short of officers.

1 and 3 Platoons made their way to Pegasus bridge and linked up with the 6 Airborne troops holding the bridge.

So ended the 'longest day'. Caen had not been taken, and was never in any danger of being taken, but a bridgehead 4 miles wide and 5 miles deep had been breached.

CHAPTER EIGHT

Expanding the Bridgehead

'Don't Shoot, Jock, We're the Paddies'

It was difficult to realise that the day for the invasion of Normandy – for which many of the Iron Division had been waiting for four years – had come and gone at a high cost. Over six hundred young soldiers were dead or wounded. But the news from neighbouring 50 Tyne Tees Division, attacking Gold beach then taking Bayeux, was good, and the Airborne were more than holding their own. No one gave a thought to the German coastal defenders' amazing courage in the face of the huge overwhelming naval and RAF bombardmants and the iron monsters coming out of the sea – flail tanks, DD tanks, flame throwers, AVRE petards. The command of the air was very soon taken for granted. The RAF dominated the skies except for desultory Luftwaffe Fockewulf sorties and insignificant bombing of the beaches at night. Sgt. Charles Packer, 1 KOSB, whose company was riding off the beach on their bikes: 'We had a Junkers 188 trying to strafe us but two Spitfires saw him off.' However, 92 LAA shot down seventeen German planes in the next few days mainly round the bridge at Bénouville. Nevertheless, German pillbox defences, with dug-in tanks and minefields everywhere all round Caen, would soon prove that Rommel was going to defend that vital city – the anvil – come what may. Indeed a strongpoint in Lion-sur-Mer was held tenaciously for another two days. The garrison of 716th Division had been reinforced by 22nd Panzer Regiment tanks and 1st/192nd Panzer Grenadiers in their counter-attack in the afternoon of D-Day. Gen. Rennie ordered 9 and 185 Brigades to thrust aggressively south towards Caen with Cambes and Lebisey as the main objectives.

The First Battle for Cambes

On the right flank 2nd RUR and 1 KOSB started their advance towards Cambes-en-Plaine, leap-frogging up the centre line: Periers–Mathieu–Le Mesnil. The RUR reported the village of Periers clear, and 1 KOSB moving through found Cazelle (i.e. Mathieu) clear, though Padre Wilson noted: 'six Heinkels suddenly appeared out of the clouds prepared to attack us, but a swarm of our fighters quickly engaged them and drove them off. Half a mile further on we reached a fairly large wood – Le Mesnil – when we were

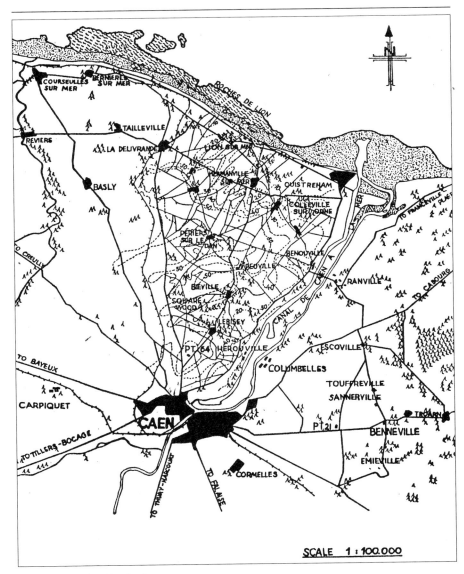

Plan of Operation Overlord

ordered to halt and dig in, much to Colonel W.F.R. Turner's chagrin. As we were digging, heavy and accurate mortar concentrations came down inflicting bad [eight] casualties on 'B' and 'C' Companies.' At one stage 1 KOSB appeared to be surrounded and a break-out was ordered, while the Pipe Major struck up 'Blue Bonnets'. But the heavy small arms fire and tracer were from a recce party of British tanks. 'We laughed rather nervously, heaved a sigh of relief and went back to our trenches.' Maj. R.B. Moberley, 2nd Middlesex, wrote:

> At Le Mesnil Wood, Brigadier Orr's carrier [now commanding 9 Brigade] was hit and brewed up and a nearby carrier of 5 Platoon was popping away with 9000 rounds of ammunition. Behind the Brigadier who had hopped out of his carrier briskly and strolled into the orchard, came Col. Weston on the back of Sgt Davis' m/cycle. The m/c was hit by shrapnel, the CO and Sgt Davis had a long crawl and run to the wood being fired and sniped at throughout from the exposed flank. Sgt Davis said to his CO 'If those chaps had been in our Army, Sir, they'd have lost their bloody proficiency pay.'

By the end of the day Sgt. Davis had earned a bar to his MM, but 2nd Middlesex suffered fifteen casualties supporting 1 KOSB in Le Mesnil woods.

Cambes village, 1,000 yds ahead, was strongly held and the forward platoons were heavily mortared. But 2nd RUR were now ordered to take Cambes with 'D' Company under Capt. Aldworth. There were 10-ft stone walls around the two woods, which thwarted both the tanks of East Riding Yeomanry and the Ulster infantry attack. Four Messerschmitts attacked the rest of the battalion. The attack on Cambes failed with heavy losses, including Capt. Aldworth among 15 KIA, 12 wounded, 4 missing and 2 stretcher-bearers killed. A heavier artillery plan was now needed.

The First Battle for Lebisey

From Blainville the Royal Warwicks were ordered to attack Lebisey wood, 3,000 yds to the south-west, on the northern outskirts of Caen. Across the road on the west side was the village of Lebisey, the next objective. The wood was to be captured by 'B' Company on the right and 'A' on the left, 'C' to pass through and clear the right half. A natural anti-tank ditch would make tank support ineffective. It was thought that the opposition would be light, but the previous evening 125th Panzer Grenadiers (of 21st Panzer Division), a formidable opponent, had arrived and dug in among existing dug-outs. Highly experienced, they laid a trap for the Warwicks, whose artillery and naval support had been called off at the last moment by Col. Herdon. 'A' Company had been delayed from getting to the start line by snipers, 'B' and 'C's rearlink communications were not working and they moved across the cornfields. At almost point-blank range the Panzer Grenadiers opened up with everything they had. Capt. John Talbot, their 7th Field Regiment FOO: 'We were pinned down all day about 100 yards short of the wood. My Pack RT set was the only link with the Division as all other sets failed to work!' Lt. Dockerley ('B' Company) and his platoon were destroyed.

'A' Company on the left was also pinned down and Capt. Illing and Lt. Adams wounded, as he relates: We eventually got into the wood where control became very difficult. I was hit by a phosphorous grenade and burst of MG fire from a hidden position in front of me. . . . The company held on to the edges of the wood until the rest of the Bn came up . . . but they were unable to move further forward.' The assault pioneer platoon CO, Lt. Wilson, was killed and the CO was caught by MG fire, shot through the head and killed. The 2 i/c, Maj. Kreyer, took over under continuous fire until 1500 hrs when 'D' Company (which had been guarding the Bénouville bridges) arrived, led by Maj. Bundock, and put in an attack on the north-east corner of the wood. The enemy now brought up some tanks. The Warwicks' day of ill fortune continued. Capt. Bannerman with his carrier-towed A/Tank guns was ordered down from Biéville to join the battalion and counter this threat. 'We had gone for about half a mile when all hell let loose. The noise was fantastic, cracking and humming past us. Luckily the banks were high . . . we pressed on up the hill . . . and fired our Bren and Stens at either side as we passed. Suddenly appeared a low bridge and a mass of rubble and broken houses that was Lebisey. Worse still was the sight of scurrying Germans as we careered forlornly into the middle of them.' An 88-mm gun knocked out his carrier, and he and his crew were captured, joining Capt. Pike the adjutant, Capt. Waterworth the carrier officer, Lt. Healey the mortar officer, and a number of men in captivity. Many guns and vehicles were lost.

The next day when the Warwicks prisoners were marched into Caen, the SS Panzer unit 'lined up along the road, men and boys in black who jeered and laughed at us'. By 1600 hrs when the rifle companies were nearly out of ammunition and under tank attack, Lt. Walton, 'D' Company, was killed. It was a very black day for the Warwicks. Their losses during the day were 10 officers and 144 ORs. Maj. Kreyer was awarded the DSO for the Lebisey battle.

Lt. Geoffrey Forrest was a LO at 185 Brigade HQ. On D+1 he had been with the Cannucks. On his return:

Brigadier told me that both the Warwicks [his own regiment] and the Norfolks had taken some medicine on D+1 and that all three Bns and the Staffordshire Yeomanry [tanks] had fought like veterans in their first battle. The result was about 200 casualties each and about 150 to the KSLI. But the Boche still held the Lebisey feature overlooking Caen. We had done jolly well to get that far – complete success of the landings. I learnt with chagrin that Pike, Waterworth, Healey and Bannerman, all friends of mine of the Warwicks were missing, one or two wounded and one of my best pals, Alan Dockerty, killed. The CO got his too as did Tony Wilson. Dickie Pratt had been hit as soon as he set foot on French soil and went back home in the same craft!

Carriers of 2nd Bn Royal Warwicks head along a battle-scarred lane near Lebisey. (IWM, B6646)

On 8 June reinforcements arrived of 5 officers and 150 men. Maj. Ryan took over 'A' Company in place of Capt. Illing and soon Lt.-Col. D.L.A. Gibbs arrived as the new CO.

The 1st Norfolks were sent forward to assist the beleaguered Warwicks. Up they went across the cornfields on the right of the Warwicks but could not make any progress against the Panzer Grenadiers with their tank support.

John Lincoln's book, *Thank God and the Infantry*, relates: 'the attack on D+1 to retrieve the situation in front of Lebisey wood cost us nineteen lives including Lts Campbell, Toft and Sharp.' Maj. H.M. Wilson: 'Hugh Bellamy (the CO) sent me back to Brigade HQ to tell the story and get orders. I found the Brigadier who told me that Hugh was the only person who could make any local decisions and wishing me goodbye as if I was going to certain death. At 9 o'clock Hugh decided to pull out bringing what there was of the Warwicks, who had lost their CO, with us.' And at last light as the last troops left the area, the enemy shelled and mortared it severely. Lt. Norman Brunning at Brigade HQ wrote: 'At about 6 pm reports of the first battle for Lebisey Wood began to come in. The Warwicks were down to about 60–80 men and very few of them had any weapons. The Norfolks were down to 300 men: the KSLI as fire support battalion had not suffered too badly. It was all very depressing. However during the night a number of men returned until the Warwicks totalled about 400 and the Norfolks 500.' D+1 had been another day of bloody fighting for the Iron Division.

The Second Battle for Cambes

On 9 June, D+3, 9 Brigade was ordered to capture St Contest, a village of great strategic importance due west of Lebisey overlooking the north-west suburbs of Caen. 2 RUR under their CO, Col. Harris, was to lead, and capture and consolidate Cambes-en-Plaine, advancing from Anisy about 1,500 yds north-west of their objective. The day before had seen vigorous patrolling around Le Mesnil by 25 Panzer Grenadier Regiment and 'C' Company RUR.

The supporting barrage from the divisional artillery and the 6-in guns of HMS *Danae* preceded the attack at 1515 hrs. East Riding Yeo Sherman tanks were also in support. 'A' Company was on the left under Maj. 'Digger' Tighe-Wood and 'B' on the right under Maj. J.W. Hyde. They soon reached the ridge 400 yds to the front and came under a heavy DF barrage. Men were dropping all round and 'A' Company lost all three platoon commanders: Lt. Hall was killed, Lt. Walsh and Lt. St John Cooper both wounded. The latter noted: 'My platoon as the Army nicely puts it "had the honour of leading the attack on the left." In the event we soon came under a barrage of shell, mortar and MG fire. By the end of the action we had lost 10 officers and 172 ORs – almost one third of the Bn. In fact in just one area of 10 sq. yards there were 10 Ulstermen and 6 Germans all lying dead (casualties from the D+1 attack).'

Sgt. John Eales, 'C' Company:

Supporting the dug-in tanks was the crack Hitler Youth Division. These had no fear. They had been trained from children to fight for the Fatherland – aged 13–17 years, they were merciless. There was no such thing as failure where they were concerned. Men were dropping all around me. It was a hard battle for Cambes, both us and the enemy sustained heavy casualties. We also discovered that the wounded from the previous attack had been shot by the enemy. We also had two stretcher-bearers killed while attending to the wounded.

Nearly 200 Ulstermen were killed, wounded or were missing in the taking of Cambes. Three MCs, a DCM and two MMs were awarded.

Roly Curtiss, 'E' Troop 113/114 Field Battery, was the radio-operator on the FOO Sherman tank under Capt. 'Nipper' Roose, with Jack Arnold co-driver, L/Bdr. Jackson gun layer/assistant driver, and Charlie Weeks driver:

Our guns of 33rd Field Reg were at Periers-sur-le-Dan. We called some fire down on some enemy vehicles. We were spotted and a large HE shell hit the top engine casing of the tank. [Two days later] On D+3 during a skirmish on the outer edge of [Cambes] wood another HE shell hit our turret. Our Capt [Roose] was killed outright, his body slumped in the turret. The driver received shrapnel wounds to his arm, having entered via his periscope. A blue flash shot through the inside of the tank and I thought we were all goners. The tank engine stopped. We gathered our wits, dropped the escape hatch below and made our way to a first aid post in a large village house which the RUR were using.

Alastair Renny, 1 KOSB: 'We attacked Cambes to support the Ulsters across open cornfield against desultory fire, also from our own tanks falling short. Enter the wood – a grisly tableau of intermingled Ulstermen and SS dead, my friend John Aldworth amongst them.' Maj. Gillies, 1 KOSB: 'Across one thousand yards of open cornfields – well-sited MG and intense mortar fire enfiladed the companies as they moved forward. Like a WWI battle called for much resolution and steel nerves as tracer bullets flicked off the corn. Casualties began to mount as we pressed forward. My Coy 2 i/c organised effective 2" mortar smoke screen to cover our open flank and we contacted the RUR.' The chaplain, Iain Wilson, continues:

After a sharp battle at close quarters with the 12th SS Hitler Youth Panzer Div – the village and woods were cleared at dusk. No sooner had darkness fallen the anti tank guns and other supporting arms were brought up against a probable counter-attack. Blundering about among a jumble of branches, trenches and bodies we flung ourselves in any sheltered spot, completely exhausted while the stretcher-bearers searched the cornfields for casualties.

In the fading light the Scots were delighted to hear the Irishmen shout, 'Don't shoot, Jock, we're the Paddies.' Fred Hartle with 'D' Company was given the order to fix bayonets at the start line and move across the cornfield in extended order.

Having cleared Cambes Wood of the enemy, we came under heavy shell and mortar fire. Several of the platoon were killed or wounded. I've never seen fox holes dug so fast. I had a Spandau bullet through one leg and a chunk of shell through the other. Brought back on top of a Jeep to our RAP our MO 'Doc' Wright, a magnificent character, sorted us out whilst our Irish padre, Father O'Brien, provided hilarious comfort. He said on looking at St John Cooper's legs, 'Ah well, Johnny, someone should tell them Jerries to put their sights up. Sure they'll never kill anyone that way thank God.'

Digger Tighe-Wood:

One platoon was now commanded by a corporal [O'Reilly] and only one sergeant and one lance-sergeant left in the company. Some enemy could be seen pulling out from the area of the chateau in the wood. 'B' Coy had come through the fire with not quite so many casualties and were advancing into the village. The enemy all had the SS insignia with the legend Adolf Hitler Jugend on their sleeves. 'C' Coy with three AVRE tanks now passed through 'A' Coy and captured the far edge of the village and wood. They took on a Mk IV tank and knocked it out with bombards but advancing beyond the village were all destroyed by 88-mm guns [firing from La Bijude].

10 Platoon of 'B' Company passed with great dash through the village to the Norman church and by 1630 hrs 'A' and 'B' had reached their objective. Having captured Cambes, the enemy retaliated with five hours of vicious DF fire and digging in was carried out with great difficulty. Maj. Brooks, the FOO of 33rd Field Regiment and a very popular commander, was killed. His CO, Col. Tom Hussey, and another FOO, Capt. Roose, were also killed that day.

CHAPTER NINE

Stalemate

War of Attrition

For four weeks the Iron Division held the front line. It was clear that Rommel intended to hold Caen at all costs with dug-in tanks, many Minenwerfers, 88 mms and massed Panzer Grenadiers. 185 Brigade was on the left flank (east) from Blainville on the Canal de Caen to Biéville; in the centre was 8 Brigade, well in front of Periers, holding Le Mesnil wood on the left of the main road to Caen. But the enemy still held a salient – the Chateau de la Londe and the two farms of La Londe and Le Landel. On the right (west) flank 9 Brigade held Cambes and part of Le Mesnil wood to the west of the main Caen road. So this front line between Cambes wood and the Canal de Caen was held until Caen eventually fell on 9 July. By the end of June no less than 64 infantry battalions and 725 enemy tanks were pinned into the Caumont–Caen sector opposite the British and Canadian armies.

On 13 June the GOC, Gen. Tom Rennie, was being driven to Cambes to visit 2 RUR RAP, by Lt.-Col. Wood, RAMC, commanding 9th Field Ambulance. Unfortunately, their jeep was blown up on a newly laid 'friendly' minefield, both officers were wounded and the GOC was evacuated back to England on 18 June.

Alastair Renny, 1 KOSB, recalls: 'General Tom Rennie on recce in his jeep with ADMS blown up on my Hawkins grenades necklace protecting our front. The GOC staggers over saying "As one Rennie to another, that was entirely my fault." But I was consoled my Hawkins had been so effective. The General was a delightful unassuming man whose nonchalant bravery reaped its sad sequel on the Rhine.'

His successor Gen. 'Bolo' Whistler, who had already won three DSOs at Dunkirk and with the Desert Rats in North Africa and Italy, arrived on 23 June to take command. His best-known nickname, 'Bolo', was derived from his 1919 Archangel expedition against the Bolsheviks. His Brigade Major, D.S. Gordon, described him: 'He had of course the presence and the personality which enabled him to win the hearts and minds of all who served under him. A decisive manner, often brutally frank and outspoken, he always had a twinkle in his eye and a most infectious grin. After every action he would always visit his field ambulance to see and offer a word of comfort and cheer to the wounded. A great Christian and a great soldier.'

Monty thought highly of him: 'about the best Infantry Brigade Commander I know [131 Queens Brigade] and later a superb Divisional Commander.' He was a tall, straight and strong man, whom soldiers would follow anywhere. Bolo wrote in his diary: '1 July have so far managed to get myself nearly killed at least twice. The soldiers did a pretty magnificent job in the assault and are going to be something quite out of the ordinary. Still not liking being a General much. It is above my standard one way and another.'

9 Brigade Front: 'The Sickening Odour of Rotting Bodies'

Jack Harrod, 2 Lincolns:

> One of the most trying periods in this, or any, war. Still eager to press forward and still confident that we could do so, we were compelled to sit and hold. Antitank guns were carefully sited, nights were spent in laying minefields and days in improving slit-trenches. Even a bulldozed track – a sort of super communication trench – was constructed as a covered supply route to the isolated forward positions in Cambes. The Brigade Commander rang the changes and at regular intervals the Bn moved into Cambes to relieve one of the Bns there or back again to Le Mesnil for a comparative rest. It was a wearing business. Throughout the day it appeared as if we just waited for those brief but devastating periods of intense mortar and shellfire which we knew would inevitably come; and by night we harassed the enemy with our patrols.

One such patrol was on the night of 17/18 June. Capt. Gilbert, CO 'C' Company, raided Galmanche from Cambes wood. One patrol under Lt. Patey attacked from the east, another under Sgt. Ward from the west. Fierce hand-to-hand fighting took place against the Hitler Jugend. Lt. Pacey was wounded and Sgt. Ward, though surrounded, fought his way out with grenades and bayonet, rescuing two wounded men. Ray Paine: 'We stayed quite a while in the Cambes wood and Galmanche area. The Channel storms played havoc with our supplies so we could only fire our mortars if the infantry company needed help. Every day at mid-day we were shelled for 15 minutes. We even dug out pits so that we could put our carriers below ground. Nevertheless we took a lot of casualties during that month.' Lt. Brown and 18 ORs were killed, including CSM Watson of 'A' Company, and 7 officers and 96 ORs were evacuated with wounds, including 3 company commanders.

Iain Wilson, chaplain 1 KOSB, wrote of the devastated French countryside:

> The trees [in Cambes] had been stripped and shredded by the furious

bombardments and the paths and lawns were littered with branches. The Chateau was blasted and gutted and the village wrecked and empty save for a few old women who still crept about in the ruins; the gardens and orchards were dishevelled and torn up and over everything hung the sickening odour of rotting bodies. Bloated cattle and horses lay on their backs with legs stiffened pointing awkwardly skywards; our own and the enemy dead lay where they had fallen, sprawling and grotesque. Trenches and dugouts were choked with the usual depressing litter of battle – helmets, bits of equipment, broken rifles, burst open boxes with long strings of bullets, respirator cases, scraps of uniform and the like. It took hours to collect the dead and their burial was a long and dangerous process under the intermittent shelling and sniping which commenced that day and subsequently never eased off for more than an hour or two. The enemy were in an arc approx. 600 yards from Cambes in strongly fortified localities at La Bijude, Epron and Galmanche. Bn HQ was established in a deep dugout built by the SS. The RAP was set up in the Chateau cellars where church services were also held and Communion administered by candlelight.

Sgt. Fred Hartle, 'D' Company: 'We were there a month. This meant patrolling in front of the Bn position. I got to know the ground quite well especially St Contest, Lebisey and La Deliverande. Led by Capt. Skinner MM we were out most nights on patrol and tried to sleep at the bottom of the slit trenches during the day but the constant rumble of artillery fire made it difficult.' On one KOSB patrol they were ambushed, so Fred carried a wounded lad back. 'He was yelling out with pain and this attracted the Germans who threw some stick grenades at us, which fell short. I crawled back with him for 200 yards, put him behind a bank.' Capt. Skinner and Maj. Donald Gray were both wounded while on patrols. On another patrol 'we cycled through narrow twisting lanes (to contact Canadian 3rd Div) and came across a German staff car. The door was open and a high ranking German Army officer was halfway out of the car. The outriders on motorcycles were layed about around the car, all killed by RAF strafing planes. We contacted Canadians at Carpiquet airbase, half held by them, the other half by the Germans.' On another occasion: 'Capt. Drinkall detailed me to take two men and enter a brewed-up Churchill tank lying between us and the German lines. We crawled up to it, yanked open the trapdoor above the bogie and tracks (the Germans were only 60–70 yards away). A huge cloud of flies rose and flew through the turret. I entered the tank. All the crew had been killed. I could not retrieve the identity disks of the crew due to the damage done to the bodies.'

From 20 to 29 June 1 KOSB went back into reserve at Le Mesnil farm, then back to Cambes. Up to 6 July they had suffered 160 casualties.

The Royal Ulster Rifles stayed in action in Cambes wood for four weeks with only four days out of the line in reserve. Charles Graves' regimental

Sgt. J.R. Hartle, 1 KOSB. (J.R. Hartle)

history records: 'The regular strafing was soon the cause of much laughter and singing of such songs as "Run, Rabbit, Run". Cambes was not liked . . . strong fighting patrols soon took up the offensive.' As a result of their ferocious battle for Cambes wood on 9 June, MCs were awarded to Maj. Tighe-Wood, Capt. Montgomery and Lt. Lennox. To Cpl. O'Reilly went the DCM and to L/Sgt. McCann, Riflemen Long and McGlenon, went the MM.

Sgt. John Eales: 'We were ordered to dig in, and dig in we did. We made ourselves nice and comfy in our trenches. We were bombed at night, carried out numerous patrols, encountered Poles, Czechs and Slavs – an understrength unit. We lost an average of five men a day from shellfire, killed or wounded.' The battle patrols were trained and operated by Maj. Charles Sweeney with Sgts. Murphy and Martin as patrol 'leaders'.

CHAPTER TEN

The Terrible Operation Mitten

8 Brigade Front

From 10 June the South Lancs patrolled for several days around Le Landel and the chateau, being shelled and mortared for most of the five days and between 7 and 15 June incurring seventy-three casualties.

James 'Smudger' Smith recalls a strange story. 'C' Company South Lancs had a young Chinese soldier in its ranks, born in East London, who 'had a right cockney accent'. Pte. Ling was a lookout in a hole in the wall of a barn at La Londe: 'We were all told not to wave our hands or make any movement to attract enemy attention. Ling waved his hands about trying to tell us there were some Tiger tanks advancing towards us. All of a sudden – a loud explosion – an 88-mm shell hit the opening. There was very little left of him.'

Lt. Eddie Jones, 8 Platoon of 'A' Company, recalls: 'On 10th June we had walked in and occupied the Chateau which is surrounded by a solid stone wall with accompanying farmhouse, outbuildings and barns. But at first light one morning the enemy brought up a troop of SP guns and shelled my platoon position for several minutes at point black range, several men were killed. The walls were reduced to rubble.' So the South Lancs withdrew and prepared for the second attack on 21 June.

La Londe battle the most harrowing – most of the original Bn officers, many of the longer serving men were lost there and the Bn was never the same again. Shelling and mortaring of Le Landel area was intensified with little respite. We had been trained in the tactics of right and left flanking movements but here there were no flanks and the enemy had to be reached by direct approach across open cornfields. Some of the older officers prophesied a stalemate, repeat of trench warfare of First World War.

Lt. Jones continues: 'After dark on the 22nd "B" and "C" Coys moved up right and left in a silent attack [on the Chateau]. "C" was held up by heavy MG fire, and "B" established itself in the orchard in SW corner of La

Londe position. Early on 23rd I moved 8 platoon ["A" Coy] forward to reinforce "B" under Capt Murison and occupied enemy slit trenches. I do not believe the rest of "A" Coy actually reached La Londe but were driven back by the intense fire.' Disaster followed. The battalion A/T guns were slow to come up, and behind a heavy DF plan of mortar, artillery and smoke, enemy tanks overran 'B' Company, crushing many of them in their slit trenches. 'Capt Greener was wounded and evacuated. We were isolated for three days under fire, several men were picked off by snipers. A night patrol led by a Scottish Sgt from "D" Coy just arrived when a salvo of shells landed on the track and blew them to pieces.'

La Londe was reckoned to be the 'bloodiest square mile in Normandy'. The 192 Panzer Grenadiers, the HQ company of 22 Panzer Regiment, backed by a score of tanks, were determined to hold the salient of Le Landel, La Londe, Chateau de la Londe and La Bijude. The GOC 3rd Division was equally determined to eliminate this salient – hence Operation

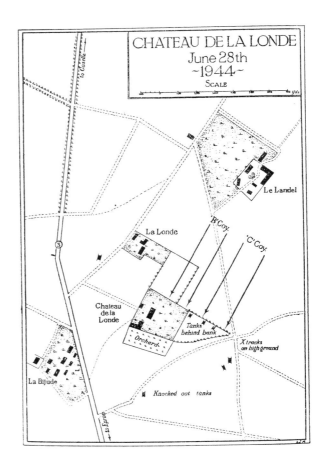

Mitten. This was to be an 8 Brigade responsibility. The South Lancs would try a third time at 1530 hrs on 27 June, supported by the divisional artillery and Staffordshire Yeomanry Shermans and a troop of Crocodile flame-throwers, but dug-in Tigers and Mk IV tanks and concealed MGs inflicted, again, very heavy casualties. Maj. W.R. Birt wrote: 'Captain Wheway, with 2 Troop "C" Sqn, 22nd Dragoons went forward to reduce the salient on the British line. The South Lancs managed to reach and hold La Londe but could not take the chateau around which the enemy had dug in more than 30 tanks supported by elements of 192 Pz. Grenadiers.' Lt. Eddie Jones, with 'A' Company South Lancs, had got to within 50 yds of the chateau:

> We were subjected to intense MG fire from both flanks and the front and at the same time we were heavily mortared. Many men became casualties at once, others took refuge in the ditch and crawled back. I and two riflemen were cut off completely from the rest of the company, the slightest movement on our part provoking the heaviest enemy fire. A Crocodile flamethrower was burning with its turret blown off . . . when dusk came we were able to return to Le Landel and report to Bn HQ where we learned that our attack had been called off and that a Brigade attack was planned a few hours ahead.

At 0415 hrs on the 28th 1 Suffolk and East Yorks attacked the chateau and the area around it, preceded by an immense barrage. In the period 21–22 June 33rd Field Regiment fired 8,700 25-pounder shells. Its historian wrote: 'By this time Victor and Uncle targets were in full swing and the names of Epron, La Bijude, St Contest and La Folie became well known to the gunners.' 1 Suffolk was to attack on the left and 2 East Yorks on the right and if successful to continue southwards. Maj. W.R. Birt's account of the battle:

> The next morning [28th] the Suffolk and East Yorks (with 1st Troop 'C' Sqn 22 Dragoons) were sent in behind a barrage of terrifying weight. But they were met by heavy shell and mortar fire which pinned them and their supporting tanks to the woods around Mathieu (Cazelle). During that long day in which advances were measured in yards and infantry casualties were grievously heavy, tanks were engaged from the direction of Lebisey and accounted for eight enemy AFVs for the loss of two of those of the Staffs Yeomanry. Though Crocodile flamethrowers were brought up to burn the enemy out of their positions, it was obviously impossible to maintain the attack. When night fell it was called off and flails were drawn back into harbour north of Cazelle, where they were heavily shelled.

'B' Company 1 Suffolk's objective was the left section of the chateau grounds. 'C' Company was directed onto the crosstracks beyond the line of trees running out from the chateau, the scene of many fierce patrol encounters. Maj. D.W. McCoffey, OC 'B' Company, took his three platoons, nearly a hundred men, through devastating fire. Twenty-four reached their objective and were then overwhelmed by six German tanks and thirty infantry.

> We had no A/Tk weapons. Things became rather bad for us in our incompleted slit trenches when the Boche shouted 'Kamerade, Tommy'. I saw the chaps nearest the tanks surrender, then others following suit. When I saw that I had lost control I took a header into a large thorn bush followed by Lt Evans who was near me. The Germans searched the area but we were not located. I then had the mortification of seeing some very brave men marched off as prisoners. After eight hours during which time our own guns put down a concentration on the area, we withdrew fifty yards and succeeded in regaining our lines.

Maj. Boycott, CO 'C' Company, was wounded early on, Maj. Philip Papillon, CO 'D' Company, Capt. Archdale and SCM Broom were killed. Maj. A.H. Claxton, then 2 i/c 'D' Company, eventually cleared the grounds, assaulted the chateau and captured nine Germans in the cellars, who were guarding some East Yorks they had taken prisoner. 1 Suffolk lost 7 officers and 154 ORs killed, wounded and missing that day. The battalion stayed in the ruined chateau for another week. There were dozens of acts of heroism. Lt. Woodward, with fifty wounds in his own body, carried another wounded man half a mile back to the RAP, and earned the MC.

During the attack East Yorks, on the right of the brigade, suffered ninety-nine casualties. Len Beevers was 13 Platoon 'C' Company's PIAT man. 'A' and 'B' Companies had reached their objectives despite withering fire from well-sited MGs and heavy shelling. An enemy counter-attack overran 'A' Company's HQ and some of them were taken prisoner, but luckily escaped in the mêlée when a defensive barrage was put down. Len fell into a slit trench on top of two Germans killed during 'B' Company's original attack. One still had a grenade in his hand, so Len got out fast. In the middle of a wood in a clearing, Len and Lionel Roebuck saw:

> a group of eight or so dead British soldiers, who had been killed in an earlier attack, all cold and stiff with their bodies in a perfect circle. Some were lying with their legs in the air, others were kneeling and a couple were standing propped up by the legs of the others. The sight was a sickening one. . . . [Later] A badly wounded officer from 'B' Coy on a stretcher was in great pain and he pleaded with us to finish him off with a bullet through his head as he didn't want to finish up as he was.

Len's PIAT team was sent to help 'B' Company, which had lost its PIAT gunners and was in trouble with a tank. They tracked it down but it was well dug in with just the hull showing, and its MG wounded Len's No. 2. Stick grenades persuaded them to lie doggo. Another German tank commander tried to persuade Canloan Lt. Jim Fetterly to surrender his platoon and was shot by Jim for his pains.

The immense cost to 8 Brigade in bringing Mitten to a conclusion – the ousting of a battalion with thirty dug-in tanks at the Chateau de la Londe position – caused the follow-up plan, Aberlour, involving the two other brigades, to be cancelled. Capt. Sperling, the 1 Suffolk signals officer, wrote:

> After the capture of the Chateau, shelling was continuous until 7 July. First World War conditions prevailed in my view for more than one month after the landing; the whole battalion in slit trenches, 100 per cent dawn and dusk stand-tos, rations brought up under great difficulty, daily losses of officers and men by active patrolling and by enemy gunfire. Our Padre Hugh Woodall allowed no dead bodies to remain without burial. The MO, Capt Robinson, had casualties collected at the double and the QM always got the rations up – somehow.

Lt. Geoffrey Forrest, LO with 185 Brigade HQ, was installed in the grounds of Cazelle Chateau:

> Roland Hobbs (Brigade TO) had wangled a grand piano. We all had some happy singsongs with it, Luc-sur-Mer for a bathe, mobile cinema in the village, some chaps had 2 days in the Corps rest-camp, comparable to Butlins and a George Formby show. Jimmy Whittle returning in his captured Daimler-Benz with the beer ration ran his chariot into a tree and was half drowned by the beer which showered over him. Monty visited us – our General, Brigadier and the COs waited for him. I must say his rows of medals looked very pretty. He chatted to me as he took off his American jacket and scarf and I walked round the Guard of Honour with him under the cameras of the two sergeant-photographers. He decorated officers and men of the Division and had tea with the Warwicks. Monty told us the Boche had lost 36 Generals, to none on our side.

But Iain Wilson, 1 KOSB, paid tribute to the opposition:

> We wondered how it was possible for human nerves to stand such an onslaught [non-stop British barrages, naval and military]. We began to realise the extreme toughness and tenacity of those Germans who lay across the wasted fields, so near to us and apparently resolved never to be dislodged . . . they had fanatical courage . . . their youth (most were 17–20) would rouse a certain warmth of admiration were it not for the fact that they were utterly ruthless and brutal.

CHAPTER ELEVEN

The 'Battle-Bruised Landscape' of 185 Brigade

Marcus Cunliffe, 2 Royal Warwicks, wrote of the battlefields north of Caen:

To the south the mood changed. The trees were splintered, the villages knocked away, the fields pocked with shell and bomb craters. The graves proliferated. After a battle they were hasty affairs with a German or a British helmet stuck on top of a rough cross or an inverted rifle. The hedgerows in this battle-bruised landscape had been burrowed in industriously and the departing enemy had left around his grubby miscellany of possessions; respirators, stick grenades, clothing, broken fibre suitcases, looted objects, private letters. About such places hovered a curious perfumed rancid smell that seemed always characteristic of German trenches which mingled with the horrible sweet smell of human dead, or the gross odour of the dead cows killed by shelling or mortar-fire that lay about in grotesque swollen attitudes. Everywhere in this nightmare zone were knocked out vehicles and tanks, most of them charred, some merely punctured, others smitten utterly.

Maj. R.G. Kreyer, now with a DSO from the Lebisey battle, was in command until 11 June, when Lt.-Col. D.L.A. Gibbs DSO took over. For a month the 2nd Battalion took five-day turns with 2 KSLI, moving from Beuville to Biéville and back again. Lebisey was subjected to daily corps artillery shoots, minefields were laid, patrols of every variety were sent out with a view to the next attack on Lebisey. Daily incoming shelling and mortaring brought a steady haemorrhage of casualties.

Harry Jones, 2 KSLI, wrote: 'By day we strengthened the defences on our right flank in expectancy of a renewed German tank attack. German snipers fully camouflaged, infiltrated our forward positions, climbed trees with heavy foliage, lashed themselves to a firm bough and proceeded to fire on any unwary soldier who might be wandering about. To counter this threat we would from time to time rake the trees with rifle and MG fire, with occasional success.' One evening Harry was quaffing a glass or two of red wine in a Beuville café. A sudden stonk from the Square wood, 2 miles away near Lebisey, caused an upset. 'I grabbed the French waitress, raced down to the cellar and flung myself and her under a heavy table. "What a way to go" I thought. The shelling eventually ceased and we made our way back to the bar. The proprietor celebrated our escape by giving those who were left a large glass of Calvados brandy.'

Harry was shocked by the difficulties of integrating the first reinforcements to replace the dead and wounded in his platoon. 'An aspect of war that had never been practised.' Having relieved the Royal Warwicks at Biéville on 17 June, Harry first encountered the notorious 'Moaning Minnies': 'with devilish ingenuity a type of siren was fitted to the tails of their mortar bombs, causing an eerie moaning sound when flying through the air'. After one successful patrol, one dead German was identified from badges of rank and regimental identification. Harry was amazed to be sent to Brigade HQ for interrogation by his brigadier. The arrival of 21st Pz Grenadier Regiment, a crack infantry unit, was now known and Harry was congratulated. As a result he wrote:

> Lying in a filthy trench
> Tired and lacking sleep
> We must stick out to the bitter end
> For the bridgehead we must keep.

Battalion HQ of 1 Royal Norfolk was predictably christened Norfolk House and 'their' no man's land, 'Duffers Drift'. 'Within a week,' Humphrey Wilson wrote, 'the bag was one marine officer, thirty five ORs, five vehicles and two m/cycles.' But the Norfolk patrols lost thirteen lives in this month. Maj. K. Fitch, OC 'A' Company, was killed on a daylight raid, as were Capt. Fearon, Lt. J.F. Williams and Maj. Brinkley, OC 'D' Company, and CQMS Thorne was wounded. Lt. Edgley-Pyshorn, 'B' Company, saw one of the first V1 rockets, which crashed to the ground several hundred yards away from him. Lt. Eric Woodhouse, Carrier Platoon: 'Wandering in front of our lines with Bobbie Parfitt and "Tinkle" Bell we were fired on by an 88 mm gun. I don't think the Jerry gunner liked us much, he kept shooting in front and behind us. Three "S" Coy officers went through a six foot hedge and back to our lines in record time.' Some of Sgt. Cutting's platoon were 'half new reinforcements, mainly tradesmen from the Wiltshires, who had to be taught all the infantry weapons; some had never thrown a grenade (after 3 or 4 years service) or handled anything other than a rifle.' The battalion operated under Double British Summertime so stand-to was an hour before dark and again an hour before daylight, i.e., 2230–2330 and 0430–0530 hrs, so no one had more than 4½ hours sleep from 6 June to 9 July. Soon the dusty roads and tracks drew immediate mortaring or 88-mm airburst, so CMPs put up large signs 'Drive Slowly – Dust means Death'. Mobile bath units quickly appeared for the whole division – usually a platoon at a time. The Colombelles factory area, half-way between Blainville and Caen, provided excellent enemy OPs. Even HMS *Rodney*'s 16-in shells could not knock them down!

From the ruined Chateau de Beuville, occupied by 185 Brigade HQ, Lt.-Col. M.A. Philp, commanding brigade signals, remarked on the number of captured German vets, since the opposition's transport was still mainly horsedrawn. He discovered a diagram of the German buried cable system. He tested it and barked into the mouthpiece: 'Achtung, Achtung! Wo ist das?' 'It sounded jolly good to me! The Regimental HQs were buzzing with the story: "I've got through to Berlin!"' He noted how regular the rum issue was, and how many cigarette packs for the troops had been pilfered and the wooden box nailed up again. Also that the Church Army mobile canteen arrived, run by two very cheerful middle-aged men in Church Army uniform, who dished out char and wads to a queue of soldiers.

The 2nd Middlesex MGs and mortars were scattered across the 3rd Division's front. Between 11 and 21 June harassing shoots were made on Epron, La Bijude and Lebisey. Fred Wiltshire, 'A' Company, recalls with some pleasure how his OC decided to have a hot bath. His batman laboriously prepared hot water. Stripped naked, the bather indulged until a quick salvo of 'incoming' caused him to jump 'tout nu' into his slit trench from which he came out 'all covered in mud and earth'. At Periers-sur-le-Dan the padre, Revd G. Fox, held a memorial service for the fallen in an orchard. As he was talking about 'true courage', the familiar noise of incoming shells rudely interrupted the service. Richard McMillan, war correspondent with the *Daily Express*, wrote on 14 June: 'I watched our massed machine gunners lay down a terrific barrage on a heavily wooded slope which the Germans held in strength.' On 20 June, 10 and 11 Platoons put 175 mortar bombs on to Epron in 2½ minutes and on 3 July, firing as a company, threw 600 bombs into Lebisey in 4 minutes. Maj. R.B. Moberley wrote:

Life in the beachhead soon developed its own pattern. The old slogan says that a soldier's best friend is his rifle. A far better friend is his shovel. The soldier soon learns in action to dig at once wherever he is and to dig deep. Then if he stays in one place for a long time he improves his hole. It probably becomes L-shaped. The short arm of the 'L' is the proper slit-trench and weapon pit, sited tactically. The long arm of the 'L' is the 'abri' or dug-out where a man can sleep lying full length. He roofs it over with planks or an old door thickly covered with earth or with earth-filled shell-boxes. This may save a man's life in an orchard or wood because shells are made to burst in the trees above and send shrapnel straight down into an open hole. Once a man has dug his hole, the next thing he learns is how to get into it very quickly. A distant 'borrum' of guns. Every ear is cocked. Every man is in his hole in a split second, in a record breaking jump, spring or dive.

Jack Prior:

When the Liberty ship SS Sambut carrying 500 troops was struck by two 16" shells from coastal batteries, she burned fiercely, the pumping apparatus having received a direct hit. After an hour the Master ordered abandon ship and by 1400 hrs the wounded and other troops had been picked out of the water by a number of small craft. 92 LAA lost 3 killed, 4 missing, one died of wounds and 14 wounded. But 317 Battery duly arrived on D+8 and soon destroyed its first FW 190. Our 2 i/c was Peter Crane who was awarded an MC for his bravery on board the SS Sambut.

F/318 Troop had joined the initial assault, 317 was to land on D+6, the other 318 troops were in Liberty ships to land on D+1. Once ashore they made for the area of Bénouville bridges. Jack Prior continued: 'I can recall attacks on most days by three or four ME 109s, FW 190s or JU 88s, particularly on the bridges area and along Periers ridge. Crews were very vulnerable when perched up in the air when on the move.'

The sappers were on call all the time for mine clearance, mine laying, bridge building and a score of difficult, dangerous engineering jobs. Sgt. Frank Faulkner RE: 'Besides patrol work we layed defensive minefields – some 15,000 mines, in addition to disarming many enemy mines and booby traps.'

Signaller David Knight of 7th Field Regiment RA reported:

In the gully before Beuville, splinters from enemy rounds had penetrated petrol cans on two of our SP guns – one about 60 yards and the other about 50 yards forward of us. One of our young officers ran to the forward gun by then well on fire, started the engine and drove it forward to a position in view of the enemy. He certainly saved the ammo dump from going up and saved several lives. The near gun just blew itself to pieces whilst we took cover in the trenches, rounds flying all over the place. I said 'Keep down, Sir' to our signals officer Lt Savile, in the same overcrowded trench. He replied 'Keep *yourself* down, Knight!' Our RSM Carden was nick-named 'slit-trench Carden'. He must have made us dig acres of trenches on training schemes but we were very grateful afterwards!'

Love Stories

Amid the noise and violence of modern warfare, just occasionally there is a moment – fortunate for the young people concerned – when love blossoms. Lt.-Col. Ian Harris met his future wife, Anne-Marie, a nineteen-year-old French girl, in Caen. Her house was being used as a billet by German officers. When 2 RUR fought its way into Caen on 9 July to flush out the retreating enemy, the French girl had eyes only for its CO. According to the

Belfast Telegraph: 'It was love at first sight for both of us. We went for a stroll in the orchard and under the trees he showed me pictures of his family back at home.' Despite Monty's lack of approval they married in 1945 and lived happily ever after.

Harold Pickersgill, 3 Recce Regiment, wrote: 'A couple of weeks after D-Day we moved into Mathieu and took over the HQ of East Yorks who had moved forward. The large house had been a private boarding school for boys – who had gone. I got to know Minette, one of the daughters of the house and after we left the area we kept in touch through the Army Post Office.' Soon after the war Harold went back to Lion-sur-Mer in the Graves Registration Unit and married Minette in Meuilly and 'lived happily ever after'.

There were other possible relaxations just behind the front line. The Divisional Club came to Luc-sur-Mer and cinema shows were available in a small schoolroom at Plumetot. The mobile bath unit also was based at Plumetot – brand new shirts, pants and towels were issued in exchange for a man's dirty washing. The Middlesex Battalion HQ fashioned a special bath in the LAD farmyard.

CHAPTER TWELVE

The Taking of Caen

'The Heavy Reek of Death'

The stalemate on the divisional front continued into early July. The Canadians had put in a huge set-piece attack against Carpiquet airfield on 4 July. 21st SS Panzers and 22nd SS Panzer Grenadier Regiment with forty tanks were subjected to immense fire plans from 428 guns plus the 16-in guns of HMS *Rodney* and the monitor *Roberts*, backed by rocket-firing Typhoons and 'Hobo's' funnies – flails and flame-throwers. Desperate hand-to-hand fighting followed, but despite ferocious counter-attacks, the Canadians held the airport – just. Operation Charnwood, Monty's grand slam operation by 1 Corps to take Caen, started with a huge RAF attack on the night of 7 July, when 450 heavy bombers unleashed thousands of tons of high explosive on the unlucky city. However, the RAF targets were 3 miles *behind* the main fortified defence positions and were timed to take place eight hours *before* the main attacks went in. James 'Smudger' Smith, South Lancs: 'Wave after wave of our Bombers passed over our position and dropped their bombs on Caen. We had a birdseye view. It lasted a few hours. One minute it was Brilliant Sunshine, next minute it was dark, the Debris and Trees being hurtled up into the air Blotted out the sun. It was a sight me and my comrades will never forget.'

The French citizens of Caen suffered the most in this holocaust. The Germans had temporarily withdrawn some of their troops and the remainder had deep defences constructed many months before. Col. Kurt Meyer's men of 12th SS Panzer had no intention of surrendering. He had withdrawn his survivors from Carpiquet airfield and sent many of his troops to the suburbs of Colombelles and Faubourg de Vaucelles, east of the river Orne. Operation Charnwood was planned for three divisions to attack with 3rd British on the left and their objectives were to capture Lebisey and Hérouville. In the centre was the newly arrived 59 Division with its objectives, La Bijude and Galmache. On the right was 3rd Canadian, partly involved at Carpiquet.

Brig. Eric Bols, now in command of 185 Brigade, was to take Lebisey and then Point 64. Afterwards, 9 Brigade was to pass through into Caen. During the night of 7/8 July 2 KSLI would push forward to secure the startline about 400 yds from the north edge of Lebisey wood. At dawn 1 Norfolk on the left, 2 Royal Warwicks on the right, would cross the startline under a massive artillery barrage.

Lebisey was held by 31st GAF (Luftwaffe) Regiment. Just before the attack Capt. R.R. Rylands, 2 KSLI, wrote: 'Came the awful news that Col Maurice had been killed at Bn HQ just down the road. Another CO in the Div described our Bn as "the house that Jack built".' An OR of 'W' Coy said: 'He was a toff – and a gentleman.' He had commanded 2 KSLI for two years and was dearly loved.

Lt. Harry Jones earned the MC during the night attack on Lebisey wood, leading three assaults on MG posts. 'I fired bursts of Bren fire into the enemy positions, shouting words of abuse in German at the enemy challenging them to "come out and fight".' Later in the afternoon of the 8th near Point 64 he was wounded in his left arm by airburst, and evacuated. 'On the hospital ship half a dozen nurses were in the Wardroom and I was given roast chicken and potatoes for lunch.'

It was a tough day for the KSLI. At 0420 hrs the barrage, 0430 hrs the assault, with 'W' Company on the left of the main road, 'Z' Company on the right. By 1600 hrs they had occupied Point 64 but had suffered considerable casualties from artillery fire as they crossed the open ground in full view of the enemy east of the river. Capt. R.R. Rylands, 'W' Company: 'The enemy held on grimly and the casualties were severe. Corporals Brown, Worrall, Ellis and Grey were killed. The CSM did yeoman service using the PIAT as an anti-infantry weapon with great effect and was a great rallier of the more faint-hearted and was awarded the MC.'

The 2nd Royal Warwick [wrote Marcus Cunliffe] 'C' and 'D' Coys reached their their startline in no mans land but tanks were delayed by A/Tank obstacles, but we pushed ahead keeping up with the barrage and by 0600 were on the S edge of their objective. 'B' and 'A' with a tank managed to get across the barrier into Lebisey village under heavy mortar fire. The enemy Bn CP in their underground warren were finally subdued; by 0730 Lebisey was firmly held. Our casualties were very heavy – a total of 153. Our Canloan, Lt Cohen, was killed and five other officers wounded including K.A. Taylor, the Warwickshire cricketer. The RSM and 3 CSMs were wounded, 25 ORs KIA and 93 wounded. We gave a decent burial to some of the men who had lain dead along the wood for a month.

John Lincoln in *Thank God and the Infantry* recalls that in their second attack on Lebisey Wood the Royal Norfolks lost 116 casualties including 25 KIA, but they captured 75 POWs, and enemy casualties were about 50. Norman Brunning wrote:

. . . the battle did not last long. All resistance was knocked out of the Germans by the heavy bombardment that preceded the attack. We dug in straightaway. About 0930 the order came through to clear the area of all dead. . . . The heavy reek of death lingered everywhere. I identified several men of 'C' Coy including Jimmy Campbell and also of the Warwicks who had been killed in the first attack. The bodies had been left in front of the enemy slit trenches to battle harden the Germans.

John Lincoln praised the close contact between the gunners of 16 Field Battery RA and his battalion. Capt. John Talbot MC: 'On the final assault on Caen I was the FOO in my Sherman tank (it had a wooden gun to accommodate an extra wireless set) with the Staffordshire Yeo, in a sweep east of Lebisey Wood. After being bombed by some American aircraft we rounded the wood just as the first Norfolks emerged from the south edge of the wood and moved on to the high ground overlooking Caen itself.'

On 8 July 2 RUR reached ring contour 60 with 'A' and 'D' Companies leading. The Boche, using OPs in the chimneys of the Colombelles factories, shelled them heavily. Maj. Tighe-Wood and all the 'A' Company stretcher-bearers were wounded. 'B' and 'C' Companies moved up also under heavy shellfire and by dusk the battalion had eighty casualties. Sgt. John Eales:

> The men were dropping like skittles but we were advancing and that meant we were winning. The medics just couldn't cope; the walking wounded had to make their own way back to the transport; the more serious wounded had to be left there after the medics had treated them. In the centre of Caen we waited for the Canadians, who didn't arrive until late afternoon. On our right 59th Div were held up and our flank was wide open. There was nothing we could do about it.

The diary of Pte. (now Revd) Jim Wisewell RAMC, medical orderly in 223 Field Ambulance 185 Brigade, has this entry for Operation Charnwood on 8 July:

> At 4 a.m. the barrage began . . . it seemed that every gun in the neighbourhood was hurling shells at Lebisey . . . . Then the infantry went in. At 5 a.m. the first wounded came back, cheerful, optimistic. We splinted fractures, covered wounds with sterile dressings and relieved each other for breakfast at 6.30 a.m. As the day wore on, sunny and scorching hot, the tide of casualties rose. Dozens and dozens were carried in. Our treatment centre always had 3 upon the trestles being attended to and soon the approaches were lined with a queue. Hour after hour we worked and evacuated and still the flow continued. Ghastly wounds there were, of every type and state of severity. Heads with skulls so badly smashed that bone and brain and pillow were almost indivisible; faces with horrible lacerations; jaws blown completely away leaving only two sad eyes to plead for relief from pain. Chests pierced through with

shrapnel and lungs that spouted blood from gushing holes. Arms were mangled into shapeless masses left hanging by muscle alone and waiting the amputation knife. There were abdomens perforated by shell splinters and displaying coils of intestine, deadly wounds. Buttocks were torn and in some cases spinal injury had followed bringing paralysis. But the leg wounds! Thigh-bones splintered; knees without knee caps; legs without feet; red, mangled flesh and blood flooding the stretcher. And others trembling uncontrollably, sobbing like children, strapped to the stretcher and struggling to be free; screaming and, when a shell landed near the ADS, shouting, 'They're coming again! O God, they're coming again.' Not heroes, but sufferers nonetheless. We ate our lunch of biscuit and corned beef with bloody fingers and when relieved by 9th Field Ambulance at 6 p.m. we had treated 466 British soldiers and 40 Germans.

Mines, huge road craters and 88-mm fire held up the supporting tanks. At dawn on the 9th patrols from 'A' Company got into Calix, an eastern suburb, and St Julien to the north-west of Caen. Lt. Burge led the Ulsters into the centre of the town – a lunar landscape – where two NCOs were killed. By 0930 hrs 'B' Company, leading into rubble and devastation, found no organised opposition left, only abandoned MG posts and rocket apparatus. No vehicle movement was possible. By 1130 hrs Maj. Hyde and his men were astride Boulevard des Alliés and were soon joined by 'D' Company moving up from Hill 60. When Lt. Palmer was wounded, L/Sgt. Bonass took command. Flags of fighting France hung from windows, the survivors of Caen greeted the Ulsters with glasses of wine. The password was 'Liberté' and the FFI guided 'C' Company along the boulevards revealing sniper and MG hideouts. Maj. de Longueuil's masterly French helped. Two people were rescued – Squadron Leader Sprawson DFC, RAF, whose Lancaster had been shot down on D-Day and who had sheltered with a patriotic family, and a Frenchman who claimed to be a habitué of Mooneys in Belfast! At Brigade HQ the BBC made a recording and by the evening the RUR had pushed down to the line of the Orne. They were a month late getting there, but get there they did!

Hérouville-St-Clair is now the northern suburb of prosperous rebuilt Caen – a mile or two south-east of Lebisey. The 2 Lincolns were placed under command of 185 Brigade (from 9 Brigade) to act as left flank protection on the river and to capture the village (as it was then) of Hérouville and explore beyond into the suburbs of Caen. The massive aerial and naval bombardment of Caen and Lebisey on the evening of 7 July made the determined assault by 2 Royal Warwicks and 2 KSLI on 8 July comparatively easy. Jack Harrod, the Lincolns' IO, wrote: 'But it was on the left flank in the narrow strip of ground between the river and the rising ground that the bloodiest fighting was taking place. Here the Bn practically unsupported and scarcely remembered in the flush of victory elsewhere, was meeting stiff opposition and stubborn resistance. It was the hardest engagement of the day.' Overlooked by the German OPs in the Colombelles factory, counter-attacked twice by enemy infantry and tanks, the Lincolns battled their way south. Maj. L.H.B. Colvin, OC 'B' Company, shot two Germans with a rifle at point-blank range. Pte. J. Thompson of 'C' Company with his PIAT knocked out a Mark IV tank and damaged two others. Ray Paine with the mortar platoon, had plenty to do: 'We were having a smoke when Capt Roll [the OC] came to see if we were OK.' A Moaning Minnie salvo landed. 'I threw myself into the mortar pit, landing on Johnny Goodson just before the explosion roared around us. My head was full of ringing bells. The blast killed Capt Roll. The bomb had landed at his feet.'

Jack Harrod: 'Nothing spectacular. The Bn just pushed the Germans back, moving forward bit by bit according to plan. By the morning of 9th July "A" Coy had reached the river beyond Herouvillette and during the afternoon consolidated, commanding the Colombelles bridge with patrols forward to the outskirts of Caen between the river and the canal.' Of the Lincolns, 32 were KIA including 3 officers, and a further 6 officers and 132 ORs were wounded – a total of 170 in the forgotten battle of Herouvillette. 3 Recce Regiment relieved them on 10 July and they went back to Lion-sur-Mer for a few days rest. An MC, a DCM and two MMs were later awarded to the Lincolns for their two-day battle.

King's Own Scottish Borderers in Caen. (IWM, B 6683)

1 KOSB soon linked up with 2 RUR in Caen, with'C' and 'D' Companies leading. The whole battalion consolidated in the centre with forward companies pushed to the canal bisecting the city. Contact was made again with the enemy, shelling from east of the river Orne, and casualties were fairly heavy. The battalion also received a tumultuous welcome from the French Maquis and the citizens, unbroken by the bombing assault and seemingly indifferent to the destruction of their homes. Alastair Renny: 'Caen was 80% destroyed by bombing. 1 KOSB led advances over mountainous rubble including cavernous hollows from 15" naval guns. The enemy rearguards were active. I met General Crocker, 1 Corps Commander, quite alone, waving us on, surely unique. But he was lucky to get away with it.' Iain Wilson observed: 'bulldozers were quickly on the scene and with amazing speed and courage set about clearing routes through the debris so that A/tank guns and armour could pass through. It was in Caen that we first experienced the genuine spirit of French resistance. . . . It was a deeply humbling experience to meet these people.'

Sgt. Fred Hartle, 'D' Company: 'My platoon advanced forward into the Abbey grounds. It was on fire and we dug in and watched as big wooden beams and rafters crashed to the ground sending showers of sparks sky high.' Some Maquis then approached and asked Fred's platoon to move forward and attack some German positions further in the town centre. 'The platoon officer said he only took instructions from his company commander and refused. The French were clearly annoyed but that was it. After two hours we received orders to advance again and we started house clearing.'

The division held Caen and handed it over to the Canadians on the morning of the 11th. 1 KOSB, wrote Iain Wilson:

> marched out with the Company pipers playing in full hearing of the enemy. As we climbed up the hill through the ruined streets we felt that a good job had been done. Outside the city we filed aboard carriers, jeeps, anything on wheels and drove back to Epron and other former centres of German resistance, now utterly ruined with their trees gaunt and stripped and their streets piled with rubble. It seemed like a dream. Tired, dirty and victorious we arrived at Plumetot where we hoped to have a rest.

CHAPTER THIRTEEN

Operation Goodwood

'Troarn, Our Deepest Tribulation'

Monty planned a new grand slam attack involving 8 Corps' three armoured divisions crashing from the eastern side of Caen southwards – just possibly as far as Falaise. 3rd Canadian Division would be right flank protection, thrusting due south from Caen towards the well-defended Bourguébus ridge. 3rd British Division and, specifically, 8 Brigade were tasked with left (east) flank protection, with the objectives of the capture of Touffreville, Sannerville, Bannerville and Manneville. Secondly, 9 Brigade would take Troarn to the east. The German opposition immediately to the east was the 346 and 711 Infantry Divisions, but to the south, facing the armoured thrust, Rommel had created over forty strongpoints in several lines of defence in hamlets and large farms, with 16 GAF Division, 1 SS Division and the remnants of 12 SS Division. Troarn, regarded as a vital position was held by infantry and dug-in tanks of 21st Panzer Division and 16 GAF Division.

Lurking in the swampy marshes, the Bois de Barent ridge and the river Dives, was yet another all-pervading enemy. Every member of 3rd British Division was vigorously attacked night and day by swarms of mosquitoes, whose bites in some cases sent men reeling back to the RAP with faces swollen and eyes and ears out of action. It is difficult concentrating on the enemy to one's front if one's body is under constant sniping by mosquitoes! Even the battalion QM's special cream failed to protect. 'Various ointments were tried as they infested the trenches in clouds. We were tortured night and day, unable to sleep or even to keep still. Gradually we became blotched and swollen from head to foot and in many cases suffered from septic bites,' wrote Iain Wilson, 1 KOSB.

The move away from Caen started on 9 July when 9 Brigade occupied the area north-east of the river Orne in Airborne country, after the infantry had spent several days out of the line. Baths, sleep, better food, football and other sports, swimming at the Divisional Club at Luc-sur-Mer and the absorbing of hundreds of reinforcements had occupied everyone.

Out of the line from 11 July, Maj. Bill Renison, 2 i/c East Yorks, wrote:

At the new Div club at Luc-sur-Mer one could buy Beverage No. 2 or

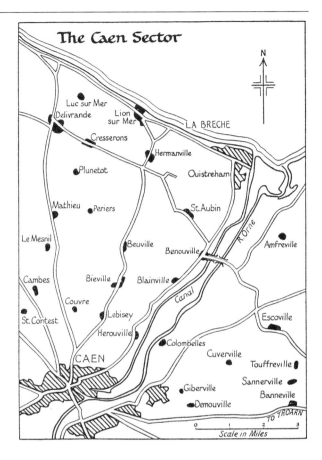

Beverage No. 3 for 5 Francs each. The mobile bath set up shop and joy of joys a Naafi issue turned up and Jack Bamford did a roaring trade at his stall in the orchard – a pint of beer per man, a bottle of whisky for officers were the highlights! Many reinforcements joined us from 9th Buffs, the band was reformed and practised stick drill but there was a shortage of bugles. I remember the look of glee on the face of one of the locals as he passed a POW cage and saw some disconsolate Boche digging slit-trenches for themselves at Mathieu.

On the 12th 1 Suffolk held a memorial service in the garden of La Londe, taken by the chaplain, Revd Hugh Woodall. The CO, Lt.-Col. J.G.M.B Gough, read out the roll of honour and the Last Post and Reveille were played. Nine officers and 57 other ranks had been killed, and another 250 in all had been wounded or were missing. On the same day the pipes and drums of 1 KOSB played Retreat in the fields outside Plumetot. 'The scene was memorable', wrote Iain Wilson, 'for the quiet evening sunshine shone over the trampled fields and on the grey walls and peaceful church tower among the trees, while the Pipers marched back and forth with kilts flying and the familiar tunes shrilling out in the French air.'

Norman Scarfe recalled that on 13 July: 'a half slice of freshly baked white bread appeared to complement the Army "dog biscuits". The three gunner regiments were in action every day. 33rd Field Regiment (and the others) supported 51st Highland Div in Operation Stack to demolish the numerous factory chimneys around Colombelles. Dawn came and the sit. rep. "No Change".'

1 KOSB moved in lorries from Plumetot on 15 July over the Orne to the Ranville area. 'Lt King our platoon officer, produced an aerial photograph which showed a group of houses clustered round a T-Junction at the entrance to Troarn', recalls Victor Campbell. A patrol of three men would be led by Lt. King to recce this junction. 'We looked at each other with something akin to dismay and wondered whether we would survive.' Under their new CO, Lt.-Col. G.C. Millett OBE, 2 KSLI route-marched from Beuville on the 14th to relieve 1 Gordons of 15th Scottish Division in the wooded area forward of Ranville, with a company due south holding Escoville. They crossed the Orne by the famous Pegasus Airborne bridge.

The adjutant of 33rd Field Regiment RA, Capt. J.A. Brymer, described the immense support for Goodwood:

The main fire support was to come from the RAF plus the divisional Artilleries of 2 and 3 Canadian Divisions, 3 British and 51 Highland Divisions. 7, 11 and Guards Armoured Divisions, 4, 8, and part of 9 and 2 Canadian AGRAs with 107 and 165 HAA regiments totalling three regiments RHA [3, 5 and the author's 13], sixteen Field, fourteen Mediums, three Heavy and two HAA Regiments. In addition HM navy supported with 21 guns. Goodwood opened with concentrated RAF bombing [8,000 bombs] on a gigantic scale during which the regiment fired on Applepie followed by Counter Battery and concentrations in support of 8 Brigade. Throughout the morning (18th July) the fire was almost continuous and was by far the most extensive programme that the regiment had been called upon to perform. During the whole day the regiment [24 Sexton 25-pounders] fired 9,600 rounds, 400 rounds per gun. Mention must be made of the superb ammunition supply by the RASC.

Unfortunately the Germans were by now expert at reading the Allied intentions. Their forward positions were thinly held and often regarded as expendable. When the immense bombardment slackened or ceased Tiger and Panther tanks and Panzer Grenadiers would be rushed forward to occupy the various strongpoints.

D-Day, 18 July

It was a pleasant sunny morning and the division, to a man, saw, heard and wondered at the air armada saturating the German front ahead. It seemed as though nobody could survive that terrible onslaught. But they did.

8 Brigade supported by 13/18th Hussars led from their start point at Herouvillette towards their objective, a track running west out of Touffreville. They cleared woodland and defended sandpits and by 2000 hrs had consolidated to allow 1 Suffolk to pass through. The South Lancs suffered forty-one casualties on the 18th, including seven officers. The East Yorks' advance is described by Pte. Len Beevers, 13 Platoon: 'With strong artillery support "C" Coy advanced in open formation to reach the first enemy strong dug-outs. Most gave in easily . . . [soon] Sgt Carter, an older senior NCO, was hit by a bullet in the arm. More annoyed than hurt he said "Look what the bastards have done to me." Small in stature, a weathered smile on his kindly wrinkled face. A father figure, he was to be sorely missed.' Len put a shot into a well-concealed dugout in the long grass. To screams of 'Kamerad, Kamerad', out came eight Poles 'made to wear their German uniforms and forced to fight with them'. But the East Yorks ran into more resistance and heavy mortaring. L/Cpl. Hall was hit and Capt. Crauford carried him back on his shoulders. Len and Frank Hodgson took the lead to help attack a farmhouse where the mortars were sited, surprised a further twenty Germans including the mortar crew and took them prisoner. Bob Spring, a tall cockney who had been a drummer in the band, showed up on his own with another large group of prisoners. 'The village of Touffreville, the main objective was taken by "A" Coy at 1800, led by Major "Banger" King. During the "Rugger Scrum" charges along the main street many prisoners and an undamaged tank were captured. Despite a lot of sniper fire "C" Coy took up a defensive position east of the village, then subjected to more heavy shelling and mortaring.' Len likened the Moaning Minnies (multi-barrel mortars) to raucous cock pheasants giving full voice or to an old rusty gate opening. The next day Len was wounded by airburst shrapnel and was sent to the RAP, then the field hospital and by boat to Portsmouth. His war had finished. After forty days in action he left his heavy PIAT behind for good.

By 1015 hrs 1 Suffolk set off for Escoville, bypassing Touffreville to the west, and by 1220 hrs had taken Sannerville with little opposition. Many very dazed prisoners were taken from 16 GAF Division. Patrols then found that Banneville-la-Campagne, 500 yds due south, was fairly clear, and 'A' and 'D' Companies consolidated round the church and chateau by 1400 hrs. A great variety of weapons were discovered – three guns, six Nebelwerfers and vehicles. The Suffolk had twelve casualties. Lt.-Col. Eric Lummis makes the point that Brigade HQ could not believe 1 Suffolk had taken both their objectives so quickly, with so few casualties. He wrote: 'The opportunity to move through a gap in the enemy's defences (S and SW to

Cuillerville and Emiéville) – but nothing was done to exploit it.' Soon bulldozers were brought up to clear the many bomb craters, and by 1730 hrs 9 Brigade was passing through to tackle Troarn.

1 KOSB was on the right and 2 RUR on the left with the tanks of East Riding Yeomanry in support, as 9 Brigade advanced eastwards at midday from Escoville towards Troarn. Maj. H.S. Gillies, OC 'C' Company, wrote:

> Cambes had been a grim and desperate experience. Troarn will ever be the symbol of our deepest tribulation. We passed through the ruins of Escoville. In open fields west of Sannerville we were ordered to halt. From our left flank we were observed from the Bois de Bavent and suffered numerous casualties. Thirst and heat were beginning to trouble us. Several men collapsed. On our advance towards Troarn the going was difficult with huge bomb craters. Utter fatigue set in, tortured by thirst, soaking with sweat, borne down by the weight of our equipment, we clambered over great piles of rubble that had once been streets. Although the enemy was considerably disorganised, 'C' Coy leading was held up by MG fire on a sunken road on the outskirts of Troarn.

The CO, Lt.-Col. G.D. Renny, was twice wounded but refused to go back. By 1900 hrs 1 KOSB were dug in at La Croix de Pierre.

> Our casualties by now extensive. We were cut off from our transport [and tanks] by the craters, running very short of water and food. We dug in as we were to resume the advance in the morning. The night was most unpleasant. Most men too exhausted to dig trenches just lay down in the orchards and tried to forget their hunger and thirst in a few hours of disturbed sleep. Our wounded in a desperate situation, short of medical supplies: no ambulances could get through. Walking wounded had to stay: no hope of negotiating the miles of craters in the darkness. During the night, the enemy shelled and mortared our positions. They brought up fresh reinforcements, sent out patrols which inflicted more casualties on 'A' Coy. 'D' Company HQ was hit several times by shellfire, 'B' Company had several casualties in a booby-trapped farmhouse and 'C' Company came under fire from a railway signal box.

During that long scorching day 2 RUR attacked Troarn from the north-west starting from Le Mesnil, 1 mile east of Sannerville. Their first objective was a brickworks north-east of Sannerville. A scissors bridge over the stream, Cours de Janville, enabled tanks to support Maj. Hyde's 'B' Company. By 1730 hrs the battalion was established in and around the brickworks and the advance continued to a T-junction a mile from Troarn despite two 75-mm German guns, which caused casualties. Lt. R. Lyttle, L/Cpl. Sharpe and Rifleman Charles McNally distinguished themselves and captured both guns. By nightfall contact was made with 5th Cameron Highlanders of 51st Division on the north-west outskirts of Troarn.

The southern attack by 185 Brigade was started at 0930 hrs by 2 KSLI mounted on Stafford Yeomanry Shermans; they had orders to capture Le Quai, Manneville and Cuillerville. They advanced through Hérouville, Escoville and out into the flat country towards Lirose, which was strongly held by 14th Nebelwerfer Battery. On the way Capt. R.R. Ryland, 2 i/c 'W' Company, remembers: 'We were bombed accidentally by American planes going over to "soften up".' Pte. Barber, a great character, was one of the casualties. On one of the Shermans a man fired his Sten by mistake, setting off a phosphorous grenade which caused more casualties. 'Y' Company cleared Lirose under heavy fire, and Maj. R.L.N. Dane was killed. In the woods and orchards on the way south to Manneville, 2 KSLI suffered heavy casualties mainly from MG fire, but also from dug-in Tiger tanks that had escaped the aerial bombing. The artillery HQ of 16 GAF Division was in Manneville, held by considerable strength. Maj. Wheelock MC, OC 'Z' Company, was badly wounded and died three days later, and Capt. Kelly, a newly joined Canloan officer, was also killed.

Capt. Rylands:

Another open space stretching to the chateau [of Manneville] proved to be the limit of our advance. A sunken ditch and hedge was full of infuriating Huns who picked us off in the open, until we got close, then they surrendered. CSM Knox MC was wounded here. His blunt determination and courage – and his droll utterances passed into legend. The chateau avenue proved to contain dug-in Tigers. Major Slatter was wounded again, Lieutenant Archie Emmens killed, and the popular L/Corp Alf George, for long the company cobbler, and there had been a steady trickle of wounded, including Sgt Croft, Bn footballer in happier days.

2 KSLI reformed along the line of the railway as the Warwicks came through.

The brigadier ordered 2nd Warwicks and 1st Norfolks to attack Manneville from the right (west) via Le Pruie. Their first objective was Cuillerville wood, which was attacked at 2100 hrs under an artillery barrage. But the Warwicks were held up by a 20-ft wall and it was dark before a way through was found. Confused fighting took place in the thick woods but forty prisoners and two 88-mm guns were captured. Later on twenty German tanks were found abandoned in the many bomb craters. The Warwicks then dug in for the night. The 1st Norfolks had a similar experience, except that they called the same wood 'Manneville' wood, and were held up by the same high wall. Maj. H.R. Holden's 'D' Company was unable to secure the wood before nightfall – so the Norfolks dug in.

Goodwood, D+1, 19 July

Jack Harrod, briefly 9 Brigade Intelligence Officer, could see and hear how Goodwood was faring.

> We had again made the most popular of mistakes: in the flush of immediate success, we had under-rated the enemy, forgotten his discipline and staying power, his fighting qualities and proneness to hit back. Across the plain [south-east of Caen to Bourguébus] the enemy fell back . . . to a strongly prepared line and our armour seeking battle with the German Mark IVs after a Libyan pattern found the way barred by an impenetrable screen of powerful antitank guns. . . . He had no intention of giving ground in the wooded country round Troarn where he had been untouched by the bombing and could not be reached by the tanks. Troarn was to be held to the last possible moment. . . .

9 Brigade was directed to continue the attack on Troarn. During the night the 3rd Battlion, 731 Grenadier Regiment, arrived to reinforce the defenders of 16 GAF Division, and a squadron of Tiger tanks arrived to bolster the defences. At 0600 hrs on 19 July 'D' Company RUR, under Capt. Bird, first took a small wood half a mile from the outskirts of Troarn, but 'C' Company came under severe fire from a church. Cpl. Brown's section with bayonet and grenades then killed seven of the enemy, captured thirteen others, and also took four machine guns. Nevertheless, 'C' Company was pinned down. Capt. Alexander led 'A' Company from the south towards the church, and Sgt. Sharkey with great gallantry killed a MG crew with his Sten gun. So, helped by the East Riding Yeomanry tanks, the church was taken by midday, and a barn set on fire. Unfortunately, 'A' Company now withdrew and the enemy infiltrated back into the position in strength. Lt. Brian Burges was killed trying to rescue a wounded ERY tank officer. Two further attacks failed to dislodge the enemy from the church. Sgt. Sharkey with a depleted platoon backed by two ERY tanks captured or killed over twenty enemy, dashing from slit trench to slit trench with tremendous courage – for which Monty later pinned a DCM on his chest. Lt.-Col. Harris consolidated the RUR in the western fringe of Troarn.

On their right flank 1 KOSB's plan was related by Maj. Hugh Gillies: '"A" and "C" Companies were to lead and secure a road junction on the outskirts of Troarn, which was to be taken by "B" Company whilst "D" secured the bridges and eastern exits. At 1030 hrs the gunners put down a 15-minute concentration on the line of the sunken road.' And Maj. Alastair Renny, 'D' Company: 'so vital was the accuracy of the barrage that the Battery Commander insisted on accompanying the leading companies but fierce defence inflicted heavy casualties with 80 killed including the BC.'

Maj. Gillies again:

The attack failed. Well entrenched and tenacious German machine gunners held their fire and then poured a hail of bullets into 'C' Coy. On the right 'A' Coy ran into heavy mortar fire and could not make progress. Our own tanks unable to get beyond the first orchard fired blindly and caused casualties to the leading platoons. A tragic situation . . . so the CO ordered a withdrawal to the original positions. The Brigadier arrived and instructed the Bn to dig in and hold. The RAP was littered with wounded. The MO had his arm blown off and the Padre took over.

Sgt. Fred Hartle, 'D' Company: 'A German soldier was laid directly in my path. His leg was blown off. He said "Give me a cigarette, Tommy." His face was as grey as his uniform. I gave him a cigarette, but I had no matches. An officer reprimanded me for this act. I could see that on my right "D" Company was being absolutely destroyed.' L/Cpl. Hardman was hit in the back. 'I whipped out my field bandage but it wasn't any good. He died 20 minutes later. Corporal Clark jumped into a slit trench – a bullet went through his chest. Everyone was shouting for stretcher-bearers. There was a burst of m/g fire and both stretcher-bearers were killed.' On the 19th 'word got round that the Germans had asked for a ceasefire . . . both sides were allowed to pick up their wounded. L/Corp Bobby Laing was a stretcher-bearer [awarded the MM later] put the Red Cross satchel on his head and together with the German stretcher-bearers tended the wounded.' In the two days of Goodwood 1 KOSB lost 12 officers and 140 ORs were casualties.

A mile further west 2 Lincolns were ordered to create a diversion pushing towards the main Caen–Troarn road just east of Sannerville. 'We moved off into the devastated area of Sannerville encountering heavy shellfire on the way,' recounts Ray Paine. 'The mortar platoon dug in amongst the trees of an orchard well away from the rest of the company. We were never very popular anyway as we always attracted German mortar counter-fire.' And Jack Harrod: 'The Bn entering the orchards between the railway and the road encountered successive concentrations of heavy shell and mortar fire. The enemy had concentrated his guns including a number of Nebelwerfers in an area SE of Troarn. The Bn hung on grimly and dug as it never dug before. Eventually it was ordered to withdraw across the railway to its former position.' By then the CO, Lt.-Col. Welby-Everard, had been wounded by a mortar bomb and casualties included three officers and eighty-six ORs. The following day, 20 July, 'heavy-eyed through lack of sleep, soaked to the skin by a series of thunder showers and plastered with the greasy Normandy clay, they edged forward again.' From 1830 hrs to 2230 hrs they dug in under endless concentration of fire. During Goodwood the battalion lost ten officers and two hundred ORs in and around Black Orchard. On 22 July they were relieved by 1 South Lancs and moved back to Escoville to reorganise, where sixty reinforcements joined

The rear of the building in Troarn which was used as 1 KOSB 'B' Company HQ, taken in 1993. What was left of 11 Platoon dug-in in the area adjacent to the outhouses. (Victor Campbell)

The building in Troarn which was used as RAP, taken in 1993. The tall building at the far end was 'B' Company HQ. (Victor Campbell)

them. When Capt. Jack Harrod rejoined his battalion as adjutant he found it nineteen officers and nearly four hundred ORs below strength.

Lt. Eddie Jones, South Lancs, recalls how shortly after the relief in Black Orchard:

we took over from the Lincolns under fire while in close contact with the enemy. Our 2 i/c approached our CO, Colonel Bolster, to report the completion of the handover. As he saluted a shot rang out and the CO fell mortally wounded. The command vehicle, a M 14 half track, visible to the enemy was mortared until they hit it and set it on fire. The Bn stayed there for a week of unremitting hazardous shell, mortar and sniper fire. Our 4th CO since D-Day, Lt Col Orgill, joined us on 26 July bringing two Canloan officers, Alfred Cope and Eric Fryer, both later killed on the Escaut–Meuse canal battle. Eric, who was built like a good prop forward, went out on his first night patrol, returned carrying under one arm a German NCO he had captured! Sannerville was like a set from H.G. Wells' 'War of the Worlds'. The village was completely destroyed, the whole area pitted with huge craters. The ground was pulverised into a sort of coarse grey flour, imposssible to dig a slit trench as the sides just trickled into the hole. The rain turned the earth into a sticky grey slime which made transport movement impossible. Our QM Billy Burke, a short puckish individual with a quiet but irrepressible sense of humour, had the unenviable task of bringing up rations and ammo to the Bn each evening, without showing a light, threading his way through minefields, barbed wire and shell holes. Our padre Paul Corin and MO, Larry Collier RAMC – most brave and dedicated men.

In nearby Banneville 1 Suffolk spent eleven days in waterlogged dugouts and trenches under fire from Nebelwerfers. Some soldiers were buried in the deep mud and had to be dug out at great speed, not always successfully as Eric Lummis wrote in his journal, '1 Suffolk in Normandy'. The Luftwaffe dropped anti-personnel mines causing many casualties in the pioneer platoon. Lt. John Perrett led several aggressive patrols, but Maj. Copinger Hill led his patrol of five men out to try to locate 10 Platoon. Only Pte. Lovewell returned. The QM, Capt. P.W. Spurgis, a big man, had constructed the largest dugout in Normandy, reputed to be fitted up with a billiard table!

Maj. Bill Renison, the new 2 i/c of the East Yorks, recalled: 'What a nasty mess where a mortar bomb had burst plumb in the middle of a party of 40 Boche prisoners. In the Chateau La Touffreville the MO's RAP contained a plentiful supply of home-brewed cider. The MO was reported to have accounted for a sniper in the church steeple. The spoils of war included two A/Tk guns, four undamaged 12 cm mortars, HQ equipment, telephones, typewriters, files etc.' Renison went out with a carrier and some pioneers and brought in the bodies of eighteen dead Yorkshires. His mail brought an

Income Tax demand. He and his driver, Mabbitt, had brought 'debussing under fire from their jeep to a fine art'. Under one stonk he saw his CO dive into a slit trench filled with water. Mosquito bites caused battle casualties: swollen fingers so that rifles could not be fired and swollen eyes so that the victim could not see. Bill Renison continued:

> The 18th July was a very hot day with dust kicked up by the tanks – unbearable – only sucking boiled sweets relieved our thirst. The CO [Lt.-Col. Dickson] and I decided that the 2 i/c should stay at Bn HQ instead of further back LOB and this took place throughout the campaign. In the Troarn battle 'C' Coy did well bombing their way from trench to trench, rolling up the enemy trenches with considerable dash. Tony Swinburne organised a rest room in his 'A' Coy area and there played the piano! Our Gunner BC, Sandy Lyle of 302 Bty, kept the noisy gunner radio open 24 hours a day. He was a delightful Scot with a slight stammer. We were relieved by the Lincolns on the 25th.

The Royal Norfolks spent nine days in Manneville wood with their HQ in a well-appointed Le Quai racing establishment, where there were some race horses, alive but frightened. Humphrey Wilson recalls: 'conditions were so frightful, we had our first cases of "exhaustion", so the "slit-trench quiz" was started. This proved most popular, kept the men's minds fully occupied.'

The 2nd Warwicks spent a week in the woods round Cuillerville. On 19 July Maj. T.G. Bundock MC earned the DSO by crippling a Tiger tank which was counter-attacking with a PIAT, and Cpl. W.J. Millard knocked out a Spandau with his Bren, only to be mortally wounded. On 21 July a patrol found Emiéville unoccupied, so 2 KSLI moved in. The Warwicks were under heavy fire all the time and in the Goodwood week lost 34 dead, 202 wounded and 12 missing. The worst day was the 23rd when the MO, J.H.T. Lawson, and the IO, Capt. A.D.R. Smith, were killed along with many other casualties. The enemy left behind snipers, 'suicide boys', usually Russians or Poles and one Turk.

From the grounds of the Chateau de Manneville, 2 KSLI fired a captured Minenwerfer against their tormentors, 21 Company Nebelwerfers. There were many casualties and several company commanders were killed (Maj. C. Griffiths, Maj. Dane and Maj. P.H. Wheelock) and Capt. R.R. Rylands took over command of 'W' Company for the fifth and final time. In the fog of war, on the night of 22 July a lost patrol of 51st Highland Division killed a corporal and wounded another man before their identity was discovered. 2 KSLI stayed in the grounds of the chateau until 25 July, when they were relieved by 11 DLI of Polar Bear Division.

Maj. R.B. Moberley, 2nd Middlesex, described the captured German dugouts near Touffreville: 'beautifully made wooden walls, floors and ceiling lined with sheets and curtains, full of wines, butter, fruit, children's shoes, crockery, cutlery, cameras, binoculars, fountain pens, excellent Dutch razor blades from the G. Air Force division recently arrived from Holland.' He found four wrecked Tiger tanks north-east of Emiéville and at Cuillerville, four more Tigers, one Panther, seven PZ KW IVs, three PZ KW IIIs and seven 20-mm SP AA guns among the bomb craters. He also found a 2 Panzer Div Memo to 326 GAF Division, which took over from them:

> The incredibly heavy artillery and mortar fire of the enemy is something new both for the seasoned veterans of the Eastern front and for the new arrivals from RHUs. The enemy has complete mastery of the air. They bomb and strafe every movement. They recce our area constantly and direct their artillery fire from air OPs. The attacking enemy simply beats down the forward battle area with his artillery and aircraft. Our supply of ammo is insufficient . . . .

Gen. 'Bolo' Whistler wrote in his diary: 'July 20. Grand news from all parts, and Hitler nearly bumped off. A pity it failed as it would have been a satisfactory ending to an evil man.' But Bolo was not happy with the command of 9 Brigade and put in his GSO1 Dominic Browne to command them. The GSO 2, two GSO 3s and the LOs were ALL changed too!

south of Bény-Bocage, attacked the enemy in La Bistière, but 'A' and 'D' Companies suffered casualties. By the morning of the 5th the enemy had gone. Near Forgues the KSLI was attacked by a Tiger tank and infantry, but 'X' Company knocked it out with a 6-pounder A/T gun. The Warwicks, having occupied Presles, were subjected at noon to a Nebelwerfer salvo, which killed RSM Lewis and wounded several others. During the afternoon a 2-mile advance down one small road to relieve 8 RB, 11th Armoured, cost them more men from shelling. Near Le Bas Perrier the battle group (now including 23rd Hussars' Shermans, a troop of SP A/T guns and some Churchill AVREs) was squeezed onto a very small feature overlooked by a higher ridge.

Lt. Geoffrey Forrest of the Warwicks, a liaison officer with 185 Brigade, wrote:

> Truly bocage country, fields rarely larger than 100 yards square. Trees were good hideouts for snipers and MG posts in hedgerows. The Brigade came under command [of] 11 Armoured Div and a most unholy jumble took place with regard to command, in filling up the gaps in the ground that 11 Armoured had taken. We had one of the AD's regiments – about 50 yards – in our HQ area. They would give us no peace at night. We could hear all the fire orders and see the gun teams in action.

The author's 13 RHA Sextons did make a lot of noise in this particular battle.

The three infantry battalions of 11th Armoured Division were 4 KSLI north of Presles, 1 Herefords at Forgues and 3rd Monmouthshires forward at Pavée. They all had Sherman tank support from their own 29th Armoured Brigade. From Vire, 9th Panzer Division struck hard along a wide front on the 11th Armoured Division salient – Montchamp, Estry, Le Haut Perrier, Chênedollé, Pavée, Burcy, Forgues and La Bistière. On 4 August 3rd Parachute Regiment joined 9 SS PZ and on 5 August 185 Brigade was ordered to relieve the hard-pressed 159 Brigade (11th Armoured). Very heavy fighting was taking place along the two key ridges, Perrier to the south and Estry to the east. Indeed 10th SS Panzer Division was sucked into the battle from the Mt Pinçon battle to the north-east. The key main road from Vire east to Vassy (D 512) was vital to the Germans' 7th Army and they were fighting desperately to keep it open. Their main counter-attack came in on the 3rd Divisional front late on 6 August. Now the GOC ordered up 9 Brigade on the right flank.

Just to the west of Burcy is the hamlet of Montisenger, which was occupied by 1 KOSB early on the 6th, while American troops were still engaged in savage fighting with German paratroops 4 miles south-west in Vire. At the same time 3rd Recce scout cars were ambushed and almost annihilated, probing around the outskirts of Vire. 'C' Squadron suffered the most, but Lt. Snelling earned the MC.

Bill Renison:

August 6th was a Sunday and the Padre of East Yorks had a communion service, nearly 200 turned up: the bread was dipped in wine, and he offered the two together like the Russian Orthodox Church. Arthur Riall 'B' Coy ran a very popular game of Housey, the proceeds going to the Regimental POW Fund. We had to keep a look out, for the Pioneers found booby trapped road blocks, even a bed in a farmhouse booby trapped. [Later] Near Vire we had a US tank destroyer unit in the next field. It was now the old 'approach to contact' battle that one had fought so often on exercise in England.

A two-battalion attack with 2 Lincolns and 1 KOSB was now planned to gain a bridgehead over the little river Allière at Pont de Vaudry, and finally push through to cut the Vire–Vassy road.

Jack Harrod, 2 Lincolns, described how the battalion had received a hundred reinforcements mainly from 7 Battalion East Yorkshires and four new officers. As lorried infantry they set off from Biéville to St Martin-des-Besaces (which now has an excellent 11th Armoured Division 'museum'): '9 Infantry Brigade debussed about 6 km NE of Vire and advanced on foot. 2 RUR led, followed by 1 KOSB and again 2 Lincolns in reserve. [After 1 KOSB took Montisenger] We were ordered to push through and force a bridgehead over the river. By now the bridge had been blown.' There were five hazards: the river, steep high ground beyond it, the minor road north-east to Aunay, the railway line from Vire running east, and the straight main Vire–Vassy road.

Ray Paine with the mortar platoon met five young 'Yank' soldiers just arrived from England, 'We sat with them round our mortar pits helping them finish their few remaining bottles. One of them was a Dodgers fan from Brooklyn. Another, a Texan, asked Johnny Goodson about a gun of *ours* which made a moaning sound. We explained that when you hear a "Moaning Minnie" you had 7 or 8 seconds to get into your slit trench before the explosion. One of the GIs looked at us and said they had taken casualties as they had never bothered to take cover.'

Jack Harrod:

The action began at 1630 and by 1715 the two assault companies, 'C' on the left under Major Gilbert, 'B' on the right under Major P. Smith, were across the river, but hard fighting had been entailed and casualties suffered. The failing light and the thick woods on either side of the road decided the CO, Lt-Col D. R. Wilson, to put the remainder of the Bn across and consolidate. The enemy was strongly placed in a sunken road (Vire–Aunay) astride our axis of advance. But HQ remained just south of Montisenger and during its shelling the MO, Capt Little, and Padre, Capt Strutt, were wounded. During the first day of this battle there were

45 casualties including Lt Hempsall and 5 ORs KIA. During the final stages the CO was hit by a mortar bomb fragment. The Bn spent the night alone in enemy territory under Major L.H.B. Colvin. The following day [7th] with a new CO, Lt-Col Firbank, the attack started again towards the railway line. 'A' Coy were caught in the open cornfields and pinned down. 'D' Coy on the left managed to get a section across the roadway but were blasted back by mortars. The attack petered out with the loss of 35 casualties.

Meanwhile Maj. Hugh Gillies, OC 'C' Company 1 KOSB, reported their attack parallel to the Lincolns. The bridge at La Houardière was blown and no tank support had arrived:

The attack was launched at 1830 when 'A' and 'C' Coys crossed the start line. The Germans spotted us immediately, opened up with concentrated mortar fire which caught us on the forward slope. After we had pushed on about 400 yards beyond the stream, MG and small arms went into action and a call was sent for tank support. Only one troop (of 44 RTR) managed to cross the stream but with their assistance 'C' Coy managed to reach the railway line. The light was failing. The Lincolns on our right had not succeeded in crossing the stream so the forward companies had no flank protection. Casualties were heavy and a platoon of 'A' Coy had vanished without trace. The operation came to a standstill and during the night it was decided to withdraw the remainder of 'A' and 'C' to form a strong perimeter around the stream crossings. These positions were held during the following day (7th) while the enemy continued to shell and mortar us.

The sappers of 253 Field Company RE built a new bridge called Hawick over the stream and lost nine casualties in the process.

Three miles east, 185 Brigade was soon to be in desperate trouble. 'Around midnight [5 Aug] I made contact with Brigadier Jack Churcher [of 159 Infantry Bde, 11th AD] who pointed out a burning ridge in the distance and said [to Maj. Humphrey Wilson, Royal Norfolks] "There are the Monmouths or what is left of them, be careful how you go as we are only in wireless touch with them. Be prepared to take over from them at first light."' Heavy mist on the morning of the 6th initially hid the Norfolks take-over moving south-east through Burcy towards Sourdevalle. When the hot sun broke through, 'B' Company under Maj. Cooper-Key were spotted and became an easy target for intense mortar fire from 10th SS Panzer Division. 'A' Company under Maj. MacGillivray made a detour to avoid Burcy, but suffered seventeen casualties. 'C' Company under Capt. H.J. Jones were also badly hit as they followed up. By 1700 hrs, however, the relief of three of the Monmouth's rifle companies had been achieved. Half an hour later, though, a very heavy artillery stonk fell on the rear of the relieving Norfolks, setting most of 'F' echelon's vehicles ablaze. The two battalion COs pooled forces (called Nor-Mons) totalling only 550 men but supported by the Shermans of the 2nd Fife and Forfar Yeomanry. At 1815 hrs 'B' Company was attacked and partly overrun and by 2030 hrs 'C' Company was down to thirty-five, all ranks. The desperate situation was not helped by friendly US Thunderbolts firing their cannon on the hapless 'Nor-Mons'.

'One evening 12 [US] Thunderbolts flew over our area. Three of them peeled off and after circling dropped three bombs in the field by 319 Bty', recalls Jack Prior, 92 LAA, 'attracting some of the strongest language of the campaign. The unwritten rule was "If attacked, shoot first and ask questions afterwards."'

'The scene was indescribable,' wrote Humphrey Wilson, 'blazing vehicles, dead men and cattle. The Thunderbolts gave us a good strafing. "B" Coy "got on the air", told Bn HQ by wireless that it was being heavily counter-attacked. In this attack Corporal Bates won the Victoria Cross.' Known as 'Basher', Bates was commanding the right forward section of the left forward 'B' Company and, seeing the situation was desperate, seized a light machine gun, charged the enemy through a hail of bullets, firing the gun from his hip. Although hit three times, he went on charging and firing until the enemy started to withdraw. It was a truly brilliant, heroic effort. He died of his wounds two days later.

A Tiger tank moved through 'C' Company, 3 Mons killing many men in their slit trenches. 'The enemy came on and on out of the sun. Our artillery worked wonders and everyone had a shot at the Boche,' recalls Humphrey Wilson. 'At about 1930 some twenty Shermans of the Fife and Forfars arrived and everybody took on a new lease of life. By 2130 hours the last of the enemy had disappeared, a great number had been killed, a large number wounded and the rest just went back.'

Sourdevalle had cost the Norfolks 176 casualties including 32 KIA. For five more days the Norfolks stayed there licking their wounds often under heavy Nebelwerfer fire. 'After a time the whole area reeked of death.' In the battle of Sourdevalle, Sgt. C. Hopkins won the DCM. Though wounded in the leg, he engaged and hit a Tiger tank with a PIAT; CSM T. Catlin, Sgt. G.A. Smith, Cpl. C. Thirtle and Maj. W.E.G. Bagwell, among others, won awards for gallantry.

Jim Wisewell RAMC:

From August 6–9th our Advanced Dressing Station was set up in a cornfield near Sourdevalle, receiving casualties from the 1st Norfolks who were having a rough time at Pavée, a mile or so away, losing about 40 killed and many more wounded. A corporal was brought in badly wounded, and we did all we could for him before evacuating him to the Casualty Clearing Station. His name was Sidney Bates; he died of his wounds and is buried at Bayeux. He was awarded a posthumous VC and

I had the honour in 1986 of sharing with the Revd Jim Green, Padre to the 1st Norfolks in 1944, in the dedication service of a memorial to Corporal Sidney Bates VC, at the place where he won it.

Jim Wisewell again:

He was about 16, a Panzer-Grenadier from the 12th SS Division. Badly wounded, he needed an urgent blood transfusion to save his life and the MO ordered it to be set up. The boy pushed it away. 'Nein', he said, 'Nein'. We asked him 'Why not?' There was a fanatical gleam in his eyes as he said 'It may be Jewish blood. I would rather die.' We evacuated him but I believe he died on the way to the CCS.

Lt. Geoffrey Forrest, CO at 185 Brigade HQ:

The Mons had taken a beating. In the close country work, man-power began to be a bit of a problem. The Norfolks who had combined to make a Bn strength with the Mons were down, but their spirits were high. The Warwicks out of our command had driven off several counter attacks, sustained a lot of casualties. The KSLI although at about ¾ of their strength, were the best off. The value of DF and SOS tasks smashed up a counter-attack about regimental strength on the Norfolks front. A scene of great slaughter, the screams from the Boche were eerie: I don't think one German got out of that concentration alive. It was terrific. The guns of the Field Regs were red-hot after the shoot, fired for about 20 minutes steadily. In the bocage one met numerous small teams of say one Tiger, one or two MGs, at crossroads or tracks. The SS boys were really tough, quite ready to die rather than give up. They never bother to bury any dead either, British or Boche, however long he may sit looking at them. The Major commanding the [Middlesex] 4.2" mortars managed to get hold of some multi-barrelled affairs (Minenwerfers), gave the Boche some of his own medicine. The Boche is a really tough and efficient soldier, but no better than the Tommy.

The 2 Warwicks were also in trouble around Le Bas Perrier, a mile due east of the Norfolks. A brigade of 9th SS Division attacked 'B' Company at close range in the high bocage hedgerows, inflicting thirty casualties. Maj. T.G. Bundock DSO tried to save the crew of a burning 23rd Hussar Sherman and was killed when the tank exploded. At 1600 hrs enemy mortar and artillery fire intensified and despite intense DF and SOS fireplans, tanks and infantry got into 'B' Company's locality causing many more losses. But 'C' Company stood firm and the Germans tried to work their way round both flanks. For another four hours the battle continued before the Panzer SS withdrew at nightfall. The next day it was less parlous, but very unpleasant. 'C' Company in Le Bas Perrier shared the vicinity with an enemy tank, later disabled by a patrol, and several more 23rd Hussar tanks were knocked out. On the 9th the Warwicks were relieved and went back to Presles, having suffered 23 KIA, 143 officers and ORs wounded and 30 ORs missing. Six officers had been wounded and one killed among the almost two hundred casualties incurred during Bluecoat.

CHAPTER FIFTEEN

Operations Walter and Wallop

'Just Like Africa Days'

Eddie Jones, IO South Lancs, described the new battlegrounds of southern Normandy:

> This was open country of rolling hills, somewhat similar to the Cotswolds, and very different from the close 'bocage' countryside in which we had been fighting. We were obviously entering a new phase of war; the fighting was more fluid, though we did not at this stage realise that the Germans in France were in full retreat and the Falaise pocket was only days ahead. Certainly, there was every appearance of an enemy withdrawal. We were moving across the grain of the country, i.e. up and down the slopes, rather than along the valleys, and the enemy to our immediate front were covering the withdrawal of their main forces to Argentan and beyond. At the crest of each hill along our axis of advance the enemy would station a 75 or 88 mm gun or a tank, supported by a few infantry with automatic weapons. Skilfully, with a minimum of troops and few casualties, they slowed our advance and bought time for their main body. Their anti-tank gun would destroy one or two of our leading tanks, forcing the remainder to leave the road, whilst their automatic fire obliged our infantry to deploy. Mortar or artillery fire would then be brought down on our troops. By the time we had concerted an attack on their position we would find it abandoned, the enemy having withdrawn to the next bound.

Lt.-Col. W.F.H. Kempster became the new GSO 1. His first operation was Operation Walter (named after him), described by 'Bolo' Whistler as 'a tidying up "op" with 185 and 9 Brigades'.

The Ulster Rifles, who had been in 9 Brigade reserve, were given the task of capturing Vaudry, a mile or so due east of Vire. So via La Gallonerie the attack went in at 0600 hrs on 9 August, only to find the village abandoned. Shelling wounded RSM Fleming, later awarded the MC.

Operation Wallop would be a two-brigade attack to take Tinchebray, 10 miles south-east of Vire, and was planned to start on 11 August. 3 German Parachute Division was in Viessoix (east of Vire) and Roullours (south-east of Vire) and 10th SS Panzer Division was still holding Chênedollé (north-east of Viessoix). 3rd Recce Regiment led and reported Viessoix clear, predictably 'Old Socks' in radio code. Brig. 'Copper' Cass's 8 Brigade followed. The South Lancs started at 0900 hrs in dense mist and advanced unopposed for 3 miles, but at 1300 hrs they met heavy fire at Point 272 and were pinned down. The carrier platoon was fired on by four Spandaus and surrounded. Maj. Neville Chance and CSM Coombes were wounded, but the former fought his way out single-handedly and crawled back 2 miles to Battalion HQ. The East Yorks reported a 'small' counter-attack. The Lincolns made contact with the Americans in the suburbs of Vire. Lt. J.R. Bush led a patrol with bravery and panache, and earned the MC for it, but was wounded for the second time. Sgt. Wilcock died of wounds in the action.

1 Suffolk called Operation Wallop, Operation 'Grouse' and by 1600 hrs had reached l'Oisonnière as support battalion.

185 Brigade also started off at 0930 hrs with 2 KSLI directed on Roullours, which by 1000 hrs was found to be empty. 'The enemy in small MG parties was roaming about in copses and lanes, firing bursts at close range and then nipping away. This was annoying,' wrote Capt. R.R. Rylands, 'W' Company, 'especially as I was still genuinely lost. [Later] We reached the top of Pt 262 and decided that further warfare could wait until we had brewed some tea.' But the final objective, Point 312, was more difficult. 'Several Scots Greys tanks were hit or stuck, and both companies, "W" and "Y" were held up by shelling and by roving machine-gunners, impudent and effective. "W" Coy's casualties were mounting to little purpose, included the well-known figures of Sgt Whyle and Pte Wood. It had been a particularly tiring and hot day, delighted when CQMS Francis and Pte Lineton brought up stores and food. Our "A" Echelon never failed.' The KSLI lost thirty-five casualties that day. The Warwicks followed up and were ensconced in La Maslerie by dusk.

Lt. Eddie Jones, IO South Lancs:

I accompanied Lt Col Orgill to the Bd 'O' Group presided over by Brigadier Cass. It was a fine evening [1900] and the 'O' Group was in a farmhouse with cobbled courtyard. The Brigadier sat in his camp chair, back to the farmhouse facing the courtyard. Col Orgill's orders were to occupy Pt 279 at first light and allow 1 Suffolk, 2 E Yorks to pass through. We left the 'O' Group to enter the brick barn where our jeep was parked. A loud explosion. All the 'O' Group except the Brigadier were lying on the ground either dead or wounded. The Brigadier looked around, shook himself, shouted 'Send for the seconds-in-command!' There was no warning whistle, perhaps it was a mortar bomb.

Bill Renison's views:

> I was ordered to report urgently to Brigade HQ. I found Orgill, S Lancs, Allen the 2 i/c Suffolks, Val Lloyd the GSO 3, a tank brigadier and Cass sitting unconcernedly on a box in the middle of the 'O' Group. No sign of Dickson [Renison's CO], no explanation given. Apparently Col Goff of Suffolks, Digby Shatterwaite the BM, Donald Fraser the Staff Capt, and a tank major had just all been wounded. A bit of a shock to find myself in command. The CO 76 Field Reg [Lt.-Col. Mervyn Foster, the East Yorks gunner regiment] was killed on his way between the Suffolks and East Yorks. The Boche left a note on his body saying apologies for not having time to bury such a high ranking officer. We captured a German Sergeant Major [early in one action] with his company roll in his pocket, so we were able to check the tally of prisoners taken, and check the strength of the Boche garrison. We had a complete lack of trained snipers, so essential in the bocage country. Their snipers had made a variety of alternative posts [in the hedgerows].

The advance continued on 12 August with South Lancs astride the main road south-east to Tinchebray and East Yorks on the left. The vital Point 312 was now occupied by five gunner FOOs – British and American – and by the GOC and the Corps Commander, Lt.-Gen. R.N. O'Connor. 1 Suffolk made a firm base at La Villonière and 8 Brigade's objective, 'Pepper' – the crossroads by Coquard and Point 279, half-way to Tinchebray – was reached.

Lt.-Col. Eric Lummis in '1 Suffolk in Normandy': 'It was the 11/8th Parachute Regiment (of 3rd Parachute Division) that the Bn was to be fighting against for the next 48 hours.' In the Vire–Tinchebray 'Operation Grouse or Wallop' 1 Suffolk suffered 168 casualties (4 officers and 25 ORs KIA and 10 officers and 129 ORs wounded). The 2-mile line of objectives south-east from the Coquard crossroads, across 'Pepper', 'Oil' and 'Vinegar', from the hills of Points 279, 247, 259 and 251 would take nearly three days, supported by Guards Armoured Churchill tanks. In close country – 'bocage' of small fields and high hedgerows – the 1 Suffolk had to fight tenaciously against rifle, MG and mortar fire. 'B' Company was practically wiped out, losing Maj. Duxbury, Capt. Calder, all three platoon commanders and the CSM. By 0300 hrs on 14 August they had reached Point 251, 'Oil', and had taken nearly four hundred prisoners. 'A' Company under Maj. Jack Prescott, made several successful attacks and counter-attacks, for which he was awarded the MC. Farmyard hens and ducks appeared in one defensive position. Maj. Prescott's orders were crisp: 'Twenty minute break. Keep the white duck for me.' One new, very new, reinforcement, spotted a German leaving his position and asked, 'What do I do now?' And Robert Moberley, 2 Middlesex, wrote: 'At Etouvy Major Langley adopted a small pig named "Monty". The Bn signwriter painted the Div Triangle and the Bn 64 on its rump.'

The attack by the East Yorkshires on the left was held up. The very popular Maj. Gaskell, 'B' Squadron 3 Recce, was killed by the bridge at Montsecret.

17 Field Squadron RE built a reinforced concrete bridge on the Tinchebray–Vire road. The work was carried out underneath an existing Bailey bridge built by 3 Troop. Sgt. Frank Faulkner notes that the same stone bridge is used today. Called Le Pont du Madeleine, there are two engraved stones inset describing – in French and English – who made the bridge and when.

On the eastern flank with 185 Brigade, the Warwicks had reached Creuley, 2 miles south of Viessoix, by 13 August, and in the evening 'D' and 'C' Companies with a squadron of tanks, took on 3rd Parachute Division's rearguard under a hail of mortar and shellfire. Three company commanders were wounded almost immediately (Maj. T.L. Brock, Capt. M.L.B. Hall and Capt. J.A. Clarke), and though a bridgehead was made over the little river (a branch of the Noireau), ten men were killed and over fifty, all ranks, were wounded. On 14 August two officers and ninety-seven ORs arrived as reinforcements, but the Warwicks sadly were much understrength. 1 Suffolk sent two fighting patrols, John 'Perrett' Force and Ken 'Mayhew' Force, eastwards towards St Quentin des Chardonnets, which was found to be empty, so a full-scale attack by the South Lancs was called off. As Lt.-Col. Gough had been wounded at the Brigade 'O' Group, Maj. Freddy Allen was in command of 1 Suffolk. Brig. Cass sent him a letter to congratulate him. 'Please inform all ranks that it was a very good show and really shook the Boche.'

On the morning of the 15th the Recce Regiment put their scout cars of 'C' Squadron into Tinchebray 10 minutes ahead of the US 102 Mechanised Cavalry, although technically the 1 Suffolk water-cart appeared to have arrived first – by mistake! The river bridge was blown and the enemy was in full retreat towards the bottleneck of the Argentan–Falaise pocket. Overnight the South Lancs and East Yorks got over the river without opposition, and the following morning 'C' Squadron 3 Recce scout cars and Ken Mayhew's carriers of 1 Suffolk raced east for 10 miles to enter Flers just ahead of the Northants Yeomanry of 11th Armoured Division.

Flers greeted the Iron Division warmly, they were 'showered with bouquets and flowers and kisses', wine and calvados flowed and the whole town was *en fête*. The Divisional Intelligence summary noted that Flers was actually taken *before* the BBC announced its capture.

The GOC wrote in his diary:

August 17. Quite a definite period in the operations. 3 Div captured Flers yesterday with considerable speed and a lot of vigour. But oh what a business to get things going and then keep them going. Dominic Browne (new CO of 9 Bde) a success, if perhaps a little slow starting. Anyway 185 [Brigade] got on top of a monster hill [312] eventually. SE of Vire, 9

1st Bn South Lancs move past 'Big Friends' between Vire and Tinchebray. (IWM, B 9019)

Bde got up where they had failed the day before, and 8 Bde struggled along. 4 Armoured Bde taken from me in the middle of the action. There was a lot of close fighting and we got a bit hurt. . . . 185 and 8 Bdes had a small advance to help US Div (2nd under General Robertson). 185 had nil success and Warwicks were a bit slaughtered but 8 Bde had a first class little action and knocked hell out of the Para boys in front of them – killing plenty and getting 130 prisoners. Things began to ease up and finally the Hun pulled out. Fearful difficulty in getting anybody to get after him. Managed eventually and we beat the US into Tinchebray, then on and on again, just like Africa days to Flers, a considerable town smashed up completely. And in poor Vire there is hardly a house left. This Hun has something to answer for, although it is us who are bashing the towns and villages. The dead cattle and humans stench the place and there are some pretty gruesome sights.

In his Order of the Day 'Bolo' praised his Iron Division: 'I am most grateful for your efforts and very, very proud of your achievements so far.'

2nd Middlesex [wrote Maj. Robert Moberley] was used to make a survey of part of the Falaise battlefield to count the guns, tanks, vehicles and weapons abandoned. A loathsome but rather fascinating job. Falaise itself was the most devasated town yet seen, a holocaust of dead German horses and horsedrawn transport. Cider was swilled by the gallon, calvados by the pint. Flers became the recreation centre with cinema and ENSA shows and the Div club. Officers trips were made to Brittany and Paris, also leave to Corps Rest Centre at St Aubyn-sur-Mer. The Naafi issue came up with long overdue double issue of beer. Plenty of football until the weather got too hot.

Flanagan and Allen, Kay Cavendish and Florence Desmond were popular performers.

Training started quickly and Maj. Ted Kilshaw ran the Divisional Training school. Initially the emphasis was on river-crossing as it was expected that the river Seine would be heavily defended, but soon it changed to tank/infantry close cooperation. On 25 August 1 Suffolk had a memorial service for those who had lost their lives in the break-out from the bridgehead. The Royal Norfolk HQ even had Britannia flying from a flag-pole.

Jim Wisewell, RAMC private, 223 Field Ambulance:

When the fierce fighting at Sourdeval was over, Lew Williams, Mickey House, Jack Heyworth and I went bathing in the River Vire at Etouvay. It was boiling hot and we dried off in the sun before exploring the Mill – the Moulin d'Etouvay. This had been left in a hurry. Supper was still on the table, plates with a half-eaten meal, cheese growing whiskers, glasses half-emptied of wine. We wrote a note of sympathy from 'quatre simples soldats' and stuck it behind a picture.

For the Iron Division the Normandy campaign was over, but eight thousand young men of Monty's Iron Sides were already casualties. And there was northern France, Belgium, Holland and the Fatherland still to go!

CHAPTER SIXTEEN

In Limbo

Waiting for the War to Start Again

For a month the Iron Division, to quote Maj. M.J.P.M. Corbally's history of the Royal Ulster Rifles: 'found themselves in the rear of the Naafi and the ATS'. The 2 RUR CO, Lt.-Col. Harris, at Heuqueville, met the charming young lady who became his wife. The move from Flers 150 miles north-east to the river Seine area took place between 1 and 3 September. Many reinforcements arrived, counter-mortar, infantry-tank cooperations and house clearance training courses were arranged. Pipe Major Doyle of the King's Irish Liverpool Rifles appeared with five pipers. Capt. R.R. Rylands, 'W' Company 2 KSLI:

> Very squashed in TCVs we moved on Sept 1st to the pleasant little village of Villers-en-Vexin, across the Seine, the whole area steeped in Anglo-French history. We did some useful training, absorbed reinforcements and changed remarkably rapidly from a gang of piratical roughs into a smart and well drilled military body again. We presented arms in the village street, inspected kits in the village hen-lofts and cow byres. Some of us even washed and went to Paris. And 'W' Coy looked well when the Bn was inspected by the GOC General Whistler. We made many friends in Villers. We ate as well as ever we did, with a profusion of eggs and mushrooms. We danced and sang. Musicians like L/C Foweraker found pianos to torment and farmers like Pte Matthews tried their hand at ploughing with oxen. In short we enjoyed ourselves.'

'In Etrepagny we enjoyed considerable comfort,' wrote Iain Wilson, 1 KOSB, 'dances were held, dinner parties given and the locals challenged at football and basketball. The performances by the Pipes & Drums sealed the popularity of the Bn. The only drawback – the local girls brought their whole family with them to the dances from aged grandparents to children in arms.' Pipe Major W. Denholm had a new tune, 'The Caen March'.

Bill Renison, 2 i/c East Yorks:

> I went back to Army HQ, had lunch there. Cottage pie, jam tart and real tea without sugar. I bought whole Camemberts at 11 francs each. I organised more 9th Bn Buffs reinforcements inc Chris Pemberton and magnificent

stuff they afterwards turned out to be. The Army Post Office now changed our address from British Western Europe Forces to British Liberation Army. . . . One minor horror of war occurred when 'B' Coy killed and ate Bob Laird's pet rabbit, strayed through the hedge into their area. . . . I found the Brigadier [Cass] very friendly and complimentary about our share in the recent operations which was most unusual for him. A few days later however Cass visited the Bn and delivered a tremendous rocket to Victor Leach, the Padre, whom he met wearing a top hat borrowed from the house where the RAP was. Dickson [the CO] came back on the 16th. We both agreed that being 2 i/c is a dreadful job, waiting for dead men's shoes.

The adjutant (and historian) of 33rd Field Regiment RA, Capt. Brymer, recalls how after using SP 105-mm guns for fourteen months, the Americans now needed them back. On 14 August the regiment was reorganised with towed 25-pounders. But all their drivers with AFV (Armoured Fighting Vehicle) experience were now needed elsewhere and most of their 3-ton lorries were loaned to the RASC to help build up forward ammunition dumps. 'However on 3rd Sept we left St Clair d'Halouze with the good wishes of the village, laden with flowers and fruit and not a little calvados . . . and arrived after a 160-mile journey at

Royal Norfolk 'S' Company officers' picnic at Villers. Left to right: Capt. W.J. Smart, Capt. T.P.K. Oakey, Lt. P.W. Buckerfield, Capt. J.A. Allen, Capt. P.G. Baker, Lt. E.A. Gray.

CHAPTER EIGHTEEN

Operation Market Garden

September

As part of 8 Corps with 11 Armoured Division, the division was to protect the right flank of the famous, daring drive to link up with the three Airborne Division drops from Eindhoven to Arnhem. On their way through northern France, Sgt. Fred Hartle, 1 KOSB, writes: 'East of Louvain was the area where the Bn had met the invading Germans in 1940 and had to retire with our backs to the sea at Dunkirk – but that's another story!'

On 18 September the flank advance started with an assault crossing of the Meuse–Escaut canal to seize the main road and railway on the north side. From Lille St Hubert, 9 Brigade led with a midnight attack. The canal, 40 yds wide and with 10-ft high banks, would be spanned later by a Class 9 and a Class 40 bridge. 2 RUR was on the left of the original blown bridge, 2 Lincolns on the right and 1 KOSB in reserve provided the storm-boat carrying parties. From 0030 hrs 474 Searchlight Company provided the new night-time tactic of 'artificial moonlight' and at 2345 hrs the divisional artillery programme started.

The RUR had an uneventful crossing, but, while boats were being launched, lost casualties to mortar fire and later to counter-attacks on the far side. Capt. Laving and 2nd Lt. Morgan were killed, but the enemy lost nearly a hundred men, killed, wounded and captured, plus a large quantity of guns, bazookas, mortars and machine guns. Maj. de Longueuil's 'C' Company distinguished itself; Sgt. Peel threw thirty-six grenades shrewdly, and Rifleman Greene, 'B' Company, earned the MM. And an accolade must go to Capts. Gaffikin and Baudains of 'B' Company who, heavily disguised in 'civvies', had carried out a daylight recce before the attack. So the village of Broek was taken, a bridgehead established, 'bridging and rafting went ahead with great gusto, anti-tank guns and jeeps were shipped across. The sappers Class 9 bridge was built and by 1000 hrs the RUR were firm, secure and prepared for any eventuality,' wrote Ken Bradshaw.

The bridge at Lille St Hubert allowed the 11 Armoured Division, in which the author served, to cross over without much thought of gratitude! However, for the Lincolns it was rather different, as Maj. Glyn Gilbert, OC 'C' Company, recalled:

Up the bank we scrambled lugging our boats and easing them down the steep slope into the water. The enemy response was immediate and fierce. Very heavy mortar fire opened up directed at the canal and village and several MG and a 20 mm were firing on fixed lines down the canal. We immediately suffered heavy casualties crossing the bank. The boat on my right received a direct mortar bomb hit. We left two sunken boats and over 70 NCOs and men killed and wounded in the canal and on the banks. George Bennett had most of his jaw shot off. Peter London and Denis Querky, two platoon commanders, were dead. The Germans had fought a good action at little loss to themselves.

By 0215 hrs all the rifle companies were across and digging while Battalion HQ consolidated in Broek. George Bennett wrote:

The canal was very low, a drop of some 6 ft to get into the assault boats. All the time during the crossing there was intense mortar fire and the crossing was most uncomfortable. Once we gained the further side we were ordered to advance some 100 yards and dig in. A house on fire nearby was burning fiercely, silhouetted me against the flames. A sniper manning an Oerliken picked me off. Not a nice weapon when used in a ground role and the bullet that hit me didn't do my face much good. I spent two years in and out of hospital. End of my war!'

'9 Platoon had a new officer, Lt Taylor. Sgt Goode had been acting Pln commander and I [Fred Hartle, 1 KOSB] was acting Pln sergeant. We crossed the canal in little canvas boats. A farm on the other side was on fire, lit up the whole area. At dawn, heavy mist and in poor visibility Lt Taylor told me to take a point section up in front. [Later] I could hear the platoon coming up behind us. Their rifle butts were catching against their shovels. I could also hear them talking a mile away.' Fred spoke sharply to them! Subsequently Lt. Taylor was killed in his first action, along with three or four of Fred's platoon.

The pioneers, under Lt. Pogson, built two Class 5 rafts and ferried all the battalion transport across. 246 Company RE built their 160-ft Class 9 bridge in record time between 0100 hrs and 0700 hrs, and 17 Field Company RE built their Class 40 bridge, which was finished by 1700 hrs the next day, the 19th. Now the GOC ordered 8 Brigade to cross the canal on the right of Lille St Hubert and two Canloan officers in the South Lancs, Alfred Cope and Eric Fryer, were killed during the crossing. The East Yorks linked up with 'A' Company of the Lincolns to battle with young SS officer cadets in a wood, and thirty-two of them surrendered the next morning.

Next, 185 Brigade came up and Capt. R.R. Rylands, 2 KSLI, remembers: 'I went forward to see the South Lancs Coy attempt a crossing. It was rather noisily done and their first Pl. fell into a trap, some being ambushed behind the high bank where they had got over, others being

The old faithful half track which carried its crew from D-Day to VE-Day. Although knocked out several times, the vehicle was recovered on each occasion. To allow room to carry more explosives, the top was boxed in with strong timber by Sapper Lofty Stevenson, who also provided the shuttering for the bridge at Tinchebray. (Frank Faulkner)

caught in the boats. We helped to extricate some of the latter and offered fire support, but this was refused . . . . 'W' Coy moved up and took over from the remaining South Lancs who withdrew. Some cross-canal sniping ensued.' At 1945 hrs on 20 September 'X' and 'W' Companies crossed in assault boats 1 mile north of the blown bridge on the main road from Caulille to Weert, established their bridgehead and advanced south down the canal against heavy opposition. By the night of the 21st they had suffered over thirty casualties. Meanwhile, 1 Suffolk took sixty prisoners in Hamont for the single loss KIA of Pte. Hollis. He was given a slap-up funeral with full civic honours, as huge crowds formed a cortège to his grave.

Maj. Robert Moberley, 2 Middlesex: 'Several million German rations were captured in Hamont, the pork and beans and cheese were quite good. But we all hated the ersatz coffee, biscuits, "knackebrot" and the cigars were quite amusing.' On the other hand the gunners of 33rd Field Regiment RA reported: 'The honey biscuits and frozen vegetables were approved but the meat was not popular.' Cheese in 'toothpaste' tubes was an edible novelty. Ray Paine, 2nd Lincolns, had strong feelings too: 'We lived off German frankfurters (a small smoked sausage) – very spicey. Ugh!' Oss was another huge German supply depot which supplied 30 and 8 Corps with Wehrmacht rations for two weeks until the Normandy bridgehead supplies caught up.

Unbeknown to most, the Airborne troops fought and died in Arnhem 50 miles due north.

The GOC's diary of 20 September: 'The Div is now concentrated – or rather it has curled its tail up and thrust its head over the Escaut. Damn fine Div! To do the crossing 9 Bde were the clever boys – and my staff! Anyway the job got done quite brilliantly. It was about a 250-mile move up to begin with and we were very short of equipment, ammo and also food. This Army under Monty and Dempsey is a pretty remarkable show. Their plans and conceptions are quite staggering.' 'The Div Club', Norman Scarfe commented, 'made a determined effort to establish itself in luxury in Brussels, but was prevailed to move to the village of Peer.'

On the evening of the 19th a company runner, Pte. Charles Ramage from Townhead, Glasgow, got lost. He saw a village, made a canny recce and was spotted by the villagers who flocked excitedly out of their houses to hail the bewildered liberator – it was Achel, just inside the Belgian border! But the battalion suffered many casualties from small arms fire as the Borderers moved into the village. Iain Wilson, the KOSB padre: 'The villagers were rapturous, wept on our shoulders, drew us to their hearts and kissed us, pressed fruit and flowers upon us.'

Sgt. Fred Hartle's 9 Platoon KOSB was now commanded by Canloan Lt. Rose. Fred was ordered to take a Bren carrier with crew to check and clear a village ahead: 'Some shots were fired at us from a wood, and a salvo of shells whistled over our heads and landed in the village behind where the remainder of the platoon was positioned. Lt Rose was wounded in the eye, taken away to hospital, so another officer was lost in such a short time.'

On the morning of the 20th 8 Brigade moved due east and 1 KOSB advanced towards Achel, north-west of Lille St Hubert, after crossing spongy fields and boggy countryside. Capt. J.B. Cranston reported: 'A determined German M. Gunner, he was a deadly shot, held us up for more than an hour.' The opposition was partly SS of 12th Panzer Division – old Normandy foes – part airborne and Luftwaffe.

On the morning of 21 September 8 Brigade crossed over the Dutch frontier and occupied Weert with 1 Suffolk leading, followed by East Yorks and 76th Field Regiment RA. Maj. Claxton led 'D' Company across the Dutch border at 1230 hrs; it was a desolate area of sand, scrub and fir plantations and they were met by heavy Spandau fire as they approached the railway from the dune. Shielded by smoke from their own 3-in mortars they pressed on, but at 2200 hrs heard explosions east and south-east as the canal bridges and ammo dumps were blown. Lt.-Col. Craddock kept 1 Suffolk going across the sandy wastes of Boshover Heide and by 0315 hrs on the 22nd had reached the Weert canal.

In Weert itself the streets were soon decked with orange flags and beribboned portraits of Queen Wilhelmina, Princess Juliana and Prince Bernhard. They sang a shrill nursery song rather like 'Aye, aye, ippy, ippy aye'. The Dutch newspapers rebuked the kids for asking 'Tommy' for cigarettes and chocolates: 'Remember your manners, Dutch children don't scrounge,' and schoolmasters taught children how to sing a well-rehearsed 'God Save the King'. Windmills received new coats of paint in honour of the liberation, with red, white and blue sails and a strong splash of orange on the base of the mill. Little girls wore orange frocks or pinafores, and little boys wore orange shirts. Even the monks and nuns wore orange 'favours' to show loyalty to the royal family. The embarassed Jocks danced on the village green.

The Belgian and Dutch resistance movements were invaluable. Besides beating up and arresting suspected collaborators, they telephoned around the countryside, finding out and reporting back the local German troop dispositions. And they rounded up German stragglers. Their courage over the last few years was indisputable; the underground movement had sheltered Allied airmen shot down over their country and devised intricate escape systems.

Bill Renison, CO East Yorks, noted in his journal:

We made ourselves very comfortable and very popular in Gemert – the Bn home station during the long winter campaign. Battle dress was pressed up again with female assistance. The troops wore soft hats off duty and could walk freely round the town. We played Retreat on the 27th in front of the town monastery. We billeted the troops in garages and barns. The Boche always turned people out of their own homes. A great temptation to the troops was the price of 1 cigarette, a Dutch guilder!

Near Weert, Lt. Eddy Jones, South Lancs:

At dawn we passed in an industrial estate, a large scale battery hen farm. As the coys went past men took off their helmets and filled them with eggs. I said to my batman 'Cook a dozen or so of those for our breakfast'. We liberated two million eggs – a month's quota for delivery to the Wehrmacht. The divisional gunners soon found that the great church belfry tower made an excellent OP until an unfriendly German 88 mm gunner thought otherwise!

Marcus Cunliffe, 2 Royal Warwicks, described the countryside which had effectively destroyed any chances that Guards Armoured and 43rd Wessex Wyverns had of relieving the beleaguered Airborne in Arnhem: 'Desolate sandy heaths, belts of pine trees, meagre little farms, the roads were mere tracks, mines were difficult to detect, vehicles were constantly bogged, the fields were water-logged and the causeways stood nakedly above the fields.' Very difficult for armour and infantry to progress against a determined enemy.

For a week in cold wet weather 8 and 185 Brigades plus 3 Recce Regiment patrolled the eastern axis of 8 Corps from Weert, 20 miles north to Asten, Liesel, Deurne and Helmond. 1 KOSB moved from Achel to Budel in Holland, where the troops quickly disposed of the watery beer left in the cafés, then on 24 September moved to Liesel. Here patrols went out to Meijel and the line of the Deurne canal. The Scotsmen (and others) were given the freedom of Helmond with its clubs, cinemas and theatres. During the last three days of September the battalion was guarding the important crossroads at Milheeze, 5 miles north of Deurne. The Middlesex sent No. 6 platoon carriers into Helmond, where they were mobbed and soon had twenty Dutch on each carrier. The drivers wore orange jockey caps, orange ribbon and orange tricoleur favours. The local liberation committee organised dances in the railway buffet room. Frank Neuerberg, a Dutch nephew of Lt. Clarke, South Lancs, joined the battalion as interpreter and served until the end of the war. Lt. Eddie Jones met a unit of 82 US Airborne. Their HQ was in a charming villa. The rather overweight American general, without a jacket, in his braces, was smoking a large cigar. Eddie duly saluted the rather surprised general, who called all his staff by their Christian names, as they did to him. 'Lesson of democracy in action!'

2 KSLI moved up to Zomeren and relieved the Herefords of 11th Armoured near Asten. Guy Radcliffe: 'Most depressing place, the weather was vile, pouring rain, the country low and waterlogged, the roads and tracks covered with mud and the ditches full of the decaying bodies of the enemy dead.' On 29 September the battalion moved back to Zomeren, then to Asten to allow US 7th Armoured's attack through Overloon and Venraij to Venlo.

CHAPTER NINETEEN

Operation Aintree

October

The 43rd Wessex Wyverns Division had fought their way to the outskirts of Arnhem/Oosterbeek and eventually rescued 2,500 of the doomed Airborne – but it was a glorious failure. 30 Corps in the centre had tried their damnedest, so too had 8 and 12 Corps on their flanks. Lt.-Gen. Brian Horrocks wrote in his memoirs: 'The failure at Arnhem was primarily due to the astonishing recovery made by the German armed forces after their crippling defeat in Normandy.'

The Iron Sides now had a new problem on their doorstep. The American 7th Armoured Division (known as The Lucky Seven) had ventured into the marshy Dutch Peel country to try to take Oploo, Overloon and the town of Venraij. In the first six days of October they took 452 casualties and had 35 tanks and 43 other vehicles destroyed. Operation Constellation was the name of the 8 Corps' plan to take over from the Americans and complete the job they had failed to do. Operation Aintree was the task for 3rd Division – initially to capture Overloon and then to take Venraij – by attacking south-east from Oploo. This would draw in enemy reserves while 11th Armoured and 15th Scottish cleared the remainder of the pocket.

The enemy, having seen off the American armour, were well dug in and ready for trouble. The German 180 Infantry Division was boosted by battle groups Paul, Hoffman, Kerutt and Walter. A stream called the Molen Beek ran north-west/south-east half-way between Overloon and Venraij, which were well defended by minefields. The muddy fields and farm tracks made tank support difficult. It was going to be a very tough and difficult battle.

8 Brigade was to lead, with Overloon its objective, by exploiting south-west down the road to Venraij; 9 Brigade would clear the Laag Heide woods 2 miles north-west of Venraij and then cross over the Molen Beek. 185 Brigade was initially in reserve to reinforce the final attack. 8 AGRA plus three divisional artillery groups (3rd British, 11th Armoured and 15th Scottish) would bring down huge barrages. AVREs from 42 ARE, flails of the Westminster Dragoons and most of the 6th Guards Armoured Brigade were in support.

'We had protected the bridge at Lille St Hubert and destroyed one of the new ME 262s as well as ME 109s,' recalls Capt. Jack Prior, 92 LAA

Regiment, 'and in the 8 Corps fire plan "Constellation" we fired 1800 rounds in support of the attack on Overloon. We also put to good use our trained minelifting squads, particularly at Overloon and Venraij.' Just before noon on 12 October USAAF Marauders and RAF Typhoons joined in the attack on selected targets, called 'Joker', indicated by red smoke.

The East Yorks were directed down the left flank through a dog-shaped wood towards the north-east part of Overloon, backed by Churchill tanks of the 4th Coldstream Guards. Pte. Ernie Goozee 'B' Company:

> A troop of Crocodiles went into the attack, 'C' and 'D' Coys in the lead, were held up in the woods suffering from small arms and mortar fire. 'D' Coy lost its officers. Major Pemberton and the only other officer wounded, the CSM and many others were hit. At one time the company was commanded by a corporal. The whole area was mined, most of the tanks and Crocs were unable to get forward. The Germans were well concealed, covering the wood clearances, held their fire. It was 'very sticky'. 'A' and 'C' reached their objectives.

Lionel Roebuck had just rejoined 13 Platoon of 'C' Company:

> Lt Hallam was still in command and welcomed me back. We reached the woodland fringe, start line for the attack. The heavy rain had cleared. The damp and misty conditions would give us some cover when we crossed the wide expanse of open ground. As the barrage of shells forming the protective curtain fell just in front of us, we set off walking and running with rifles and fixed bayonets at the ready, keeping in line, close up to the creeping barrage [100 yds per five minutes]. An artillery spotter plane flew over Overloon. Suddenly it just disappeared from the sky, hit by a shell from one of his own guns. Sam 'Sunny' Rigby was a recent recruit from the disbanded 6th Bn Duke of Wellingtons, being new to us had been put with me.

When 13 Platoon was held up, Sunny slipped off his equipment and slumped on the ground, back against an oak tree. Lionel told him sharply to 'Dig in – or else!' Three young German prisoners were 'persuaded' by CSM Pullen to dig his slit trench for him!

'Typhoon rockets skimmed over us to explode on a multi-barrelled mortar position – frightening so we put out our yellow silk reflective markers. . . . It was heavy going, just like the Chateau de la Londe battle all over again, the fanatical opposition leading to many nasty bloody encounters in the woodland glades.' By dusk the East Yorks were in the northern half of Overloon having lost fifty-one casualties. 'Lt-Col Dickson, shocked by a near miss shell burst was once again a casualty. The Brigadier [Cass] gave him a direct order to report sick. He gamely carried on but later Major Renison once again resumed command of the Bn.'

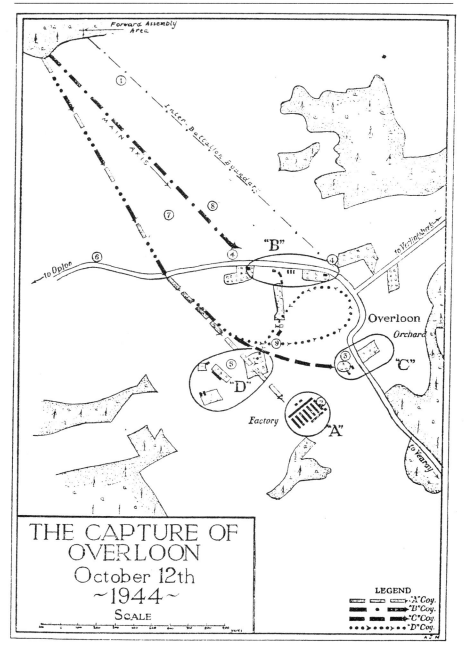

1 Suffolk attack on Overloon.

Lt. Eddie Jones attended the early morning 'O' Group of 8 Brigade:

Brigadier Cass gave out orders in a very peremptory manner. Our Bn [South Lancs] in reserve. East Yorks up left, 1 Suffolk on right, to be crossing the start line of the Molen Beek at 0645. The CO from East Yorks just back from being wounded in Normandy, said 'Do you mean I am to be across the Molen Beek with my Bn by first light tomorrow, when the leading troops of 9 Bde are still some 400 yards short of it?' Cass ordered his 2 i/c Major Renison to take over.

Bill Renison was disturbed to learn that in 185 Brigade the Brigadier, Eric Bols, held a conference for all his COs at 0800 hrs every morning. He was also disturbed that 'Swazi' Waller was now acting CO of the South Lancs as John Orgill had somewhat 'mysteriously' been removed.

On the right flank 1 Suffolk, under Lt.-Col. R.W. Craddock, were directed south-east to take the southern half of Overloon village. Like every battalion in the Iron Sides they had recently received reinforcements, as Maj. A.C.L. Sperling related: 'In Oct '44, one draft consisted of 2 Corps Military Police, 5 RAMC stretcher bearers, a dozen Gunners and 4 tank drivers. Officers were drafted from a dozen different units.'

1 Suffolk marched out of Rijkevoort at 0730 hrs on 12 October and while drinking hot tea in the assembly area, watched medium bombers and Typhoons attacking targets ahead. By 1400 hrs nine prisoners from Parachute Battalion Paul had been sent back by 'B' Company, but 'A' arriving at a burnt-out windmill, were held up by small arms fire. All three officers were casualties, Maj. Ellis being killed by sniping, and CSM Leatherland assumed command. A new attack went in at 1530 hrs and two hours later all objectives were taken including a large factory on the outskirts of Overloon. Twelve enemy had been killed and sixty prisoners taken, but 'A' Company also had heavy losses during the day.

Some idea of the scale of the support available was that 33rd Field Regiment fired 6,926 25-pounder shells in the 12 hours from 0600 hrs to 1800 hrs, and 2nd Middlesex fired 3,800 mortar bombs and 300,000 rounds of MMG Mk VII Z bullets during the day!

At 1700 hrs South Lancs passed through the East Yorks and 1 Suffolk, and Overloon was firmly in the hands of 8 Brigade.

Friday 13 October was to be another nasty day, mainly spent clearing pinewoods south-east of Overloon, preparing the way for the eventual attack on Venraij.

2 RUR went south-west from Overloon at 0900 hrs, with 'A' Company under Maj. Sweeney and 'D' under Maj. Bird advancing slowly through very thick woods. German positions and abandoned equipment were soon found and Sgt. Schofield captured several snipers' nests. All objectives were taken despite two prowling Mk IV tanks in the forest rides.

Padre Iain Wilson, 1 KOSB, wrote:

We stood and shivered in the biting wind watching batches of prisoners coming past, with hands clasped behind their heads – the types that Grimes featured in the 'News Chronicle' – long coats flapping about their heels, dirty old scarves round their necks – a wretched looking crew . . . the abandoned German trenches in the wood still littered with helmets, ammo, welfare items such as gramophones and records. Tanks roared and slithered past us skidding in the mud or sinking in the sand . . . all the farms were burning – a dismal sight – the dank waterlogged area was dismal – stinking to high heaven with the scattered corpses of cattle, pigs and horses.

1 KOSB were on 2 RUR's right, working their way through Laag Heide woods under heavy artillery and mortar fire. The new wooden cigar-box Schu mines were encountered and caused many casualties.

When 'C' and 'D' Companies emerged from the woods into the heather they were met by MG crossfire. L/Cpl. W. Harmon of 'D' Company crawled out into the open under heavy fire and flung two hand grenades into one MG, then rushed it firing his Sten, killed the machine gunners and immediately did the same with the next MG post. He deservedly won the DCM. And Cpl. Forrester with his Sten knocked out a bazooka team, killing two and capturing another five.

By nightfall 1 KOSB were dug in again as the QM brought up warm food under a hail of shell and Minenwerfer shells, which was as bad as at Troarn.

Sgt. Fred Hartle, 1 KOSB, has vivid recollections of Operation Aintree: 'In the woods near Smakt the slit trenches were only two foot deep. Any deeper and they filled up with water.' He got into trouble by firing a captured Spandau MG (with plenty of ammo) at night to confuse the Germans. But he also confused 9 Brigade. 'When the CO got to know, we all got a rocket!' When the QMS brought the rations up at night the truck was distinctly audible: 'several of our platoon were killed or wounded making a run for the hot meal'. His friend Cpl. Bill Tannock was hit by a mortar bomb. 'I tried to lift Bill clear of the mud but he died in my arms. . . . Two or three days later Sgt Paddy Shaw took his platoon towards the village of Smakt. Five minutes later there was heavy firing. Then silence. I don't think any of the platoon got back.' Fred's new 'A' Company CO, Capt. Boyd, sent him off to spy out the notorious Molen Beek – how far away, how deep, how fast the current and whether a tank could cross or not. On their way back from the recce, Fred and the others were trapped in a cottage, but sneaked their way back at nightfall. 'Capt Boyd was very pleased to see us back, especially with the information about the Molen Beek. He assumed from the firing we had run into trouble. A few days later Capt Boyd was blown up and lost one of his legs.'

185 Brigade had been directed south-west from Overloon, as Maurice Cunliffe, 2 Royal Warwicks, wrote: 'The advance was through a complicated patchwork of woods bearing little relationship to those shown

on the map. Clearing them was a tedious job that swallowed up men. On our left was 2 KSLI. We advanced behind artillery fire shortly after noon [13th] to reach the southern fringe of the woods to allow 1 Norfolk to come through and attack Venraij itself.' Once 'A' and 'C' Companies moved out of the woods into open ground casualties mounted and by nightfall they had lost twenty-one including Lts. Brown and Merryweather.

Apart from the Churchill tanks being bogged down or delayed by minefields, radio communication while in thick woods was predictably abysmal. Capt. R.R. Rylands, 'W' Company 2 KSLI, which was parallel to the Warwicks, wrote:

The woods were so vast that no copybook wood clearing drill was possible, especially as the map did not 'fit'. The job was done – with considerable casualties particularly on the forward edge of the wood facing Brabander and Venraij. Lt Mike Bellamy who had rejoined after being wounded on D-Day, was killed by a concealed MG. L/Corp Stout and Pte Hook with our jeep evacuated our casualties swiftly. A berserk Nazi charged up a ride and so confused our sniper, L/C Luscott that he escaped.

On the next day, 14 October, it was the turn of the South Lancs to drive east of Overloon to capture Halfweg (the north–south railway line) a mile short of the Maas at Vierlingsbeek. 'C' Company did well and took 83 (out of 102) prisoners. By 1800 hrs the objectives were taken. Maj. Johnson and Capt./QM Burke earned MCs and Cpl. Horrocks and L/Cpl. Knight, MMs on that day. But as Lt. Eddie Jones reported: 'The Brigadier came up and took Lt Col Orgill to one side for consultation. When the Brig. left the CO intimated to me "He would be piping down in the future and leaving things to Major Waller." He left for England the same evening. We were sorry to see him go – a gentleman who had a concern for his men.' Lt.-Col. W.A. 'Swazi' Waller MC became the new CO.

The Lincolns, who had recently received fifty reinforcements from the Bermuda Volunteer Rifles under Maj. A.J. Smith, suffered a bloody nose, as their adjutant, Jack Harrod, related: 'The Hun was playing an old game and a safe one. The fire from small arms in the wood, though it took its toll was but the bait to catch the fish. As "A" Coy approached the Molen Beek ditch which ran across its axis, the defensive fire of the German artillery and mortars came crashing down. In a few minutes "A" Coy suffered so heavily it could not continue . . . it was a disastrous start to a day's fighting.' But worse was to come. The brigadier ordered a full-scale battalion attack towards Kleindorp. Supported by the divisional artillery and a troop of tanks to attack at 1530 hrs, 'D' and 'A' were to lead. 'And then there followed one of the most magnificent examples of courage and determination in the history of the regiment. The enemy fire came down even more intensified and more prolonged. But there was no faltering this time; the orders were to take the wood . . . of cover there was absolutely none, only the soft sandy soil to minimise the effect of the murderous rain of shells.' The wood was taken. Twenty-eight Lincolns were killed including Majs. Smith and Dawson, and 115 were wounded. As Ray Paine recalled: 'every open piece of ground between the woods was under observation from the enemy OP in the Venraij church tower.' The Lincoln CO, Lt.-Col. Firbank, was awarded the DSO, CSM Shaw the DCM and Pte. Bristowe the MM.

Still on the 14th, the Norfolks had a similar task, with 'B' and 'D' Companies leading to cross the open country from the thick woods south-east of Overloon down the Venraij – and somehow get across the Molen Beek stream. Supported by Churchill tanks, flails, AVREs and M-10 SP A/Tanks they set off at 0700 hrs under a divisional barrage. Lt. John Lincoln, 'D' Company, related:

Within minutes some of our tanks had become casualties, the rest retreated into the shelter of the wood, leaving us on our own. I was all too aware of the din of mortar and gunfire about me, of our own mortars and artillery engaging forward targets, of the enemy resisting our advance with MG and 88 mm together with Nebelwerfers, 'Moaning Minnies' producing a distinctive and frightening sound when fired . . . our Piat man had been killed . . . Barney Ross my batman/runner was badly wounded in the jaw. L/Corporal Stork i/c the 2" mortar section was killed outright by a shot in the head.

Maj. Ian MacGillivray, 'A' Company, was wounded while bravely trying to dislodge a Tiger tank which was holding up the battalion advance, and his replacement, Capt. D.W. Glass, was hit by a tracer bullet which tore his New Testament Bible in half.

The divisional artillery was in action almost continuously. Lt. A.C. Jeffery, 33rd Field Regiment RA, passed back many of the Mike targets, Scale 5, which were engaged during the day. For a time his set was the only communication between leading companies and Brigade HQ.

On 15 October the Iron Sides' action was limited to patrolling, as plans were made by Gen. Whistler for a two-brigade attack to get bridgeheads over the Molen Beek and thence into Venraij. Although only 10-ft wide, the stream's high sloping banks produced a real gap of about 25 ft, which necessitated the CRE, Lt.-Col. 'Tiger' Urquart's divisional sappers, putting box girder bridges (mounted initially on Churchill AVREs) into the Beek to form tank crossings. Floating Kapok bridging would produce infantry crossings.

185 Brigade, led by the Norfolks and Warwicks, would attack on the left, with Brabander, the northern suburb of Venraij, and St Servatius monastery, as their objectives. 8 Brigade on the right, led by 1 Suffolk and the East Yorks, would pass through 9 Brigade in Laag Heide wood, cross the

Royal Norfolk A/TK section in Malden woods. Left to right: Pte. White, Pte. Read, L/Cpl. Pratt.

Royal Norfolk 'O' group before Aintree. Left to right: Sgt. W. Paskell, Capt. E.H.T. Ridger, Capt. J.A. Allen, Capt. T.P.K. Oakey, Maj. F.H. Crocker, Maj. I.A. MacGillivray, Capt. R.W. Hodd, Maj. H.R. Holden, Maj. E.A. Cooper-Key (extreme right).

Beek and enter Venraij from the west. The 4th Grenadier Guards tanks would support 8 Brigade, and 4th Coldstream Guards, 185 Brigade.

Gen. Whistler wrote in his diary:

> As the job had completely foxed the 7th US A Div I rather wondered what it was going to be like. . . . Bags of mines and desperate mud, Churchills bogged down everywhere. Bridges collapsing – in fact every bloody thing quite bloody. Desperately gallant soldiers with a wonderful spirit. Even better than I had hoped for and that was saying a great deal. Infantry went forward without tanks which was a particularly good show.

The Taking of Venraij – 185 Brigade

The barrage started at 0700 hrs on 16 October and lasted for two and three-quarter hours. 33rd Field Regiment fired no less than 294 rounds per gun in that period. But well before that – silently – the Warwicks and the Norfolks each had two companies across the Beek using Kapok crossing 'bridges'. The brigade plan was for 2nd Warwicks to take Brabander, 1 Norfolk then to advance and take the wood just east, and finally 2 KSLI to come through and take St Servatius monastery.

Marcus Cunliffe, adjutant 2nd Battalion Warwicks, wrote:

> The bridging equipment arrived at 0300. In pitch darkness at 0430 'D' and 'B' in silence lowered the pontoons (Kapok) and slipped across under heavy enemy DF fire all along the Beek which was sown with mines. Major F. Bell 'D' Coy earned the MC by taking farmhouses with 30 POW, and driving off counter attacks in hand to hand fighting. The supporting tanks only had one successful tank bridge for the next 24 hours. [Sgt. Finan of 617 Squadron RE drove his AVRE with its box girder bridge and released it into the stream – the other two AVREs came to grief.] By 1200 Major Brooks's 'A' Coy was established on the crossroads in the middle of Brabander. There Corporals Mobley and Bowman and Pte Garland all did well. 'D' and 'B' followed up in the steady rain. By evening Capt Gilbert's 'C' Coy had fought its way into Ste Anna's Hospital to the east. The hospital was an asylum for 1700 incurable female lunatics. The FOO with the Warwicks radio'd back '2000 bad women, etc' which caused some speculation.

The Warwicks had had an excellent day but it cost them sixty-two casualties including six officers.

'By 0600 "B" and "D" Coys of the Norfolks had crossed unwittingly through Schu-minefields without a single casualty; such are the fortunes of war,' wrote Humphrey Wilson. 'Both bridging tanks had failed – all our

Churchills had been knocked out. It was now 0700 and both sides were slogging each other with all they had.'

John Lincoln's *Thank God and the Infantry* gives graphic accounts of the day's action by Sgt. Carr, Maj. Searight, George Dicks, Lt. 'Friar' Balsam, L/Cpl. Ernie Seaman and Nevil Griffin.

'Despite attacks by Tiger tanks', Humphrey Wilson continued, 'by the afternoon the enemy was feeling it badly and it became possible for "A" and "C" Coys to push on about a thousand yards south (and across) the Beek. We had at least secured the crossing and forced the enemy to withdraw but that night called for special vigilance.' The Royal Norfolks lost 211 casualties in the four days of Aintree including five company commanders and three captains.

2 KSLI was in support, as Guy Radcliffe wrote: 'We moved up behind the Warwicks but it was impossible to continue the attack, both because there was little daylight left and the AVRE bridge could not take our tanks until it had been repaired. The rifle companies crossed [the Molen Beek] and spent a simply appalling night. The shelling was very heavy.'

Capt. R.R. Rylands:

Our 'O' Group was immediately mortared most accurately and at very close range. There were a lot of casualties. I have a confused memory of chicken coops leaping into the air scattering dead and live fowls in a flurry of feathers: of the disintegration of a man standing next to me: of the CO continuously and quite composedly stuttering into an 18 set: of lumps of steel appearing in Pte Bennion's helmet and my haversack: of an attempt to take cover behind a disembowelled pig.

Fortunately jeeps could cross the Beek and CQMS Francis brought up hot rations.

At 0330 hrs on the 16th 1 Suffolk marched out from Overloon under 'artificial moonlight' and by 0700 hrs 'B' Company, carrying Kapok bridging equipment, was approaching the Molen Beek, clearing mines and under heavy MG fire. A flail tank got bogged. One AVRE with a bridge was bogged, another got stuck in the Beek and the third was inadequate to bridge the stream for tanks. By 1045 hrs 'C' and 'D' Companies had passed through 'B' and over the Beek without tank support, carriers, or A/Tank guns!

Unfortunately, the CO, Lt.-Col. Craddock, was blown up on a Schu-mine across the Beek and had his foot blown off. So for the second time the 2 i/c, Maj. F.F.E. Allen, took command. It was raining hard, the wireless sets were waterlogged, 'A' Company had no officers and his battalion was ordered to push ahead against a strong and determined enemy. By 1300 hrs the company commanders of 'C' and 'D' were wounded and the two Churchill tanks, having crossed the Beek, were at once bogged down. But struggling away, 1 Suffolk made a new attack at 1500 hrs and by nightfall they were

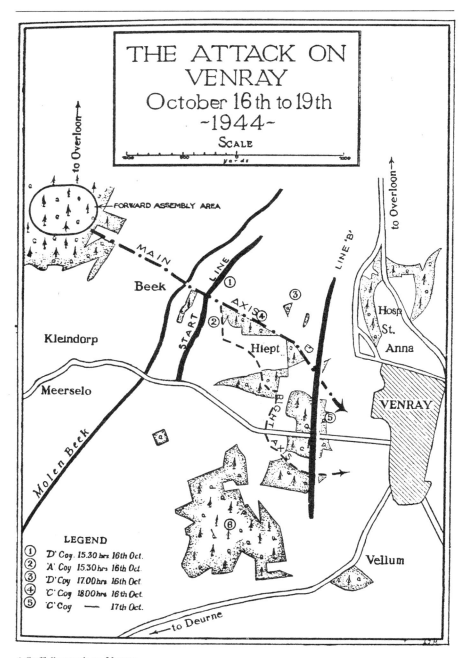

1 Suffolk attack on Venray.

dug in around the hamlet of Hiept, 1,000 yds west of Venraij's suburbs. Pte. F. Barrett distinguished himself by bringing back wounded men under heavy fire. By the end of 16 October 1 Suffolk had lost forty-nine casualties including their CO and three rifle company commanders.

The East Yorks had crossed the Beek during the day through the Suffolk positions and remained on the left flank. Now under command of Lt.-Col. D.D.W. Renison, with the famous Maj. 'Banger' King promoted to 2 i/c, by nightfall they reached an area just north of 1 Suffolk in Hiept. Pte. Peter Brown was platoon PIAT man: 'We formed up and advanced through a creeping artillery barrage across the fields and into the woods. The going was very difficult. By mid afternoon I was so exhausted that I threatened to throw the Piat into the nearest ditch if someone else didn't take a turn to carry it!' Lionel Roebuck described the plight of the tanks:

In the boggy area near the stream were a number of Churchill tanks, all hopelessly stuck. One was in the stream, one in the soft ground near the track and another was settling down in boggy ground leading up to the stream. Shells and mortar bombs were raining down on the struggling crews of recovery men. A grim task for them. Bales of beech or chestnut paling had been placed in the water to form a bridge and we in 13 Platoon quickly got across away from the heavy stonking.

On the night of 16/17 October 426 Field Company RE constructed a 40-ft trestle bridge at 1 Suffolk's crossing point and 253 Field Company RE built another where the Overloon–Venraij road bridge had been previously. REME recovery worked through the night to free the score of bogged Guards Churchill tanks.

The next day, the 17th, the two brigade attacks continued. By 1300 hrs the East Yorks on the left of 1 Suffolk had two companies involved in street fighting in Venraij. The Germans had rushed Battlegroup Hardegg from Maeseyck to help defend the town. Ernie Goozee wrote: 'We pushed into Venraij itself, very heavily mined, intense street fighting developed, German snipers and Spandaus very active. Major Crauford, CO 'C' Coy was badly wounded during this fighting. The Bn's MO with a Sgt looked for the RAP, wandered too far and was taken prisoner. The Germans continued to shell the town, sent out patrols which complicated mopping up in the darkness.'

Pte. Peter Brown, 'C' Company, was 'involved in street fighting, entered one house, found a Dutch family who insisted I had some of their bread and ham. Great people the Dutch.' Pte. Lionel Roebuck was next to Maj. Crauford:

the crack of the discharge from the high velocity gun exploded in the road between us. He was hit in arm and stomach, lay on his right side by a doorway. He was fully conscious and in some pain. [Later] The rubble from the damaged buildings made progress difficult. As the section

'Five Yorkshire Tykes', including Lionel Roebuck and Arthur Littlewood.

rounded the next bend, a MG opened up. Backerville, the leading man, got a full burst at close quarters, more or less cutting him in two. The German gunner, ungainly, ugly-featured with ape-like face and arms then surrendered.

Lionel's section spent the night in a café-bar near the town centre, a dead German in the doorway with the Bren gun on the bar counter directed towards the street window.

1 Suffolk spent the 17th combing the woods to the west of Venraij. Sgt. Albert Pattison, 1 Suffolk, recalls: 'Our platoon was reinforced so many

South Lancs advance on Venraij after the capture of Brabander. (IWM, BU 1212)

times, I didn't know the names of half of my men. After the battle I was called to Div HQ to meet the General who offered me a commission in the field, which I turned down. I did not have a very good education. I didn't think at that time I was officer material.'

The South Lancs had moved up behind the East Yorks with orders to enter the town at dawn. The Warwicks consolidated in Brabander and 2 KSLI supported by Coldstream tanks cleared several woods on their left through thick minefields. 'W' Company cleared the area of the hospital on the edge of Brabander. Capt. Rylands: 'The leading coys had got on so fast, they had left a strong party 30–40 strong behind with spandaus and bazookas. Col Millett took me to have a look at the job. [Later] The assault was highly successful, though confused. The enemy drove out the unfortunate Dutch in front of them. A good many Germans were killed, 30 prisoners. Our casualties were few and Lt Denham and Sgt Mann particularly distinguished themselves.' The veteran pioneer officer, Lt. Bert Aldridge, guided the Coldstream Guards' tanks through a minefield with no cover from stonking and was awarded the MC. 'Z' Company in reserve suffered heavy casualties from an intense stonk that reduced one platoon to twelve survivors.

The seventh and final day of Aintree, 18 October, began with two hours of Victor (Corps) target, starting at 0400 hrs. At 0645 hrs the South Lancs passed through the East Yorks in the centre of Venraij into the north-west corner of the town, as Lt. Eddie Jones recalls:

By 0830 'A' Coy fought its way into the northern suburbs: the enemy was pulling out, but rest of Bn was greeted with very heavy defensive fire and numerous mines were encountered. The noise was particularly intense re-echoing in the built-up area. The effect of shells bursting in the narrow streets enclosed by buildings especially devastating. Major Eric Johnson, CO 'C' Coy (wounded at La Londe), shouted out that he couldn't see, caused by blast or shock. He recovered, awarded later the MC. Captain Ted Fenton i/c A/Tk platoon was killed by 75 mm field gun fired over open sights. A Liverpool policeman, tall, dark with a splendid glossy, black Sam Costa type moustache. He and others KIA in Venraij were buried in Venraij War cemetery. A special service was held by Padre Paul Corin. St Anne's Hospital appeared undamaged. Johnny Longland Signals Officer and I occupied one room with real beds in it. It rained heavily and water streamed through the ceiling.

The East Yorks took over from the Warwicks defensive positions east of the town around St Servatius monastery. Maj. 'Banger' King was put in charge of the evacuation of the black-robed elderly nuns, whisking them to safety in his jeep, ambulances and lorries.

Apart from the indomitable courage shown by all the Iron Side rifle companies against very tough opposition, there were three features that everybody will remember about Aintree. Firstly, the prompt deluge of 'friendly' shells as the divisional artillery responded to frequent instant DF

Divisional sappers and flail tank advance through Overloon. (IWM, B 10818)

targets. The seventy-two 25-pounder guns were in action day and night for a week. John Foster was bombardier gun fitter, 'B' Troop 101 Battery 33rd Field Regiment RA:

> All through the actions from the beaches right through to Holland I never once had to remove a jammed shell in the barrel from a [25-pounder] gun. Then it happened twice to the same gun in 24 hours at Overloon.

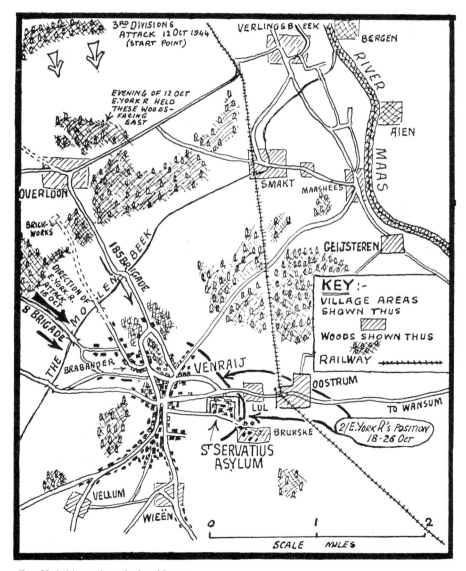

East Yorkshire actions during Aintree.

The wet sand had stuck to the shell and caused it to stick so far up the barrel. A bit scary. There was a good garage in a deserted hamlet which I used to repair a recuperation system. The job took about four hours. Each time it had to be swept for mines and booby traps.

Secondly, the huge-scale defensive minefields sown across the Peel landscape by the Germans. During Operation Aintree Sgt. Frank Faulkner estimated that a quarter of a million mines had been laid by the Germans around Overloon and Venraij. 'We – 17 Field Squadron – lifted about 30,000 of them.' The author's FOO carrier was demolished by a Teller mine on the Oploo road, his driver was killed, and he was taken to Eindhoven and subsequently to hospital in Brussels.

Finally, the cold, constant teeming rain which soaked everyone to the skin, filled slit trenches as soon as they were dug, bogged down 'friendly' tanks, and did nothing for morale.

Operation Aintree was over at last – Overloon and Venraij had been taken in a week of intense, savage fighting. The Iron Sides earned their battle honours, for the month of October had cost them nearly 1,400 casualties. 8 Brigade now faced due east out of Venraij and on their left 9 Brigade and 3rd Recce held the river line up to Cuijk – a 16-mile front.

The Corps Commander, Lt.-Gen. Richard O'Connor, sent a special

Maj. Peter Crane, 92 (Loyals) LAA Regt. RA, receives his Military Cross.

Order of the Day on 16 October (two days before Venraij was captured by 8 Brigade), mainly congratulating 185 Brigade on their magnificent performance in bridging the Beek 'with all the elements against them'.

'After all,' Bill Renison pointed out, 'the East Yorks had been the first troops actually to enter the town of Venraij. All the Bns in 8 Brigade were now commanded by 2 i/cs, Allen of 1 Suffolk, "Swazi" Waller South Lancs, and me. The GOC was trying to get commands for us but there are large numbers of unemployed Lt Cols available.' He reflected on Aintree: 'Overloon marked our return to the utter devastation of the Normandy battlefields, after 2½ months of comparative peace and beauty.'

During Aintree the Warwicks took 158 casualties and even when the town of Venraij was finally cleared, St Servatius monastery's eastern wall marked the front line for some time to come. Lt.-Col. D.L.A. Gibbs earned a bar to his DSO, as Marcus Cunliffe wrote: 'for the 2nd Bn's own exemplary performance when it broke through the final ring of German defences in the Venraij struggle.'

The division had lost three commanding officers and no less than sixteen company commanders. The GOC wrote in his diary: 'Fighting continued until today – 18th – when we finally cleared Venraij – liberated is, I suppose, the right word. I had no close shaves during this battle. Getting cunning and careful, I suppose. But definitely not so brave as I used to be – dammit.' From D-Day to the end of October, Monty's Iron Sides had lost ten thousand casualties. No wonder a German POW described the black and red divisional sign – three black triangles on a field of red – as 'the sign of dripping blood'.

awarded and SM Webb received both the DCM and the MM. And Gen. 'Pip' Roberts sent Lt.-Col. Renison a personal letter of thanks: 'You occupied an unpleasant area, never a grumble, carried out some excellent patrols,' and on 19 November FM Montgomery paid a visit to the East Yorks to present personally the many awards for bravery. The South Lancs reorganised themselves with three rifle companies and 'B' Company became the training company. On 4 November Lt. Wright MM led a patrol at Rioolerings Reservoir, east of Venraij, and was awarded the MC. Later that month Lts. Rennie and Wright trod on Schu-mines on patrol and lost a foot each. At the end of November the South Lancs went back to a rest area near Gemert.

1 Suffolk also transferred its 'B' Company into a battalion training cadre for all incoming drafts, and on 7 November Lt.-Col. Dick Goodwin DSO returned after five months absence to resume command. Lt.-Col. F.F. Allen, who had commanded the Suffolk for four and a half months, was posted to 53rd Welsh Division. On 18/19 November Divisional Counter-Mortar had pinpointed so many active enemy mortars that a divisional artillery target known as 'Melrose' was fired twice on the offending Minenwerfers.

Brig. 'Copper' Cass went out partridge shooting in November and had the bad luck to be blown up on a mine; he was badly injured and evacuated. A Grenadier Guardsman, Brig. E.H. Goulburn DSO, succeeded him. In the first week of November 8 Brigade relieved 9 Brigade.

9 Brigade's Autumn

Jack Harrod, 2 Lincolns, wrote:

> There were three battalion positions, each of which was occupied in turn by the three Bns of 9 Brigade. A semi-tactical area, east of Overloon on the road to Vierlingsbeek: the thickly wooded country south of Overloon, flanked by the Boxmeer–Venraij railway (with the enemy still holding Smakt across the railway), and an area near St Anthonis regarded as a rest area. We had the honour on 9th Nov to be chosen as 'the typical fighting county regiment' to take part in an Armistice Day broadcast service. It took place at Oploo under the direction of Chester Wilmot of the BBC. Our Padre Capt (Rev) Wynne Jones read the prayers, the CO Lt Col Firbank DSO read the lesson and an address was given by Revd J.W. Steele, the Hampshire cricketer.

Ray Paine took part in a night patrol with the Lincoln Pioneers to load mines and take them to the front line of woods. 'We left the Pioneers to lay the mines. We began to feel lost and uneasy on the return. All the woods and trees seemed the same.' Fortunately, Ray located the Plough and the Pole Star in the moonlit sky, 'so I knew where north was. We had needed to go west but had actually been travelling east!' When the battalion was ordered to send a patrol across the Maas, Lt. H.J. Pacey MC took twelve eager volunteers, but Ray said, 'he could have had a hundred more!' Once he and his mate, Charlie Smith, were ensconced in a farmhouse. Charlie brought in a little square wooden box. 'Look what I've found,' he said. The young innocent had found a German Schu-mine. There were many more on a slope to the river bank, 'the sergeant formed a line to pick the mines up. Usually a four foot stick called "prodders" was used to prod the ground at arm's length.'

Monty invested 1 KOSB at Oploo on 14 November and Maj. H.S. Gillies was awarded the MC. However, Padre Iain Wilson wrote:

This Smakt position ranks high in our less pleasant memories. It was uncomfortable, dangerous and boring. The Germans had relatively comfortable positions while our companies strung out over a two thousand yard front were condemned to live in damp, sandy trenches. The enemy had excellent observation – proceeded to shell and mortar the Bn with annoying persistency and effect. We lost many valuable men in

Pte. Ray Paine, 2 Lincolns.
(Ray Paine)

this way . . . we were thoroughly bad tempered and engaged in agressive patrolling.

Pte. Victor Campbell, who had been wounded on 6 August at Montisenger, rejoined 1 KOSB at the end of November:

> Everything was so different. There were so many new faces and a lot of the old ones had disappeared, some for ever. I felt that my Battalion had died in France and those who had survived and those, like me, who had come back would have to try to re-establish the old spirit. [Later] We went out on patrol in our new snow suits with bags of straw encasing our legs and boots. A bit cumbersome but at least it kept our feet and legs warm. When not on patrol we manned OPs along the river line. We had to report back to Company HQ anything of interest either to Intelligence or to the Gunners.

Once, Victor's section had to lay an ambush: 'I spent a reasonably warm night lying on top of a manure pile.'

Norman Scarfe related how: 'on 1 November, All Saints Night, "A" Coy 2 RUR saw in the darkness an enemy patrol. Unhappy with their reply to his challenge, the Ulster Rifles sentry opened fire with his Sten gun. One of the German patrols – obviously a fluent linguist – shouted "Tommy, Tommy come out". His body was found in a ditch in front in the morning.' Late in October the battalion went into reserve at St Anthonis with leave parties to Deurne and Helmond, cinema and ENSA shows. And, yes, more training. Most of November was spent at Veulen, a mile south of Venraij.

Major Mike Quarmby's recollections:

> After Guy Radcliffe's return (mortar wound in Normandy) as Adjutant, Lt Col Millet of the DCLI now commanding 2 KSLI after Jack Maurice, the CO, had been killed, recommended me for Staff College. But within a month I was posted as GSO III to 9 Brigade in November. I had known Dominic Browne the Brigadier when he was in the Hampshires. Then I worked with Walter Kempster (KSLI) who took over – found him admirable in every way. I used to accompany him in his scout car used as TAC Bde HQ. On several occasions in the appalling conditions of the Reichwald battle we were isolated both from main Bde HQ *and* the battalions!

185 Brigade's Autumn

On 22 October the Corps Commander, Lt.-Gen. O'Connor visited 2 KSLI but four days later the battalion moved to the St Servatius monastery area of Venraij. 'A vast building with an astonishing amount of glass in it', according to Capt. Rylands. 'After one look I felt no desire to throw stones.' However, the drink ration now came up regularly, 'a most solemn and philosophic evening followed over a bottle of Scotch during which Capt Carey, CSM Thomas, CQMS Francis and myself settled the fate of nations.' 'W' Company shared its farm with a Dutch family, their cattle and some exotic birds. Pte. Forbes was suspected of reducing their number and L/Cpl. Evans led a sniping expedition into Bruxhe village. Everyone got a bit depressed with 'cellar-itis'. 'X' Company was stationed at 'Death Corner', the north-west corner of the monastery, and the carrier platoon occupied the centre front of it to deter infiltration. Guy Radcliffe: 'There would be four or five simply imperial stonks in our area some time in the day. The enemy valued his bridgehead [west of the Maas], enabled him to mount his counter-attack towards Asten.' The RAP received a direct hit on 10 November, killing the new MO, Capt. P.A. Robinson, and causing ten casualties. Now promoted to major, R.R. Rylands left to become chief instructor at the Divisional School.

In the first fortnight of November enemy shelling of the Venraij area steadily increased. 2 Warwicks lost a dozen casualties despite having three companies in cellars, and one back. However, they also received about a hundred reinforcements including Maj. P.J. Albery and Capt. D.A.L. Pile.

Bob Basshan, 1 Norfolk, recalls how one crossroads in Venraij was known as 'Stonk Corner' for obvious reasons. 'One morning the Church Army canteen visited us, parking on the tarmac'd road near the gas works and opened up for business. The chappie managing the canteen must have wondered why he was getting no customers! Eventually one bold squaddie scooted across to the van and put him wise!'

John Lincoln wrote about how Capt. Robin Wilson was appointed 'Patrol Master' of 1 Norfolk, to plan and coordinate all patrol activity.

A recce patrol seeks information, not trouble, so we were only lightly armed. We wore black plimsolls so that we could move without noise, our faces were blackened with burnt cork, woollen cap comforters on our heads, over our battledress leather jerkins turned inside out so that there would be no shine from the leather . . . . A revolver was tied to my thigh and small pouches contained compass and revolver ammo. We each carried a Sten with a spare magazine and the odd grenade in our pockets.

On 14 November FM Montgomery decorated his Iron Sides. Lt.-Col. Bellamy received the DSO, Maj. D.W. Smith and Capt. Robin Wilson the MC, and Sgt. Allen, Cpl. Thirtle and L/Cpl. Shingfield the MM.

The gunners were on call all the time for DF plans, but on 28 October 33rd Field Regiment RA was on the receiving end. Enemy counter-battery fire had been increasing and a hundred shells fell in the gun positions of 109 and 113/114 Field Batteries causing ten casualties. Mijnheer De Blaauw joined them as official interpreter, as did young, brave Dutchmen for every unit of 3rd Division. On occasions 25-pounder ammmunition was rationed down to 30 r.p.g., later reduced to seven and even to four.

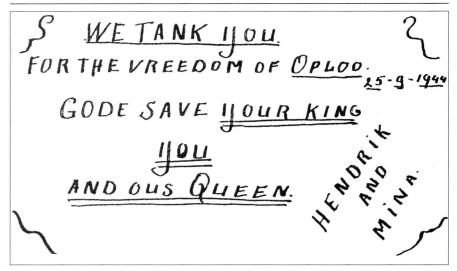

A touching note of thanks given by a young Dutch couple to Jack Prior, IO of 92 (Loyals) LAA Regt. RA.

An unknown member of 185 Brigade workshops of the British 3rd Division wrote these verses during the 1944–5 campaign:

When this bitter war is over and the guns have ceased to roar
And the gallant lads who fought and won are marching home once more,
When the tattered flag of freedom proudly tops its mast
And the tyrants who besmirched its name have met their doom at last
When the graves of fallen heroes in liberated lands
Are tended with special care by sympathetic hands
Then will be told the story of the deeds of fearless lads
Who made the British Third Division 'Monty's Ironclads'.

They sailed away on D-Day, they left their native land
To be among the first to set their feet on France's shingled sand
For them began a bitter fight on the beach at Ouistreham
Yet yard by yard and mile by mile they fought their way to Caen
Where round that fair city they faced a fearless foe
They fought the best the Germans had and gave them blow for blow
They fought and died as heroes do, ignored the Hun's derision,
And proved the worth and greatness of the British Third Division.

From Warwickshire and Lincolnshire, these men so strong and true,
From Middlesex and Shropshire, from ancient Norfolk too
From Lancashire and Yorkshire, no Wars of Roses here,

But all together, side by side, their path of duty clear,
Stout lads of Bonnie Scotland have fought and made their stand
With the fearless sons of Ulster, who came from Shamrock land
Their courage and tenacity, their boldness of decision
Writ large the name in history of the British Third Division.

Then on to shattered Caumont, to Vassey and to Vire
Their courage was magnificent, an example to inspire
No thought of self, no holding back, no resting could they take
They simply did their duty, their honour was at stake
From victory on to victory, they trod the hardest road
Their comrades falling round them, yet on they grimly strode.
Theirs is a glorious epic, they forced by bold incision
The withdrawal of a brutal foe from the British Third Division.

When finally their enemies held fast within the trap
Were doomed and cut to pieces in the famous Falaise Gap,
Our heroes rested, paused a while, to heal their many scars
And then began the chase once more of those whose God is Mars.
Through Belgium with great skill and speed, they helped to smash
    the Hun
With lightning stroke and counterstroke, they kept him on the run
'Cross Holland's dykes, canals and streams, they fought their bitter way
The British Third Division to the Arnhem men at bay.

CHAPTER TWENTY-ONE

Winter Patrolling on the River Maas

'Wacht am Maas'

'Bolo' Whistler's diary for 26 October: 'My battle front is well stretched and seems moderately quiet at the moment. I have been a Major-General for four months and feel pretty aged.' And on 7 November: 'Bloody cold these days, rotten for the men – bagged one partridge, one pheasant and several Germans – a good shoot! Now having many changes in staff and commanders including CRE "Tiger" Urquhart.' Indeed Gen. O'Connor, GOC 8 Corps, who was posted to India, came to give a farewell talk at Oploo on the 23rd emphasising the problems of countering battle exhaustion.

But on 22 November patrols indicated that the Germans were no longer holding their front line in strength. Guy Radcliffe, 2 KSLI, writes in his history:

> On 23rd we moved forward, with the Norfolks also advancing on our northern flank. Strong patrols were sent out ahead. . . . At 0745 'Z' Coy moved out to Brukse, found unoccupied and 'W' and 'X' moved up at 1300 into Oostrum, found to be heavily mined and booby trapped. The whole place stank to high heaven, there were dead cattle in every direction . . . patrols that night found Oorloo, the next village 3,000 yards SE, also unoccupied. 'Z' Coy sent Sgt Gillett's 17 platoon into Meerlo, a small village on the Groote Molen Beek.

A heavily defended strongpoint there was destroyed. For this action Maj. Read, Sgt. Gillett and L/Cpl. Jones were decorated. The bridges over the Beek were, of course, blown.

Lt. George Dicks in *Thank God and the Infantry* describes 'D' Company 1 Norfolk's patrol towards Wanssum: 'We sallied through the streets of Lul and Oostrum with Friar [Balsam] leading followed by me and Ray [Hilton]. Wanssum was a long narrow village running north and south, split in two by the canal and the western half was soon occupied.'

To the north and left of the Norfolks, 1 Suffolk was sent forward to the area between the railway and the river Maas, which was clear except for the castle of Geijsteren on the river banks. A battle then ensued for the next four days. The castle was covered by extensive river flooding. The attack on 25 November from Maashees failed because of heavy enemy shell and MG fire, 600 yds from the castle entrance, and 'D' Company could not deploy because of the deep flood water. Despite divisional artillery barrages, Typhoon attacks and tank fire, each attack broke down. Eventually at 0150 hrs on 30 November 'C' Company attacked in assault boats to find the defenders had flown the coop! 1 Suffolk lost fifty casualties in the four-day fight. Capt. Thomas, 'D' Company, won the MC and Pte. Jaggard, the company runner, the MM for conspicuous bravery. Cpl. Fordham distinguished himself in the collection and evacuation of the wounded.

Guy Radcliffe, 2 KSLI, again: 'The civilian problem now was perfectly frightful. The Germans had evacuated a large number of the inhabitants of Venray and Overloon to the other side of the Maas to work on the defence works. In twenty four hours there were several thousand in St Servatius monastery waiting for transport and in a pitiable state of exhaustion. The scene in the pouring rain and the deep mud as they made their way back was too tragic.' The Master Race had every reason to be hated by their Dutch neighbours.

185 Brigade were now moved north to assume responsibility for a vast river front while 8 and 9 Brigades took their place. A strong enemy pocket

The shattered village of Blitterswijk.

had been identified in the Wanssum–Helling–Blitterswijk bridgehead. 9 Brigade sent in the Ulster Rifles. M.J.P.M. Corbally's history states: 'It was a bloody business: the low flat country was traversed by fire, the attacks on two successive dawns were illuminated by bright moonlight. The enemy held every advantage and the attacks were not successful.' The German defences were marked by a single Dannert wire with mines and booby traps attached. It ran from the canal across the Helling–Meerlo road 750 yds south of Helling, then north-east towards Blitterswijk and then north to the Maas. 'C' Company under Maj. E.M. Murphy had a terrible time; their leading platoons were pinned down and the pioneers under Lt. Shimmin were killed, wounded or captured. 'C' Company lost six KIA, four wounded and twenty were taken prisoner. On their right Maj. Bird's 'D' Company was more successful and with great dash got through a wood and with brisk grenade throwing captured two windmills. The second attack at 0100 hrs on 1 December was not helped by the enemy using two captured Bren guns and Capt. Gaffikin's 'B' Company lost six men KIA and thirteen wounded. 'D' Company was caught by Spandau fire – L/Cpl. Rossiter picked up the wounded Cpl. Carroll under fire and brought him back to safety. Rifleman Irwin, 'D' Company, helped deter an enemy patrol with his MG and after breakfast went on leave to Brussels. Capt. W.E.S. Sturgeon was captured from his HQ house, but Maj. Bird was awarded the MC. The enemy

Royal Norfolk 'char up' at Hooge Heide, 18 Platoon, 'D' Company. Left to right: Sgt. Crichton, Pte. Woods, Cpl. Simpkiss.

eventually withdrew across the river and Wanssum was at long last occupied. The Ulsters suffered seventy casualties in the two-day battle. Shortly afterwards Lt.-Col. Harris left and was replaced by Lt.-Col. Drummond from 1st Battalion RUR.

The gunner regiments were always on call. Roly Curtiss, 'E' Troop 33rd Field Regiment, with his FOO Capt. Taylor, set up their OP in Blitterswijk on 28 November:

> The church was in ruins so we used the house next door which had skylights. The thick morning mist lifted and we saw two likely enemy OPs across the river. Our guns erased one and whilst dealing with the second our house roof and attic wall received a direct hit. Captain Taylor told me I'd received a 'Blighty Touch'. I was lying on a bloody soaked golden coloured eiderdown in the cellar. The enemy had blown the bridges behind us and evacuation had been delayed awaiting 'Weasels'. I awoke in Eindhoven and again later in Brussels hospital with the inevitable lifesaver bottle of penicillin drip.

In the operation to clear Wanssum Capt. H.S. Taylor supported the 2 RUR and 1 KOSB and was awarded the MC.

Censorship of troops' letters back to their families was a pointless chore, always given to junior officers. George Dicks, 1 Norfolks, remembers: 'Some soldiers are incapable of writing a letter without sealing it with a series of letters which may, to the uninitiated, seem like censorable codes.' No doubt readers will be familiar with SWALK, ITALY, BOLTOP, GUTS and BURMA – but NORWICH?

1 KOSB had celebrated St Andrew's night with a party held in a loft on 27 November. They had reasonably comfortable billets in and around Kastenraij. Radio security was still strict and code words abounded particularly 'Sunray' jargon. A staff officer was heard shouting into a radio transmitter: 'I don't want to talk to your Uncle Flo. I want to talk to your Aunty Joe and I want him NOW. Over.' The 2 KSLI received a V2 aerial bomb hit on 2 December which damaged many houses, but there was no loss of life.

Bill Renison wrote: 'East Yorks back to Gemert, we had the pick of the billets. 1 Suffolk did quite well at Bockel but the South Lancs were scattered in muddy farms off the Oploo road.' Also Renison wrote in his diary:

> 3 Dec. 76 Field Regiment gave a magnificent dinner party for 56 officers [including many Yorkshires] in a pub parlour in Oploo – champagne, brandy and cigars. The songs grew bawdier well into the night.
>
> 5 Dec. Feast of St Nikolas equivalent to the Dutch Christmas Day. To my surprise the daughter of the house gave me a plate of ham and fried eggs, bread, fresh butter, slice of lovely home-made cream cake.

8 Dec. Bde HQ gave a cocktail party and dance in a hotel imported a number of society ladies from Helmond. The standards of beauty higher than anything we had been able to raise in Gemert!

10 Dec. Sunday. Divisional Commander came to our church parade. First time head of Bn on ceremonial parade and march past.

11 Dec. Monty came to present medal ribbons, gave a good address, plans for UK leave and how we would win the battle of Germany *this* side of the Rhine.

Guy Radcliffe, 2 KSLI, then based mainly around Rijkevoort, Voekel and Lottum, wrote:

In the line the patrolling was far and away the outstanding factor in our lives. The long winter nights, the wide front which we invariably held and the generally aggressive character of the enemy made this a formidable task. The life of the companies was centred round the patrolling on which all else had to be based. If the forward company held a village the cellars and groundfloor rooms would be used for all the platoon and by HQ and for sleeping accommodation for the men by day. The outside slit-trenches were always roofed over with doors or wood and earth to give protection against shell fragments or airbursts. These were successively improved with oil or coal stoves, lined walls and solid roofs. But the long hours of standing about in the cold or huddling in ill-lit dugouts was a great test of moral . . . south-eastern Holland in winter ravaged by war, ill kept, dour and rather dirty inhabitants, level as the sea, held no attractions at all.

On 20 December the CO, Lt.-Col. C.G. Millet, and three ORs were killed by a booby trap and a mine, and a week later Lt.-Col. P.D. Daly assumed command. By the end of the year 2 KSLI had suffered 638 casualties including 123 KIA since D-Day.

The Warwicks were stationed at Heide from mid-November 'in a sea of glutinous mud', according to Marcus Cunliffe, and by 3 December were holding a 6,000-yds front along the river from Vierlingsbeek to Vortum. They had two companies up, two back, since the ground in front was heavily flooded. Despite one of the wettest Novembers for many years, morale remained high. 'There were civilians to look after, observation posts to maintain, shoots to be carried out whenever enemy movements were noticed. There was digging, wiring and minelaying. Out of the line at Gemert dances were held with enthusiastic local girls, despite disapproval by the priests.'

Bob Moberly, 2 Middlesex, noted: 'Single sentry on each post during the short days, double sentry during the long nights, stand to at dawn and dusk and whenever an enemy patrol was expected near at hand. It was usually very quiet at night and ears and eyes were strained for any sign of movement. Now and then a trip flare would go up but they were often false alarms, set off by the wind or by a stray cat.'

1 Suffolk reported 18 inches of snow on their front on 12 December. When their CO, Lt.-Col. R.E. Goodwin fell off a bridge into an icy swollen river, the onlookers included his brigadier and at least one company commander! Four years back in the retreat to Dunkirk, the regimental drums had been cached in Roubaix, so a search party was sent back to find them. Capt. Breach, L/Cpls. Hutchinson and Masson, and Pte. Whitman returned in triumph with three of the drums. The battalion was billeted in the villages of Hegilson, Megelsum and Blitterswijk. Capt. Skelding organised several good concerts and the Corps Rest Camp, Divisional Club, leave to Helmond, cinemas and ENSA shows kept up the spirits of the Suffolk.

Ray Paine, 2 Lincolns, was on leave in Brussels during the Battle of the Bulge in the Ardennes:

> The passengers in the tram car enquired if we thought that the Germans would re-invade Brussels. The war situation was tense with the Germans breaking the American lines. Freddy and I said that Monty wouldn't let them down – and hoped we were right. Just as we said this, the sirens started and overhead a doodle bug or flying bomb came chugging over. Its motor cut out and went off two or three streets away with a deafening roar.

His hostess, Greta Morritt, gave him a copy of *As You Like It*.

Jack Harrod, the adjutant, described their front: 'Eight tiny Dutch villages on or near the banks of the river Maas, pleasant and prosperous in the smiling days of peace, broken and forlorn now, with every church and tall building an utter ruin. Each a daily target for the enemy guns entrenched among the Siegfried defences.'

Leave, starting in January, was on everybody's mind. The GOC had gone back for two weeks – who was next? Capt. G.A. Binney, 2 Middlesex, wrote:

An Offensive Ode

Why does Hitler make Von Rundstedt
Start these wild extravaganzas
When he knows he can't afford to
Lose so many of his panzers?
Probably his one good reason
Was to stop our festive season
Should you fail to grasp these stanzas
Ektually – the object was to
Ask him if his future plans as
C-in-C would interrupt MY LEAVE.

The 2 Middlesex produced a Christmas magazine in their RHQ office called *Diehards' Digest*, which raised 732 guilders for their POW fund. They also published this 'Dutch' limerick:

> As I sit on the banks of the Maas
> I reflect that its really a Faas
> At my time of life
> And miles from my wife
> To be stuck in the mud on my Aas.

All units celebrated Christmas in some style. The Recce Regiment history by Lt.-Col. J.K. Warner recounts:

Christmas celebrations went off excellently and everyone much enjoyed themselves. 'B' Sqn were unlucky to be moved down to a backstop position behind Vierlingsbeek but they had their Christmas dinner a few days later after they had been relieved. The QM said he had never seen so much Christmas fare even in peacetime. An excellently arranged Christmas party was held for the children of Meerselo at which large numbers of children ate sweets and other food very voraciously. The Padre (Capt Fox), the QM (Capt Adlard), the Doctor (Capt Matheson) and the Dutch CO (2/Lt Fluijt) helped to make it a great success.

The 2 Middlesex had a first class dinner at Grubbenvorst and Lottum, the platoons decorated their billets with greenery, RAF silver paper and streamers bought in Helmond. On the menu was pork (of course – every Dutch pig was at risk), turkey, Christmas pudding and fruit. Hardened old sweats said it was the best Christmas dinner they had had in the Army. It was a fine day with a hard, crisp frost. John Lincoln, Norfolks, wrote:

The CO [Lt.-Col. Bellamy] offered a prize of a hundred bottles of beer to the Coy which provided the best Christmas dinner. The moment we settled down at Horst my job was to make sure 'D' Coy won the prize. . . . We planned an entertainment in the evening of the 30th and with Eddie Hastings I wrote a script following the pattern of a popular radio show, 'I want to be an actor'. The villain was called Count von Spitzenfarz. . . . Never has 'Nellie Dean' been sung so loudly. And the CO awarded us the prize.

Maj. Mike Quarmby, GSO 3, recalls:

On Christmas Eve 9 Brigade was holding the west bank of the Maas with 1 KOSB and 2 Lincolns forward and 2 RUR (whom Brigadier Walter Kempster always called the Micks) in reserve around Bde HQ at Horst. At about midnight we heard more and more shots being fired, so we ordered the Defence Platoon to stand to. In the village street we were surprised to find most of the RUR officers, after a convivial evening, taking potshots at the village church tower weather-vane. The Brigadier had of course to tear a strip off Tommy Harris, the RUR CO. . . .

Part of Gen. 'Bolo' Whistler's Christmas message to the Iron Sides was: 'I wish to say a special word to the Infantry. Splendid as has been the support given by all arms of the Division, it is that small number of men in the Rifle Companies of the Infantry Bns who had to take ground and hold it. In spite of heavy casualties they have never failed to take their objective and retain it.' So ended 1944.

CHAPTER TWENTY-TWO

New Year's Resolutions

'Spitting Distance of the Boche'

1945 started with a bang – a series of loud bangs as the written-off Luftwaffe staged a fierce noisy comeback. Jack Prior, 92 LAA, recounts: 'We were beginning to believe our A-A role was over but we were proved dramatically wrong. In less than an hour on New Year's Day the regiment shot down seven German aircraft raiding 3 Div positions. [In addition] we had five probable kills and shared in two others, a total of 14. During the action the guns fired 1765 rounds and the CO Peter Henderson commented "Sheer good shooting, entirely visual."' Maj. Bob Moberley, 2 Middlesex, recounts: '40 to 50 Luftwaffe planes came in at very low level. Our LAA had a field day. I myself saw six come down between Deurne and Venraij.' 'Bolo' Whistler wrote in his diary for 31 December: 'The Boche is by no means defeated yet. At the moment his counter-attack in the Ardennes is on its way – a thumping big one which caught the Americans on the hop. I have had 6 months of being a Major-General, and a lot too much war generally. It started as a Great Adventure and it will finish as one – but it is a very long one.' Padre Iain Wilson, 1 KOSB, agreed: 'Here on our front the enemy acted very foolishly as the new year dawned. They sang and shouted all evening and then at midnight made a brilliant display of flares and tracers. The sky was illuminated and the celebrations were rising to a crescendo when our guns interrupted with heavy shelling which effectively terminated the evening's merry-making. Silence reigned.'

The first action of the New Year took place on the night of 1 January, when an aggressive German fighting patrol crossed the river from Well to the wood north-east of Wanssum, held by 'D' Company South Lancs, and attacked the village of Wanssum. Lt. Ken Baxter was with his mortar OP Ack Cpl. Spink of 10 Platoon 2 Middlesex. 'We saw a mob of 25 Germans shuffling up the road in a disorderly manner. Their leader took our sentry's rifle and shouted "Heil Hitler".' The South Lancs were out on patrol so Ken's party of seven opened fire and dispersed the attackers. Their Bren jammed, of course, but Ken shot a German through the head as the enemy tried to rush the OP house, backed by bazooka fire. After a twenty-minute firefight, the enemy withdrew. Baxter earned the MC, but 'Oxo', the platoon dog, went AWOL for two days. Alan Candler was the South Lancs carrier platoon signaller:

Regimental cartoonist's
lifelike impression of Jack
Prior. I.O. 92 LAA Regt.

Around midnight a fighting patrol of about 50 enemy attacked our section under Sergeant Lewis on the north side of the Beek. One huge Panzer Grenadier was riddled by a burst of gunfire from Corporal Gooch, who later received the MM. The fighting patrol then crossed the Kapok Bridge killing a number of 'D' Company and taking a number of prisoners. When they withdrew they fired 110 rounds of artillery/nebelwerfer fire into the village and devastated it. All signal lines were severed. Yours truly had the onerous job of restoring line communications. I went out into the freezing night. A few hours later the IO [Eddie Jones] and the CO South Lancs were half way through breakfast when a young dapper, beautifully turned out Royal Signals captain came in, saluted smartly. 'I have been sent by the Brigadier to investigate the failure of your communications during last night's op.' Col 'Swazi' Waller bristled, said nothing, slowly ate his compo sausage. The Brigade SO went on and on, stressing the importance of communications etc. The CO fixed his gimlet eye on the BSO. 'Young man. You speak more balls to the square inch than anyone I have met for a long time. Go back and tell the Brigadier that if *I* want to conduct an enquiry into *my* signals set up, *I* will do it. Goodbye.'

The winter on the Maas.

The Germans called it 'Operation Snowman' and despite counter-attacks by the South Lancs on the 2nd, 3/4th and 6th held on to their wood tenaciously, inflicting heavy casualties on 'A' Company. So 1 Suffolk was deployed on the 8th with 'C' Company in Kangaroos, and 'D' Company in carriers to attack Wanssum wood. Although there was a snowstorm and much skidding, when seven Kangaroos struck mines, twenty prisoners were taken and the wood retaken. Lt. J.B. Smith of 20th A/Tank Regiment won the MC that day as he carried out a feint attack to draw enemy mortar fire. Kangaroos are of course vulnerable to mortar fire and infantry needed to dismount quickly from the back, sides, even the front, to avoid casualties.

Leave to the UK had started. 2 Lincolns had an allotment of 8 officers and 137 ORs for January. Jack Harrod: 'An entire novel could be written entitled "Night Train to Calais". There was a certain amount of chagrin that line of Communication troops were placed on an equal footing with the "Sharp End" soldiers.' Ray Paine, 'S' Company 2 Lincolns, arrived back at Desborough via 3-ton truck, train, boat, slow train, and then, as no buses were running, marched the last few miles home. 'Mother greeted me and was worried that I was so late. Sleeping in my own bed, thinking as I closed my eyes there would be no stand-to on guard tomorrow.' Strong gales in the Channel extended his leave by seventy-two hours. The GOC went on leave

Royal Norfolk patrol – snow suited – Wijnhoverhof.

Members of Carrier Platoon
1st Bn South Lancs Regt.
drawing names out of the 'tin
hat' for UK leave, Holland,
1944. (Alan Candler)

to the UK on 24 January and 3rd Division was commanded temporarily by Maj.-Gen. A. Galloway.

Winter had now arrived with a vengeance. White camouflage snow-suits were provided, battalion welfare groups sent out balaclavas and winter woollies of all descriptions. The 'Q' side organised self-heating soups, hot cocoa, rum rations and Valor stores for dugouts and cellars. On 10 January 27 degrees of frost were recorded!

Every night the front line battalions sent out patrols. 3rd Recce Regiment guarded the villages of Groeningen, Vortum and Sambeek. They had two Dutch Resistance Companies under command, 'Blae Peter' and 'Toni Boormann'. 'Wilforce' was a group of two carrier troops from 'A' Squadron 3 Recce under Maj. Wilson, who became expert at handling assault boats in the often stormy Maas. Lt. Hodgetts led a 3 Recce patrol on 28 January across the river to the Alferden–Heijen road. Lt. Francis, 2 KSLI, earned the MC at Pol and 'Weir' Island when his patrol house was counter-attacked by a much larger patrol on 21 January. Lt. Cray, 1 Suffolk, and Lt. Moon, 2 Lancs, were also brave and successful patrol leaders in the intense winter conditions.

Officers of 319 Bty, 92 (Loyals) LAA Regt. RA.

Harassing fire by all weapons was deployed – from 25-pounders, Vickers MG, Brownings, LAA Oerlikens, Bofors and the 4.2-in mortars of 2 Middlesex. However, these 'Pepperpot' shoots were often returned from the enemy side of the Maas! Padre Iain Wilson, 1 KOSB: 'We erected a couple of dummy Company areas where we dug positions and encouraged movement and the enemy obliged by putting down such shells and mortar bombs as he had.' On 22 January 'C' Company was attacked by a strong fighting patrol which was driven off with losses. At the end of January the intense winter snow and frost dissolved into thick mud as a rapid thaw took over. It was impossible to move transport.

Howard Marshall of the BBC visited the division and part of his broadcast said: 'Troops are living out in the mud. I have been living with them for a time, men of the Norfolks and Warwicks, troops who were living in the open "within spitting distance of the Boche" as one company commander put it. . . . It's deliberately quiet – the quietness is sinister except for the crump of a mortar or the crackle of a German spandau or the sudden wallop of guns putting down a stonk on enemy movement.'

CHAPTER TWENTY-THREE

Operations Veritable, Ventilate and Heather

February

In the first few days of February – after the great thaw on 31 January – patrolling continued. 1 Suffolk under Capt. Harris, Lt. Gray and six ORs crossed the Maas opposite Geijsteren on the night of 2/3 February. They searched two houses 1,000 yds inland, destroyed an enemy patrol and, later, two MG posts, but by mishap both officers and one OR were captured. Lts. Hancock and Beavan, 2 RUR, led successfully two patrols across near Lomm, to bring back prisoners. 1 KOSB learned that a party of six Germans had crossed the Maas in a rubber boat on a misty morning – but couldn't detect them precisely. Lt. Harry Richardson asked his CO, Maj. James Gray, for orders. He looked at the map and put his finger on a spot. 'That's where they will make for.' So Capt. Sydney Gibson and four Borderers went out to meet the German patrol. Arriving at the RV they lay quiet for ten minutes, listening hard. Pte. Conrad Linton said: 'I heard a German voice, pulled the pin out of a grenade and we took the enemy by surprise. There were six of them, five of us but they didn't even try to put up a fight. Three wore the Iron Cross, a fourth had Russian campaign ribbons. They were experienced troops.'

The Divisional Football Championship was played at the De Valk ground at Venraij and won by 2 Middlesex, who beat the South Lancs 3:1 on 5 February. On the same day Lt.-Col. Weston of the Middlesex gave his pet goat Mary to the Signal Platoon to look after. Pte. Clift was appointed Goat Major but somehow his smelly charge went AWOL – which caused little grief!

Operation Veritable, a massive Anglo-Canadian offensive sweeping south-east from Nijmegen through the Reichswald and the Siegfried Line, had now started. The American 9th Army would then move north-west in a pincer movement to link up – eventually.

The planned assault crossing, Operation Ventilate, by 3rd Division across the Maas to coincide with Veritable was now cancelled. 52nd (Lowland) Division started to relieve 3rd Division, 8 and 9 Brigades moved to Louvain and 185 Brigade was sent southwards to the Maastricht area in Belgium.

Marcus Cunliffe, adjutant 2 Warwicks: 'We were all delighted at the move.

We had seen enough of Holland in winter and were all eager to go south. No mud could stop us and by Homeric struggles [on the 8th] the Bn's transport was manhandled heaven knows how, out of the quagmire of mud which we had called home. The companies left Horst on foot, carrying mountains of kit and wading through mud in torrential rain and in the blackness of the night.' The Warwicks installed themselves in the village of Opgrimby and 1 KOSB at Herent, 'where we lived in very comfortable billets, ample facilities for amusement and recreation – during the day hard training was continued – and magnificent hospitality of the Belgians,' recalls Padre Iain Wilson.

The South Lancs took 7½ hours to cover the 12 miles to Deurne and 2 Lincolns journeyed almost 100 miles to get to Wilsele, 3 miles north of Louvain. Ray Paine: 'two sections of the mortar platoon were billeted with a Belgian family. We played cards with them. In the kitchen was an enormous stove, on top was an enamel bath tin, two feet across, in which the wife cooked the most delicious soup, full of vegetables from the garden.' Ray and the others in turn provided cans of soup, beef stew, bully beef and more bully beef. Jim Wisewell, 223 Field Ambulance, occupied comfortable billets in part of a lunatic asylum! 'Being out of action we were subjected to parades, spit and polish – and squad drill. Sidney Grundy and I saw the patients watching us, mystified as we sprang to attention, halted, banged our feet on the cobbles and saluted – no one! Sidney whispered "They're wondering just who are mad – us or them?"'

33rd Field Regiment was given the task on 8 February of firing a deception smoke screen from Haps, in support of Operation Veritable. Capt. J.A. Brymer: 'We were in action by dusk in a non-tactical setting, guns being almost wheel to wheel along the road. The one fire task in the area of Gennep at maximum range amongst the super-heavies. We eventually arrived late at night at Aerschot within easy reach of the Lommel firing ranges.' 185 Brigade had moved near Maastricht to assist 33rd Armoured Brigade (part of Gen. Hobart's 79th 'Funnies' Division) to perfect and practise assault river crossings. Marcus Cunliffe: 'We worked with the LVTs or Buffaloes, each capable of carrying a platoon of infantry, or a jeep, Bren carrier or anti-tank gun, practising on the river Maas in readiness for an assault crossing across the Rhine.' 185 Brigade cooperated with the production of landing-tables, marshalling schemes and river bank control.

3rd Recce Regiment concentrated around Lubbeck near Louvain and on the night of 7/8 February watched the heavy bombing attacks on the Reichswald–Goch area. They had a regimental tram service to Louvain, 'everyone going to Brussels, painting vehicles and overhauling equipment. Dances were arranged, football played,' wrote Maj. J.K. Warner in the regimental history. When 1 KOSB had to leave Herent to go to war again, their padre wrote: 'The sight of helmeted despatch riders sitting astride their machines while kisses were showered on them and of earnest Jocks straining out of carriers to receive a parting embrace amply justified Monty's belief that "the Borderers had a special technique in all matters of the heart".'

Operation Veritable was proving extremely difficult. The five British and Canadian divisions had struck eastward into and beyond the Reichswald in appalling conditions of rain and mud. The Germans had had years to perfect the defences of the Siegfried Line. They now mustered two Panzer divisions, one Panzer Grenadier, four parachute divisions and three infantry divisions, with 1,054 guns and 700 mortars deployed, according to a 21 Army Group estimate. New orders arrived for the Iron Sides on 21 February, to cross the Maas and reinforce 30 Corps after a fortnight of terrible fighting in dreadful conditions. Marcus Cunliffe, 2 Warwicks: 'Still more enemy units were brought in to fight the northern battle. The effect was comparable to that of the Normandy campaign where British and Canadian formations also attracted to themselves the main weight of enemy opposition thus simplifying the subsequent American advance.' The American 9th Army was delayed from 10 February by the flooding of the swollen river Roer. It was only on the 23rd that the Americans were able to launch their offensive northwards. Monty's plan had all along been to defeat the main German armies west of the Rhine.

The 3rd Division moved up to relieve the 15th Scottish Division. 2 Warwicks entered the battle zone on 25 February through Nijmegen and Cleve to a concentration area north of Goch. Marcus Cunliffe: 'Everywhere were the marks of violent struggle: splintered trees, shellshocked houses, destroyed or abandoned equipment, graves. Cleve bombed from the air was an indeterminate nightmare of rubble among which bulldozers sought the obliterated streets. Goch looked much the same. Endless vehicles crowded along the few main roads, slithering on a carpet of mud. Some roads in the sector were under water.'

The Iron Sides entered the battlefield for Operation Heather at Gennep opposite Oeffelt, with the river Niers meandering south-east into the river Maas. The plan was for 8 and 9 Brigades, which were holding the front south of Goch, to attack south-east through close, wooded country and secure the Udem–Weeze lateral road – 3 miles ahead. Then 185 Brigade in reserve would pass through and capture the small town of Kervenheim, a further 2½ miles south-east. On the immediate left was 11th Armoured Division, which had just entered the line, and on the right was 53rd Welsh Division, which would seize the town of Weeze. The immediate enemy defenders were the 7th Parachute Regiment of 8 Parachute Division. Operation Heather was aptly named. The two divisional centre lines were 'soft, saturated sandy tracks'. The whole advance through woods and heaths – with no metalled roads – would be a nightmare for the tanks and tracked vehicles of 6 Guards Tank Brigade, attendant flails, Crocodiles and AVREs under command.

9 Brigade would advance on the left through the woods to secure the eastern sector of the Udem–Weeze road, and 8 Brigade on the right would take the western segment. Capt. J.A. Brymer, 33rd Field Regiment: 'Ammo dumps were being built up to 300 r.p.g. The whole area was extremely

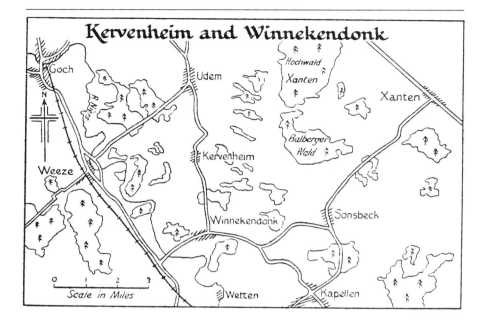

Kervenheim and Winnekendonk

soggy and OPs were issued with Weasels as tanks and carriers would be useless.' Heather began at 0700 hrs on 20 February.

8 Brigade's Attack

On the left attacking through woods were 1 Suffolk and on the right the East Yorks, whose objective was the capturing and holding of the vital Muhlen–Fleuth bridge. The plan was for the bridge to be taken on 27 February so that a brigade of 53rd Welsh Division could attack Weeze in the flank on the 28th.

'Leaning on the barrage' fired by twelve field regiments of three divisions, 1 Suffolk had taken their objective by 0900 hrs and the South Lancs came through. 'C' and 'B' Companies with Grenadier Guards tanks now had a torrid time fighting in the woods all day. The tanks were picked off by bazookas, the troops by MGs and snipers. The South Lancs had 76 casualties with 5 officers and 25 ORs killed in action. Two company commanders were killed, but 32 POWs were taken.

On the 28th the battalion concentrated in the area north of the railway. On their right were the East Yorks. Pte. Ernie Goozee, 'B' Company, wrote: "A" and "D" Coys were forward, each with a troop of Guards tanks. "A" was to attack Geurtzhof and afterwards push on to Kampshof. "D" was to take Bussenhof and then push on to seize the Muhlen–Fleuth bridge and the Schaddenhof farm on the far side of the stream.' Despite increasing resistance, the main road, a few hundred yards away from the bridge, was reached at 1330 hrs. Maj. Reg Rutherford's 'C' Company came through (Operation Donald), seized the bridge and consolidated in Schaddenhof, a group of farm buildings across the river.

Between the Maas and the Rhine, a book by the German, E. Hassi, stated that: 'the bombing and shelling around the bridge had damaged the fuses of the four huge 500-lb demolition bombs.' Lt.-Col. Bill Renison recalled: 'In the face of heavy fire and across completely open ground "C" Company moved faster than I have ever seen troops move before. "Sticky" Glen's 13 platoon crossed the bridge unblown [at 1400 hrs], and at 1615 hrs I received a signal from the Corps Commander. "Congratulations Donald taken".'

Lionel Roebuck, 13 platoon 'C' Company, had seen his friends wounded. Cpl. Ginger Smith, a keen PT man, was shot in the knee by a sniper, Sgt. Nicholson died of wounds, and 'Tabby' Barker was hit in the left leg. At nightfall 'C' Company, holed up in the Schaddenhof farm buildings, were counter-attacked on four occasions, once by tanks. 'A direct hit on the dug-out sent shrapnel crashing through my steel helmet and into my head with such a bang!' Lionel was badly wounded and was flown back to hospital in Oxford. He eventually recovered his health. Later he found out 'Jimmy Russell awarded the MM that day for gallantry and Arthur, my old schoolmate helped me on to a stretcher, while the battle raged all around us with grenades, Sten and Bren guns, hand to hand fighting and a Tiger tank belting shells into the farm walls at close range.' The famous 2 i/c Maj. 'Banger' King DSO drove a Bren gun carrier loaded with ammo through the enemy lines to reach the beleaguered 'C' Company and drove back with the badly wounded Lionel and gunner RA signaller. 'But during that harrowing night, one by one, with no attention to their wounds, many died. Johnny Vayre, one of the last to go, asked the wounded "Tabby" to hold his hand to give him some comfort before he died.'

The 7th Parachute Division and part of 190th Division were desperate to retake the vital bridge. 'B' Company had also managed to cross over from Bussenhof to relieve 'C' Company. Capt. Laurens, the A/Tank platoon commander, was killed next to Lt.-Col. Bill Renison as they moved from Kampshof into the main battle. Lt. John Ford, 76th Field Regiment FOO, fired almost the whole of the Corps Artillery into the woods in front of 'C' Company until 0400 hrs on the 28th. Maj. E.V. Hollis was another FOO with the East Yorks. 33rd Field Regiment handled 10,000 rounds of 25-pounder shells between 0500 hrs and 0900 hrs and during the two days' fighting fired 15,849 rounds, an average of 660 r.p.g. The first counter-attack was by 1st Battalion 24 Parachute Regiment and the next by 3rd Battalion of 22 Parachute Regiment. Bill Renison: 'It had been what I think Wellington would have described as a "close run thing" but we had won.' 'Banger' won a bar to his DSO but the East Yorks casualties were 33 killed, 123 wounded and 4 missing. The gunner FOOs, Lts. J. Ford and Maclean were awarded MCs. 'We took 150 German prisoners and counted 85 dead of Para Group Hubner in the battle area', recalled Ernie Goozee, 'but my platoon lost Corp. Stan Kirk, L/Corp Ginger Hamblin, Pte Bill Cuxby, CSM Biff Trowell: Gen "Bolo" Whistler ordered the sappers to place a nameboard on the bridge with the East Yorkshires' Crest and Name – "Yorkshire" bridge.'

9 Brigade's Attack

Towards their two objectives of Kervenheim and Winnekedonk the 2 Lincolns led, to cross a stream, then to exploit to a wood 800 yds beyond. 2 RUR and 1 KOSB would then pass through, cut the Udem–Weeze road, and capture the woods on the far side. Supported by a barrage from five field regiments, a squadron of Scots Guards Churchill tanks, four Kangaroos and three Weasels, 2 Lincolns set off at 0730 hrs. An hour later, to their surprise, all objectives had been taken, with sixty POWs. Much the same thing happened with 2 RUR. Their attack was at 1000 hrs with 'D' Company right and 'A' Company left moving 100 yds every five minutes, in front of a barrage of colossal intensity. The tank support was close and effective. The Germans were demoralised and well over 160 prisoners taken. Lt. Purcell, 'C' Company, captured several enemy posts with great dash, but the Ulsters took sixty-six casualties, mainly sustained by shelling before the attack began. 1 KOSB were on their right and had cut the Udem–Weeze road by 1100 hrs – a 1,000-yds advance in fifty minutes, overrunning one German position after another with excellent tank operation. At 1345 hrs Lt.-Col. R.C. Macdonald, the CO, sent back the code word 'Daffodil'. L/Cpl. Mould, Sgt. Jaggers, Lt. Simpson and Sgt. Pearson all distinguished themselves and Pte. Fulton of 'D' Company carried a 38 set, led his platoon and captured fifteen prisoners. But the final attack failed. At 1530 hrs 'C' Company tried to secure a bridgehead over the Muhlen–Fleuth. This involved crossing a stretch of open country with both flanks exposed in face of Spandau fire from a group of farms across the stream. Four Churchill tanks were bogged down in deep mud and an enemy SP gun knocked out three more in rapid succession, as the smoke screen ran out. Nevertheless, 1 KOSB had taken 140 prisoners of 1 Parachute Regiment and killed many more paratroops for the loss of 28 casualties.

185 Brigade's Attack on Kervenheim

185 Brigade was now commanded by Brig. F.R.C. Matthews, with 2 KSLI attacking on the left, 2 Warwicks on the right and 1 Norfolk in reserve.

2 KSLI had moved from Gun, north-east of Horst on the Maas, where, with the East Riding Yeomanry tanks, they had practised river assault crossing while the main brigade was at Eysden. The billets were good and the people extremely friendly, but the troops had to march 4 miles to their 'Buffaloes' and another 4 miles 'home'!

CSM Sutton was commissioned and took over the pioneer platoon and Maj. Brooke-Smith left to join 7 Somerset Light Infantry in the 43rd Wessex Wyvern Division. Guy Radcliffe, their adjutant, wrote: 'The Para troops which we were now to fight had accumulated more artillery and mortars than we had expected, but so had we, more than we had ever had before. How the enemy survived at all was something that we could never understand. If we thought our life hell, theirs was so much worse as to bear no comparison.'

2 Warwicks' first day went well through woods, waterlogged clay fields, scattered houses and no roads to speak of. By nightfall on 28 February they consolidated just outside Kervenheim. 1 March, a dismally wet day, was difficult. The QM, Capt. Williams, had just managed to bring up a meal during the night and at dawn the whole of 185 Brigade was heavily stonked. 'B' Company was attacked by seventy-five paratroops with SP guns. Lt. Guest, Ptes. Walker and Bates fought back effectively. Pte. Cook fired A/Tank HE over open sights at the advancing infantry and knocked out an SP gun, for which he was awarded the MM.

In two days 2 Warwicks took forty-eight casualties including two company commanders, but they held firm and drove off the counter-attack. 2 KSLI had to clear the 2 miles south of Pfalzdorf to Kervenheim down one sandy track through woods, supported by a squadron of Coldstream Guards' Churchills. They started at 1300 hrs on 28 February and halted

A Carrier Platoon of South Lancs in the woods near Kervenheim. Alan Candler is second from the right. (Alan Candler)

after heavy opposition in the thick woods in darkness at 1800 hrs. Pte. Hewett of 'W' Company won the MM for dashing forward to collect casualties and for taking out a strongpoint with his Bren gun. Food came up at midnight, and at 0900 hrs on 1 March the attack was renewed. Lt. Aldridge and Sgt. Fisher of the pioneer company were killed by mortar fire. 'He [Aldridge] would dodge about the battlefield in his jeep or on foot, ignoring completely either shelling or mines, helping to evacuate the wounded, carrying messages, aiding his sections or the sappers, all the odd jobs of the battle,' wrote his adjutant, Guy Radcliffe.

So 'Y' Company on the the left and 'Z' Company on the right resolutely continued the advance. The farms and buildings of Kervenheim were strongly held and 17 Platoon produced many heroes that day. Lt. Banks, who commanded, won the MC and Pte. Joseph Stokes the VC for incredible gallantry. During the day in countless attacks he was wounded eight times and later died of his wounds. He personally captured twenty-one prisoners, and refused to go back to the RAP. 'Again without waiting for orders Pte Stokes, although now severely wounded and suffering from loss of blood, dashed on the remaining 60 yards to the objective firing from the hip as he struggled on through intense fire. He finally fell 20 yards from the enemy position firing his rifle to the last. As the company passed in the final charge, he raised his hand and shouted "goodbye",' wrote Guy Radcliffe.

At 1300 hrs 'X' Company was sent up to reinforce 'Z', but between them they could not penetrate beyond the northern outskirts of the town. Here

Royal Norfolks in Kervenheim: Canadian Lt. Laurie leads 18 Platoon 'D' Company.

CSM Olden won the MM; he reorganised and led forward a platoon whose commander had been killed. At 1515 hrs 'W' Company moved up and the battalion consolidated for the night in the suburbs. Later, Terence Cuneo painted a fine scene of the dramatic action of Pte. Joseph Stokes winning his VC, which is now owned by the Trustees of the King's Shropshire Light Infantry.

Humphrey Wilson, 1 Norfolks, wrote:

At 0415 a long snake of men wound their way [from Pfalz Dorf] along the track to the assembly area. Before dawn on 1st March the Bn was dug in and by 0800 our tanks had arrived and the final link-up was completed . . . to the right were two groups of farmhouses. From these we suffered our initial set-back. 'A' Coy on the right suffered badly. Major D.W. Smith was shot through the head, all the platoon commanders were either hit or badly wounded, only the gunner FOO [Capt. George Haigh] remaining to control what was left. 'B' Coy had got on a bit better. Despite an Uncle target [fire programme] the enemy still held firm.

Sgt. E. Carr: 'At Kervenheim I was acting CSM. The frontal assault was a disaster. Very soon 4 officers and 103 ORs were reduced to only 35. The officers were all either killed or wounded. The next day we entered Kervenheim unhindered.'

Capture of Kervenheim – Royal Norfolk carriers lead.

Five hundred yards to the west of Kervenheim were the two enemy strongpoints at Muserhof and Murmannshof. 'D' Company under Capt. Robin Wilson, initially in reserve, now attacked from the left flank and fierce house-to-house fighting ensued. John Lincoln, 'D' Company, was wounded in the final attack. In *Thank God and the Infantry* he wrote: 'We had no close support, no tanks, no rolling barrage to flatten the opposition ahead of us. Just the will to get up and move forward. [Later] We had achieved our first objective and were the first troops in the town. We had unfortunately received further casualties from 88s, mortar and MG fire and from the opposition we encountered from the centre of town.'

'C' Company was able to back up 'D' Company. The fierce house-to-house fighting continued and by the evening the enemy had had enough. The Norfolks had lost 5 officers and 36 ORs KIA, and 5 officers and 115 ORs wounded. Humphrey Wilson wrote in his battalion history: 'Success had been achieved but at a heavy cost.'

2 Lincolns were put temporarily under command of 185 Brigade and 'A' Company under Maj. Larkin 'were given the honour to assist 1 Royal Norfolk; after a fierce struggle in which Lt Seabrook was killed we cleared and consolidated the factory area at the north end of the village and secured a footing astride the main road from Udem', wrote Jack Harrod, the Lincolns' adjutant. 'It was no difficult task for "A" and "C" Coys to complete the capture of the village in the morning.

9 Brigade's Attack

1 KOSB and 2 RUR now moved south with the objective of taking Winnekedonk, some 4 miles away, supported by 3rd Scots Guards Churchills. 1 KOSB started off at dawn on 4 March, found little resistance and proceeded to secure Bruch, a small village in the outskirts of Winnekedonk. 'A most impressive column we were too: a squadron of Churchill tanks led the way, followed by some SP guns and we brought up the rear in our 50 Kangaroos [bypassing Kervenheim]. The 2 RUR moved through us', wrote Padre Wilson. But 2 Lincolns were asked to make the final frontal attack on Winnenkedonk across 1,200 yds of open ground. Jack Harrod:

The Bn surged forward under pitiless fire. Many fell including Major Clarke, killed by a grenade. By 1820 the road junction at the near approach to the village had been reached. But still the enemy parachutists fought back grimly. Snipers fired from first floor windows and Spandaus shot through loopholes in the walls at ground level. Now the light was going fast and the infantry and the 3rd Scots Guards' tanks went into the village in billows of smoke, punctuated by the orange flashes of the enemy 88s and criss-crossed by lines of tracer. It was a great and terrible spectacle. The Bn had really got its teeth in and was not to be denied.

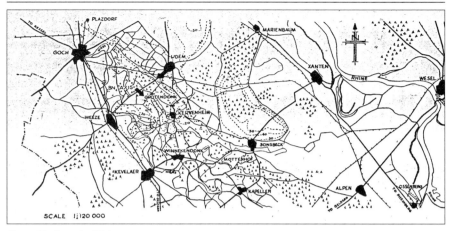

From Goch to the Rhine.

Savage fighting continued until the parachutists had had enough. Thirty were killed, fifty were wounded and eighty surrendered. When the village was finally cleared in the morning seventy more gave themselves up. Major Clarke and fifteen ORs were KIA, three officers and eighty eight ORs were wounded or missing. The CO, Lt-Col C.L. Firbank, was awarded a bar to his DSO and Sgt Boothman, Corp Spye and Pte Conner were awarded MMs.

The battered Lincolns stayed in Winnekendonk for another ten days, licking their wounds.

Maj. J.K. Warner's history of 3 Recce recorded:

C Sqn got moving and had a good run through Kevelaer [2 miles west] and Wetten [2 miles south-east from Winnekedonk], captured two demolition parties preparing charges. They were held up only just short of Kapellan by a SP, a brilliant day spoilt by the death of Lt Ferguson. The count of prisoners for the day topped the hundred mark. We stayed until 15 March in the Wetten area, clearing booby traps, removing 250 kilo bombs from a bridge, disarming the local inhabitants and acquiring a lavish collection of sporting weapons – and had some good shooting.

30 Corps now ordered the Iron Sides to capture Kapellan, a village surrounded by a natural water obstacle on almost all sides, with only one road leading into it. To the left was a large wood with a big country house – Schloss Haus Winkel. 185 Brigade was given this task and Brig.Matthews ordered a night advance of the 6 miles south of Winnekedonk to secure the last objective of Operation Heather. Mounted on Kangaroos, 2 KSLI led

with 2 Warwicks following on foot. 2 KSLI captured Mottenhof half-way and soon had patrols into Kapellan. Maj. Bell, 2 Warwicks, led 'D' Company, followed by 'A' into the village. The enemy had withdrawn and a dozen prisoners were rounded up. But heavy shelling of Kapellan started and two Guards Churchill tanks were knocked out advancing eastwards. 1 Norfolk carried out a daring 2-mile night advance through a forest, which encircled the manor house, Haus Winkel. Maj. Dye, 'C' Company, led and the whole battalion worked their way through the woods in single file. Everywhere the roads were cratered and bridges blown, but at first light all objectives had been taken for negligible loss.

On the morning of 5 March, Guards Armoured Shermans streamed through the Norfolks' position in the Winkelscher Busch over the Bonninghardt ridge, while 8 Brigade screened their left flank from Sonsbeck.

'Bolo' Whistler's diary:

We had had our most successful battle. Damn difficult country – centre line non-existent or on a mud track – yet we have done everything asked. We have captured 1,200 prisoners, nearly all paratroopers. We must have killed and wounded many more. The scenes of devastation in Germany are quite remarkable. There is nothing that has not been damaged or destroyed. We have captured Kervenheim, Winnekendonk and Kapellen of the larger places. I would say the 9 Brigade under Rennie have done best, 185 next under Mark Matthews. 8 Brigade have not had so much luck though East Yorks had a terrific night holding a bridgehead against repeated counter attacks.

'Bolo' praised the gunners under their CRA, Brig. Gerald Mears, and the sappers under Tom Evill:

The whole standard is very, very high. Am getting on very well with Jorrocks [Gen. Horrocks, 30 Corps Commander] He is a fine leader and well liked, quite ruthless but one has to be. . . . The Boche are beaten pretty badly here. We are through the Siegfried Line and very near the Rhine. I would not have missed this battle for anything – unpleasant and frightening though it has been. To fight on German soil after all this time is more than I ever expected. Now for the Rhine.

Heather was over.

CHAPTER TWENTY-FOUR

Operation Plunder

'Cracking About in Northern Germany'

'Playing' on their home ground amid the formidable defences of the Siegfried Line, the German paratroops had put up a superb effort against the Canadians and 30 Corps in Operation Veritable. The RAF had 'taken out' every town and village west of the Rhine. And the immense artillery support available to the Allies brought down avalanches of shells. To support a battalion attack on a hamlet, Mike, Uncle, Victor and Yoke targets were fired. For instance 33rd Field Regiment RA disposed of 27,515 25-pounder shells in six days – as did the supporting gunner regiments in 30 Corps. Medium, heavy and super heavy artillery regiments were deployed and Pepperpots were frequent when the LAA fired their Bofors, the Middlesex their 4.2-in mortars and MMGs, and supporting tanks joined in with HE fire. The Germans in their deep well-planned strongpoints, protected by concrete dragons teeth and huge minefields, still received new tanks, SP guns, 88-mms and ammo supplies from the Ruhr factories – despite 'Bomber' Harris' best efforts. They had another important ally in 'General Mud'. Almost non-stop rain and river flooding had produced a battlefield where it was a miracle if the armour – Shermans, Churchills, AVREs, flails and Crocodiles – could appear in the right part of the battlefield, on time. Nevertheless, Lt.-Gen. Horrocks' five divisions of 30 Corps had done a superb job in the four-week battle of Operation Veritable.

On 12 March the Iron Sides took over a stretch of the Rhine opposite Rees. 'Die Wacht am Rhein' meant a defensive role to ensure that any enemy river-patrol crossing to obtain information about the impending river assault, would be foiled.

There were now many changes of management. Lt.-Col. R.C. Macdonald left 1 KOSB to take command of 2 Royal Warwicks in place of Lt.-Col. Gibbs, who went to command an OCTU in the UK. Lt.-Col. W.F.R. Turner, former 5 KOSB, now commanded the Borderers. Lt.-Col. Hugh Bellamy of the Norfolks was promoted to be a brigadier in 6th Airborne Division and was succeeded by Lt.-Col. Peter Barclay. Brig. E.L. Bols left 185 Brigade to command 6th Airborne and was succeeded by Brig. F.R.C. Matthews. Lt.-Col. Lindsay, CO 33rd Field Regiment, was posted as GSO1 to GHQ AA Troops, 21 Army Group, to be succeeded by Lt.-Col. Hope and then by Lt.-Col. J.M. Bayley. Lt.-Col. Tapp left 92 LAA for a Far East posting and was replaced by Lt.-Col. Bazeley.

Padre Wilson, 1 KOSB: 'We moved through the badly wrecked town of Xanten and then on into a most lovely and tranquil countryside, bearing no sign of war except trench systems and occasional minefields and lying quietly in the spring sunshine. The old farms were undamaged, the orchards a soft green and there was nothing more to disturb us than the continuous lowing of unmilked cows and the cackling of geese.' The Borderers watched the town of Rees from the western river bank between Calcar and Xanten. By night three companies moved across the Bund flood bank to man a series of guard posts along the west bank of the river. St Patrick's night was celebrated. 'C' Company gave a memorable dinner to the MO, and 'C' Company captured two men in enemy uniform who were British Intelligence agents from across the river – truly!

2 Warwicks and 2 KSLI were stationed opposite Emmerich on a large and completely flat island well provided with amply stocked farms. However, it was overlooked by the high buildings in Emmerich, so that all movement had to be carried out by night. All the bridges to the island had been blown but a Bailey bridge was soon constructed. As all the German civilians had been evacuated, there were problems with cows, pigs, sheep and rather fierce large bulls. A Warwicks patrol needed a PIAT bomb to despatch one such bull. The Germans sent several patrols across the 500- to 1,200-yds river on 18 March, which were tackled by Lt. Foster, Sgt. Roberts and others of 'C' Company.

The East Yorks, which had just received a huge draft of nineteen-year-old reinforcements, very raw, but tremendously keen, now shared the small town of Calcar with 1 Suffolk. But on 15 March East Yorks moved to luxurious accommodation in Honnopel, where fringe benefits included poultry farming. Col. Renison suggested 'a daily egg was better than one chicken dinner'. Maj. 'Banger' King went to Brussels to receive a bar to his DSO and Pte. Russell the MM, from FM Montgomery.

On 9 March Col.-Sgt. Hatfield, 'A' Company Middlesex, was wounded in the left eye by a Jerry. No, not a German soldier! L/Cpl. Giles, clearing a littered room for an office, with a fine, careless gesture flung a chamberpot out of the window as the luckless CQMS was passing. It broke his glasses, cut his eye and sent him off to hospital just as he was due for UK leave!

2 Lincolns guarded Hochend and then Obermormter and, when an eleven-man patrol of 7th Parachute Division crossed the formidable river barrier, it was destroyed by a Lincoln patrol under Capt. H.J. Pacey. Each battalion in the line provided five patrols by night and five manned OPs during the day. Round about Walbech 'A' Squadron 3 Recce built a most remarkable collection of log huts 'to relieve the housing shortage' and their Capt. Brough, and Lts. Tierney and Evans extracted drink etc. – a new form of blackmail – for providing better class shelter for the troops in their area.

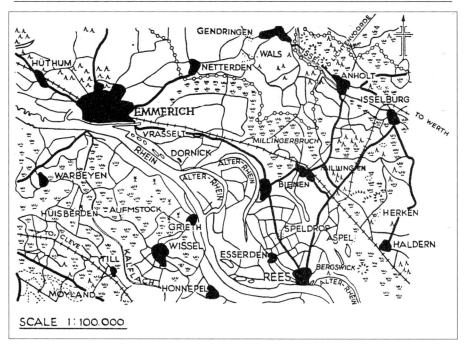

From the Rhine to the Ems.

Many curious arrivals were noted apart from the enormous amount of bridging material, such as 45 -ft long, 14 -ft wide naval ships, dragged up by road across Belgium and Holland. The statistics for the build-up to the Rhine crossing were quite staggering. Thirty thousand REs and pioneers were preparing the pontoon bridges along the two Army Corps assault areas. Thirteen thousand artillery guns – 25-pounders, mediums, heavies and super heavies backed up by Pepperpot contributors (LAA Bofors, Middlesex heavy MGs and mortars, A/Tanks M-10 fire, etc.) – would produce perhaps the biggest barrage of the war. Indeed 60,000 tons of ammunition was being dumped in readiness. Six hundred tanks were in harbour – the author's 11th Armoured, the Desert Rats and Guards Armoured, plus vital flails, AVREs and Crocodiles. Norman Scarfe's book *Assault Division* details the significant part played in this gigantic build-up by the Divisional Signals, REME, Sappers, Gunners, RAMC, and, above all, the RASC.

Marcus Cunliffe, 2 KSLI: 'For once the weather was proving kind to the Allies. The spring came early: a succession of clear sunlit days made war seem far-off. Yet the atmosphere was not that of peacetime.'

Operation Plunder – the British part of it – was to be a two Corps attack between the towns of Wesel and Emmerich with 12 Corps on the right (south) and Lt.-Gen. Horrocks' 30 Corps on the left (north). Two Airborne divisions, the 6th British and 17th US, would drop on the east bank to secure the bridgeheads. The German 8th Parachute Division was based around Rees, with the 6th and 7th Parachute Divisions on the flanks. Their immediate reserves were 15th Panzer Grenadiers and 116th Panzer Division.

To mask the immense build-up that took place in the next two weeks, the gunner regiments fired masking smoke screens above the river. Capt. J.A. Brymer, 33rd Field Regiment: 'if there was no wind the smoke hung about all over the Brigade area making many people violently sick'. On one occasion 1,300 rounds of smoke were fired to screen from Haffen to Rees for 3 hours.

The Corps plan called for assault crossings on both sides of Rees, 10 miles upstream from Emmerich. First across were to be the 51st Highland Division. A gigantic counter-battery fireplan, plus at 1900 hrs the Pepperpot opened up at H-4 (1700 hrs on Friday 23 March) and continued through the night and the next day. 33rd Field Regiment had fired 8,599 rounds by noon on the 24th. Bob Moberley also described the Rhine Pepperpot shoot with 3 MG battalions, a tank regiment, 2 A/Tank regiments and 3 LA regiments. Some of those taking part were 13/18th Hussars, the 20th and 73rd A/Tank regiments (forty-eight 17-pounders), the 92nd, 94th and 4th (Canadian) LAA (with seventy-two Bofors). By midnight the Middlesex had fired 4,833 mortar bombs and fired 304,000 MMG rounds across the Rhine. The RAF had already pounded Wesel, Rees, Emmerich – indeed every town and village on the east bank. It was Wagnerian – the noise, the flames, tracer flashing, the great Allied Airborne divisions passing overhead. Jack Harrod described the: '"Airborne armada", monsters of the air, full of incredible grace, grim purpose and deadly power. First came the Paratroops in Halifax or Stirling, then the Dakotas towing gliders. Visibility was not too good. We waved them a greeting. We had fought side by side with some of them in the old beachhead days and knew their worth.' There were 1,572 troop-carrying planes, 1,326 gliders and 1,800 protective fighter escorts.

The Airborne drops were successful although heavy losses were inflicted by the waiting defenders. 1st British commandos took Wesel, the Black Watch were the first infantry across and the two Scottish divisions, 51st on the left, 15th on the right, soon made good their bridgeheads. Rees still held out for some time, where 30 Corps proposed to build a bridge across. For several days the Iron Sides were in the unusual situation of watching and listening to the storming of the Rhine – a few hundred yards away from the war. On 24 March they were visited by the Prime Minister, who arrived at Divisional HQ at Schloss Moyland, 4 miles inland. He was dressed in his uniform of honorary colonel of the 5th (Cinque Ports) Royal Sussex and came equipped with a gold-topped cane. He addressed the troops and remembered that the Iron Sides were one of two British divisions to land on D-Day on the Normandy beaches.

Bdr. John Foster, 33rd Field Regiment, recalls: 'During the Rhine barrage a column of German POW passed through our [25-pounder] gun position. One of them stopped, asked me in fluent English if our guns were automatic. A tribute to our gunners. They looked the part that day with a RASC 3-ton ammo truck behind each gun.'

The tragic death of Maj.-Gen. Tom Rennie happened on the same day. The gallant GOC of the 3rd Division, who had been wounded in Normandy, was now killed by a mortar bomb blast as he was visiting one of his 51st Highland Division brigades in the bridgehead.

Soon 9 Brigade was ordered into the fray to cross by London, Blackfriars, Waterloo and Westminster bridges at Honnepol and then to pass through ruined Rees. 1 KOSB and 2 RUR were first to cross on the 27th and marched into unoccupied Haldern on the following afternoon. Padre Iain Wilson wrote:

White flags hung out of the windows of the smashed town and no resistance was offered. At one o'clock on the following morning we marched in a light drizzle bound for the capture of Werth. Just before dawn 'A' Coy scrambled across the river [the bridge over Oude Issel was blown] running through the outskirts of Werth, clambered over the great cement blocks barricading the main street. In the evening we received orders to press on with our third consecutive night attack. The Brigade had the task of securing the bridgehead over the river Aa, crossing a stream 1000 yds north and exploiting the line of the main Bocholt–Isselburg road.

Their pioneer platoon lifted hundreds of enemy mines, but the dreaded wooden Schu-mines were less easy to secure and caused casualties. At 0100 on 30 March, the Lincolns and 2 RUR carried out an assault crossing over the river Aa – successfully – and by 0830 the Guards Armoured Shermans were passing through in hot pursuit. In comfortable farms where there were goose eggs for breakfast, 1 KOSB stayed put until 2 April. On Easter Sunday Padre Wilson held a church parade, followed by a march past to say farewell to Brig. G.D. Renny, who was posted to 52nd Lowland Division. He was succeeded by Brig. W.F.H. Kempster.

Meanwhile 2 Lincolns moved on towards Lensing and Doing, via Haldern and Monkerath, to check if the river bridges were blown. 53rd Welsh Division was attacking Bocholt on the right and 51st Highland Division, Dinxperlo on the left.

The crossing of the river Aa warranted a two-battalion attack with 2 Lincolns on the right and 2 RUR on the left. Forty assault boats arrived promptly and from Houten Klump 2 Lincolns crossed at 0100 hrs led by Maj. Hart's 'D' Company, then 'C' and 'A'. They were totally successful with thirty-two POW taken for the loss of five Lincolns KIA and nine wounded.

The sappers then constructed a Class 40 bridge over the Aa and later 1 KOSB would establish a bridgehead over the Halttuicker Bach.

The Ulster Rifles assault crossing of the river Aa was also a great success. Thirty feet wide, knee deep with steep banks, it was crossed by assault boats in the middle of the night and sixty prisoners were taken for six wounded Ulsters. A tall, fair-haired youth claimed to have lunched with the Führer in Borholt the previous day! Everybody 'took' prisoners – the CO, Maj. Bird, the RAP sergeant, Sgt. Tipper, and Sgt. Cochrane, who, with his men captured an entire enemy patrol, for which he was awarded the MM.

On Good Friday Guards Armoured charged through 9 Brigade's bridgeheads on their way to Aalten, and a few hours later Gen. 'Bolo' Whistler went round the division (8 and 185 Brigades had now caught up) outlining the advance plan for 30 Corps.

During the first week of Operation Plunder, 3 Recce Regiment were loaned to work with and lead 6 Guards Armoured Tank Brigade in their 15-mile right hook to Borken, to link up with the Airborne drop. On 26 March from Geldern they crossed the Rhine on an American rubber pontoon bridge and entered Wesel, still shattered and smoking from the bombing and Pepperpot. West of Peddenburg by 0300 hrs on the 27th the whole regiment was concentrated and ready, as Maj. J.K. Warner wrote: 'the next eight days are so full of incidents both sad and amusing. We took 700 prisoners and were in contact with the enemy throughout the whole operation. Our objective now was Munster, "A" Sqn to lead, supported by the Scots Guards carrying one of the American Para Bns.' Through Dorsten, Schermbeck and Haldern they scuttled, pushed and probed. 'The Coldstream Guards were most impressive as they shot at anything which might be concealing a German. Farms were ablaze, prisoners coming in and it was raining hard. The Dortmund–Ems Canal protected our right flank, all the bridges having been blown.'

Maj. Rayner, OC 'B' Squadron, wrote an account of their adventures in *Seven Days to Munster*:

Our task was to recce a route to Munster [50 miles away] to enable 17 US Airborne and 6 Guards tank bridge to capture the city . . . our first sight of the Americans moving down the road in a varied collection of jeeps, saloon cars, captured three-tonners, horses and carts and one original soul in a mechanical invalid chair. Others satisfied their egos with top hats, umbrellas and other tasteful items of civilian dress, all in high spirits following their successful landing two days before.

Some old beachhead friends now turned up again. On 28 March 'B' and 'C' Squadrons of the 22nd Dragoons with their Sherman flail tanks, crossed the Rhine to support 9 Brigade who were clearing Haldern, and then moved north to cross the river Aa. Maj. Raymond Burt wrote in his regimental history:

Late in the evening of April 1 the regimental group moved off in support of 185 Brigade. It was like old times. There was a regimental order of march [the squadrons usually worked quite independently with their 'little friends' clearing minefields] and a regimental net: there were start points, report lines and map reference codes – all the once-familiar apparatus of an approach march but the jibs of the flails in the darkness of an awkwardly sited Bailey bridge . . . an exasperating struggle to coax the tanks across. At dawn we were across the border once again and in Holland.

The liberation of the Dutch towns was also described by Raymond Burt:

. . . a festival of rebirth and liberation indeed. They were out on the roads, a waving, cheering mass that surged over the [22nd Dragoon] tanks, shaking our hands or embracing our grubby faces between tears and laughter. Orange sashes, hats, hair ribbons, gloves; orange in the coat lapels and shoe buckles, orange about the windows and on the doors, orange even on the collars of frenzied dogs and the tails of sober horses.

Pte. Jim Wisewell, 223 Field Ambulance:

We set up the ADS in a school in Nordhorn and shared the room with a dead German. Corporal Mickey House took 4 of us next day to bury him in the local churchyard. The Padre gabbled through the service and a woman came over with a bunch of flowers, the children clinging to her skirt. 'For your English comrade' she said, holding out the flowers. Mickey thanked her, explained it was a German comrade. She snatched the flowers back, 'I am Dutch. No flowers for a German.' So we left him with a slip of paper in an empty 50-cigarette tin. It read 'Obergefreiter Schmidt. Shot through the lung, April 3rd 1945'. Just that. No flowers.

Behind Guards Armoured Division, 8 Brigade led the Iron Sides into Holland via Aalten and Groenlo after spending five weeks in Germany. On Easter Sunday morning 8 Brigade was established in Groenlo and Bob Moberley, Middlesex, noted: 'Some of the houses flew white flags – they were the houses of collaborators, some of whom were being marched away when we arrived. It was All Fools Day.'

Still following the Guards through Haaksbergen, Enschede to Oldenzaal, they recrossed the German border on 3 April to enter Nordhorn on the junction of the Almelo canal and the river Vechte. Now 185 Brigade followed by 9 Brigade, passed through Nordhorn towards Lingen, a town 15 miles away on the eastern side of the Dortmund–Ems canal.

Gen. 'Bolo's' diary:

March 30. What a week! The crossing of the Rhine started on 23rd and the Highland Div passed through us. All very successful but the Para boys fought awfully well. Rees was very troublesome and the bridges were late as a result but the business went on. So sad about Thomas Rennie – a great friend of mine. He had fought through all the campaigns. McMillan took his place. Two days ago 3 Div began to cross the Rhine and came up on the right of the HD. Pressing forward with 9 Bde and the guns, with minor trouble until yesterday until we bumped it with the Lincolns . . . that very excellent sapper Edward Collins killed. CRA Gerald Mears, promoted to CCRA, sad for him to go. Tom Evill, CRE, wounded. Last night 9 Bde took seventy prisoners. The whole place is mined as I had seldom seen – mines in the roads and the verges and many in the fields. Bridges blown, roads blocked and every devilish device the Hun could think of. I trust he is in for it now. I am heading for Hamburg etc. And the Yanks will yet be in Berlin before old Joe.

The Battle for Lingen: 'One More River to Cross'

Guy Radcliffe, adjutant 2 KSLI, wrote:

The area on the east bank of the Rhine had been utterly pulverised by the bombing and the artillery fire. Dead cattle surrounded every derelict farm, the debris of war lined the roads with the torn-off boughs of the trees. The Germans moved about in a dazed state . . . we had very little trouble with them . . . of repentance there seemed to be none, only a grovelling self-pity.

[On 1 April] the Bn arrived at Lichtenvoorde in Holland. We were overjoyed to be back in friendly country. One could feel the 'freedom' in the air, every house had put out the flags which had long been concealed. We reached Enschede the next day and experienced for the first and last time in the campaign what a large town did when it was liberated.

The hundred-vehicle column, which included the flails of the 22nd Westminster Dragoons in their 'proper' role as tanks, had to be stopped frequently and pushed down side roads to allow Guards Armoured through. The enemy still held Hengelo to the north of Enschede. And on the morning of 3 April 2 KSLI were ordered off towards Lingen to lead the 185 Brigade assault crossing of the river Ems and the Dortmund–Ems canal. This double water obstacle formed an obvious natural defence line on the western outskirts of Lingen, a sizeable garrison town, defended by 111 Battalion Grossdeutschland Brandenburger training regiment plus several hundred paratroops.

In a brilliant action Guards Armoured had captured intact the bridge over the river, 2,000 yds west of Altenlingen, 2 miles north of Lingen itself. Capt. Liddell was awarded the VC for this daring action. 2 KSLI then were ordered to make a night march to the bridge and advance and cross the canal. At 0230 hrs they started the attack, 'X' Company on the left and 'Z' on the right – in almost total silence. By 0530 hrs the canal was reached. Boats had been sent forward and at 0635 hrs the companies started to cross the second water obstacle. An artillery stonk was directed on the *south* side of the town to mislead the enemy. Capt. Graham Lewis, commanding 2 Platoon 7 Field Company RE, recalled: 'As dawn broke the KSLI were ready with the assault boats and shooting now started from the opposite bank in earnest. There was a whirl of paddles, the assault sections leapt ashore on the far bank and swiftly made their way forward, merged into the landscape.' Fortunately the light AA guns near the canal were not fully manned and a bridgehead was quickly formed. Pte. Medlicott saved a blazing carrier full of mortar bombs and Cpl. Coles led his section to take an enemy-occupied farmhouse. Both earned the MM.

By 1030 hrs the sappers of 17 Field Company had built a Class 9 bridge across the canal while under fire and despite attacks by two Messerschmitt 109s. Graham Lewis' company commander, 'Scotty' Scott-Bowden, was seriously wounded in this opposed landing. Across the German plains the remnants of the Luftwaffe appeared to help defend the river and canal crossings. Jack Prior, 92 LAA, reported: 'Even as late as 4–6 April the German Air Force made attacks in an attempt to halt the battle for the Dortmund–Ems canal. We were involved in 44 sorties near Lingen resulting in our destroying another ME 267 and two other aircraft.'

The Warwicks and Norfolks crossed next and turned south to attack the

17 Field Company RE. All the men are decorated, and the group includes Maj. Scott Bowden DSO, MC (centre, seated) and Sgt. Frank Faulkner (far left, seated). (Frank Faulkner)

town. Marcus Cunliffe: 'Fortified only by a hasty cup of tea (we were supper-less), we [2 Warwicks] formed up at 0900 [4 April] and began to attack Lingen from the north at 1015, "C" and "D" in the lead.' The enemy, still expecting the main attack from the south, responded slowly. 2 KSLI had taken 50 prisoners and now 2 Warwicks added another 170 for negligible cost.

The attack was pressed with admirable speed and success . . . . Field Marshal Montgomery's men fought like veterans. Many of them actually were reinforcements, youngsters who had joined the campaign at a comparatively late stage. At mid-day the 1st Norfolks came through us in the hope of accounting for the several hundred paratroops [of 2 Para Corps] that remained in the southern half of Lingen. 1st Norfolk fought through the streets, house by house and block by block until evening. Then in turn the Lincolns [of 8 Brigade under command] came through, cleared some more houses in the dark and resumed its progress at dawn the next morning. Street fighting is a laborious business – as well as a nerve-wracking one. Lingen was a large town with a good many Germans distributed in it. Lt W. Genever 'A' Coy secured with his platoon an undamaged canal-bridge in Lingen, stayed there for two days, shelled, bombed and machinegunned by occasional Luftwaffe.

Humphrey Wilson, 2 i/c 1 Norfolk, wrote:

Lingen was known to be defended by all types of Boche – Para, SS, Wehrmacht and the Volksturm (Home Guard) [Later] The whole Bn was fully extended. It was a real soldiers street-fighting battle, but we would have given anything for a squadron of crocodiles. Sgt Langford and his only WASP did extremely well [he won the DCM]. After the main square of the town had been passed the stiffer opposition was met. Major J.B. Dye, OC 'C' Coy, got hit. There were several near shaves. The CO had his batman shot one pace behind him. Major W.H. Brinkley had to pop into a doorway – rather quickly. We were very lucky, casualties were light. By 1800 things were under control, a number of houses were burning nicely. By 2000 the Lincolns came up. After dark, everyone had to clamp down. Limited patrolling, hot meals and sleep for those who could.

2 Lincolns were put under command of 185 Brigade and soon found themselves in the centre of Lingen, and within an hour committed to street fighting in the dark. 'Necessarily progress was slow,' recalls Jack Harrod:

There was no personal recce by the commanders, plans were made wholly from the map. 'A' and 'B' Coys edged their way forward, found themselves under fire from houses they had already searched into which the enemy had filtered back in the dark. A bazooka at close range firing at

Sgt Langford and his Wasp did extremely well in the battle for Lingen.

Royal Norfolks battling for Lingen.

A 2-in mortar crew, 2 Lincolns, Lingen. The crew includes Ray Paine (left) and Ptes Johnny Hudson and Fred Shufflebotham (standing). (Ray Paine)

your house is no joke. By 0600 little headway had been made but three hours later, supported by a squadron of Staffs Yeo – old friends from the beach-head – and a troop of Crocodiles, we went into the attack with a will. The Boche has no great liking for flame. They tumbled out of houses 'in bundles of ten' as the troops said. In ten minutes 90 of them were in the bag and the rest in full retreat. By early afternoon [on the 5th] Major Glyn Gilbert's 'C' Coy had actually captured the road junction SW of the town 'reserved for 1 KOSB'.

Pte Jones was awarded the MM, but Lingen cost 2 Lincolns twenty-two casualties.

Padre Iain Wilson, 1 KOSB, witnessed a dog-fight:

About twenty Messerschmitts swooped out of the low clouds to attack us. A scene of some confusion followed as the fields were crowded with

Royal Norfolks take prisoners in Lingen. Left to right: Pte. Wilby, Pte. Phillipson, L/Cpl. Gould.

civilian refugees fleeing from Lingen and every tank in the vicinity was blazing away with its BESA. In an almost miraculous manner however, a few Spitfires and Tempests suddenly appeared and drove off the enemy after a terrific dog-fight. We moved into Lingen, passed a blazing ambulance, and eventually at three o'clock passed through and cleared the southern outskirts. We spent a comfortable night in well furnished houses crammed with loot including expensive French wines, Russian vodka and jewelry, in this Nazi stronghold.

But the enemy still had some fight left. Marcus Cunliffe, the Warwick's adjutant:

On the east side of town 'A' Coy 2 Warwicks had cleared another block of houses, German shelling intensified. Then driving into 'A', 'D' and 'B' Coy areas along two of the main streets came a sharp enemy thrust by about two infantry Coys and seven or eight SP guns. Four of the latter finding a gap between 'D' and 'B' broke through. Corporal T. Rowell's house was knocked down by an SP gun and some of his men were buried. Lieutenant K. Harris stalked one, and Private W. Gibbon knocked one out with a Piat. Four SPs and 37 POW were captured for the loss of 13 Lincolns wounded.

Meanwhile the South Lancs had crossed the Ems at 0300 hrs on 6 April to clear the north-east exits from Lingen. 'B' Company (Maj. St John) on the right, 'D' Company (Maj. Percival) on the left. At 1445 hrs they seized an important bridge intact, but were soon counter-attacked; they dislodged a platoon and took some prisoners, but the bridge was re-occupied by dusk.

Signalman Alan Candler, South Lancs, wrote:

A sharp enemy counter-attack had [on the 6th] dislodged 'D' Coy from the road bridge, some were taken prisoner. A foot patrol under Capt Percival [*sic*] was sent to re-occupy the houses south of the bridge. We went forward under an accurate 'stonk' of 88 mm shellfire and the house we occupied received several direct hits. The aerials of my 18 set were blasted so I shinned up a down-comer to disentangle a domestic aerial to regain contact with Bn HQ. The building was hit again and my pseudo-aerial destroyed.

Percival had entrusted Alan with safe custody of a tin of peaches. 'During our meanderings I opened the peaches and we shared what we thought might be our last meal. Capt P. was not amused.'

South Lancs had their Battalion HQ in a railway repair shop in the Laxten suburb of Lingen. Eddie Jones relates: 'The 2 i/c Major Jack Warner came racing up in his jeep, "Come on Eddie. I've just found a railway engine with

Royal Norfolks, with 'Big Friends', on way to Bremen.

steam up. Let's see if we can drive it." Standing on the rails was a large continental type engine with steam hissing faintly. But no luck.' Eddie described how in the house clearing: 'Young 15 or 16 year old boys came out of the buildings twitching and flinching so violently they could hardly walk – suffering from shellshock.'

2 RUR were now ordered to consolidate the vital crossroads on the south-east outskirts of Lingen, to allow Guards Armoured Division to pass through. Charles Graves, their historian wrote: 'The Boche was known, however, not to have quitted the town and was expected to defend all main routes out of it.' On 5 April 2 RUR put in a battalion attack backed by a troop of Shermans and another of Crocodiles to clear the many occupied houses on the way to, and on the key crossroads – a distance of 1,500 yds. Capt. Barry, OC 'C' Company, led but vicious MG fire and sniping pinned them down. Cpl. Watkin in a fearless rush was killed, and casualties inflicted on his section. Rifleman Scott accounted for three German officer cadets, but two infiltrated Platoon HQ, killing Capt. Barry. The Crocodiles left the road and were bogged down, and a Sherman Firefly's 17-pounder shot, by mishap, wounded several Ulsters. Capt. C.G. Alexander pushed his third platoon northwards and with covering fire from the Sherman, houses were cleared and twenty-five prisoners taken. Lt. Songest of 'A' Company, throwing grenades, advanced with his platoon under intense small arms fire, and took another sixty prisoners.

2 RUR took all their objectives against 7th Parachute Division opposition: 600 yds to a triangle of roads south of the crossroads, but with heavy casualties during the day. Charles Graves: 'This phase of Lingen produced bitter, lethal fighting. The fanatical Germans asked no quarter and received none. Hand to hand fighting took place and the bodies of the Germans lying within a few yards of our own wounded and dead grimly testified to the fierceness and severity of the fighting.'

The enemy now crumbled. Lingen was a notable battle honour for the Iron Sides.

CHAPTER TWENTY-FIVE

On the Way to Bremen

The Final Swan

Brig. Walter Kempster, after sick leave, took over command of 9 Brigade on 30 March. 'The final "Swan" was in being: 9 US Army on the right were sweeping along the North Ruhr boundary with, on their left, 8 Corps, 12 Corps, 30 Corps, 2nd and 1st Canadian Corps; each Corps had an Armd Div in the lead with an Inf Div following up on the "thrust" line.'

On 6 April the Guards Armoured led again towards the north-east and 43rd Wessex Wyverns came through, advancing due east. 9 Brigade's next objective was to clear south to Bramsche. At the same time the Warwicks of 185 Brigade on their left would take Mundersheim – both about 5 miles from Lingen. On 7 April Jack Harrod wrote: '2 Lincolns led in the opening of the axis Lingen–Plantelunne, and "C" Coy in Kangeroos were on their objective within half an hour. A quiet night spent and 2 RUR and 1 KOSB in turn passed through. The latter fighting a splendid action at Polle Estringen Rottum where 160 POW and 12 Flak guns, which had fired at a murderous rate down the road, were captured.'

A thousand yards short of Bramsche, Maj. F. Holden, 1 KOSB CO, was held up by an A/A battery of 88-mm guns. So 'C' and 'D' Companies, under heavy artillery concentrations, went in with tank support at 1630 hrs and by 1715 hrs the village was taken. Lt. Peter Lloyd: 'We kept going. The usual routine of fire and movement on a Company basis and we cleared the houses. We dug in and rounded up some prisoners. Practically a whole company of them! They had been badly shaken by the barrage.'

Padre Iain Wilson, 1 KOSB:

> For those who were present, in so far as any battle can be enjoyable, this day brought us to the highest pitch of exhilaration of the whole campaign, when evening fell, we were in magnificent form. . . . The Royal Ulster Rifles watched this spectacle with some relish. [Later] Now full of aggressive enthusiasm for the attack on Bramsche, the General arrived – immensely pleased with the Bn achievement – told us to get ready for a lengthy move the next day.

In one German village Sgt. Fred Hartle encountered an English-speaking

German in a bungalow – the mayor – who greeted him with: 'It's taken you a long time to get here!' He then started to lay down the law about the Geneva Convention. Fred discovered a picture of the German in full colonel's uniform with spiked helmet, the uniform was in a wardrobe and there were scores of photographs showing Russians being hanged from trees with troops looking on. The mayor was made a prisoner and sent back to the cages. 'The non-fraternisation orders against the Germans were now in full swing. I rammed it into my platoon how serious it would be if caught.'

A couple of miles to the east Lt.-Col. Macdonald was preparing for 2 Warwicks to take Mundersheim. 'It makes a very nice Bn objective,' he said of the village, which was a cluster of farmhouses, 400 yds square. The pincer movement began from the west side at 1700 hrs, with Crocodiles and SP guns in support. Tanks and Crocodiles from the north-west, 2 Warwicks from the west. It all worked perfectly. An AA post of five four-barrelled and six double-barrelled guns sited outside the village, was taken in the rear by Maj. F. Bell's 'D' Company. A hundred prisoners were taken, and fifteen Germans were dead on the ground for the loss of Sgt. W. Groves killed, and six men wounded.

Temporarily the campaign became more fluid. 11th Armoured, the

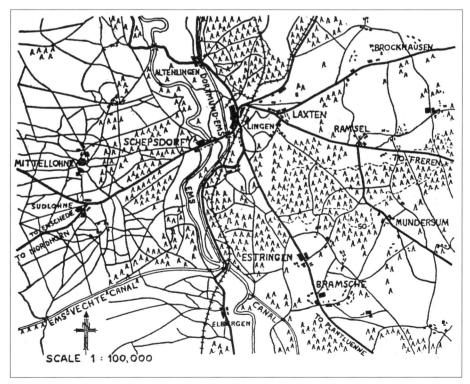

Dortmund–Ems canal and Lingen area battlefields.

Desert Rats, and Guards Armoured really were 'cracking about in the northern plains of Germany', just as Monty had predicted. 3rd Division now left 30 Corps to join Lt.-Gen. Ritchie's 12 Corps, which was now heading north-east from Osnabruck making for Bremen. 9 Brigade led and 185 Brigade followed in trucks on 9 April.

Brig. Walter Kempster:

10 April. The position was fantastic except in the North. On 30 Corps' front, Hun opposition except on certain river lines and in defended towns had collapsed. That notoriously fine fighting outfit, 86 German Para Corps (6 and 7 Para Divs) was still opposing 30 Corps, 1st and 2nd Cnd. Corps. These para boys have to be exterminated, they do not surrender easily. The Bde was deployed in a rough triangle with sides of 20 miles – however there were very few Huns, and food and drink plentiful.

2 Lincolns moved over 50 miles in convoy via Ostercappeln and pitched up in Barnsdorf, 20 miles south-west of Bremen on the Osnabruck–Bremen road. For several days they protected the left flank of 7th Armoured Division at Reckum and Kleine-Kohren. Padre Iain Wilson, 1 KOSB:

On Sunday 8th April we embussed and performed a long move which placed a great strain upon the drivers – through the night – Rheine, Osnabruck, turned east at Diepholz and at dawn halted at Wehrbleck. We had breakfast there while we watched the endless procession of released Displaced Persons streaming back towards the west – French, Dutch, Russian, Belgian and others. Also the heartening sight of several hundred German prisoners. Then through Twistringen and finally arrived at the delightful village of Heiligenloh where we secured extremely comfortable quarters.

Battalion HQ liberated the Alter Korn gin distillery, which 'quickly attracted a swarm of visitors'. On 12 April 1 KOSB took over from South Lancs at Wildeshausen. The next day 'D' Company experienced a sharp counter-attack and 'the enemy suffered a complete reverse'. The Wildeshausen railway station was the scene of a typical 'pocket' battle as enemy parachutists took part in grenade battles. The Borderers – far better cricketers – tossed grenades from the upper floor of the booking hall down the stairs, killed eight and took three parachutists prisoner. 'Our worst experience though was being bombed by our own aircraft.'

2 RUR motored 100 miles to Diepholz, where 'accommodation was excellent, town itself clean and cheerful', according to Charles Graves, and on 12 April another 40 miles to Harpstedt, where Lt. Harris led a carrier patrol. Unfortunately a disastrous explosion – possibly a naval or aerial mine – killed seven men, three more were missing and two were wounded. A complete patrol wiped out.

3 Recce had rejoined the division on 6 April and Sgt. Cottrell won the

DCM when 'A' Squadron cleared a bridgehead south of Lingen. By the 9th the regiment had made a fine run to Westerkappeln and Rheine and concentrated near Lemforde. For several days as the division moved up into the south-west outskirts of Bremen, the Recce squadrons were spread across 50 miles of countryside.

On the night of 8 April 8 Brigade leap-frogged across the whole division, an amazing unbelievable, very tiring journey of 180 miles, and relieved a brigade of the Desert Rats. By 11 April the South Lancs were in Wildeshausen, the East Yorks in Harpstedt and 1 Suffolk in Bassum. Each small town controlled a road leading north-east into Bremen, 15–25 miles away. 185 Brigade now arrived and the Warwicks moved into Syke, 1 Norfolk into Barrien and, two days later, the 2 KSLI into Sudweyhe and Kirchweyhe.

Guy Radcliffe, 2 KSLI, described the forthcoming battleground:

Bremen lies astride the river Weser, the greater part of the town lying on the north of the river. To the south the town is only some two thousand yards before the fields begin. But outside this there are a series of villages or small towns which form a suburban ring. On the west there is Delmenhorst and moving clockwise, Brinkum, Leeste, Arsten and Dreye which was only three hundred yards from the river Weser. The fields between these villages were very low and had been extensively flooded by

South Lancs at Bassum. Dick Harnby, batman; Alan Candler, signaller; Pete Baro, driver; Capt. Percival, Platoon CO. (Alan Candler)

the enemy. North of Brinkum was flooded to a depth of four feet. Between Sudweyhe and Dreye there was little flooding but the ground was so soft that tanks could only move on roads. A wide stream flowed across the front from the floods north of Brinkum between Sudweyhe and Dreye to the Weser.

The remains of the German parachute army had now reinforced the Bremen garrison. Lt.-Gen. Brian Horrocks had an expanded 30 Corps to take Bremen: from the east, 43rd Wessex Wyverns and 52nd Lowland and from the west, 51st Highland and the Iron Sides.

The German High Command – probably Adolf Hitler in his Berlin bunker – ordered the main defence of Bremen to take place in the small towns, villages and hamlets west of the river and flood barriers.

33rd Field Regiment fired 500 rounds of propaganda shells into the city. Capt. J.A. Brymer relates in his history:

Two Nazi school mistresses evacuated from Berlin were observed by 113/114 Field Bty to be behaving in a very aggressive manner. Our interpreter A. de Blaauw interviewed them and to curb their high spirits told them that the Fuhrer had been captured by the British. In dismay they asked to be shot forthwith. Their request was naturally refused. They were locked up in a farmhouse and discovered dead the next morning, having taken poison.

Personnel of 2 Platoon, 17 Field Company RE, 3rd Division, Germany, 1945. (Frank Faulkner)

Jim Wisewell, 223 Field Ambulance RAMC, who had seen enough first hand of the horrors of war, was now more fortunate.

12 April. We set up the ADS in Barrien, took over a hotel and had one glorious night of luxury. We spread a snowy tablecloth, used plates, glasses and cutlery from the kitchen, layed a carpet on the floor, sat on dining-room chairs, picked spring flowers for the meal table – pity the rations were still the same! At bedtime, luxury reached its zenith: we chose well sprung mattresses in single rooms, made up the beds with sheets and civilian blankets. We sprinkled eau-de-cologne on sheets and pillows and drifted off into dreamless sleep.

CHAPTER TWENTY-SIX

The Suburbs of Bremen

'The Enemy Broke in Complete Disorder'

The first objectives in what – just possibly – might be the last grand slam battle of the Iron Sides' north-west Europe campaign was to be the taking of the large villages of Brinkum and Leeste, then Arsten and Dreye and then the south-west suburbs of Bremen. Operation 'Bremen' was the obvious name.

It was to be a two-week battle, against a determined enemy rag-bag, 18 SS Horstwessel Training Battalion, AA crews, U-Boat and R-Boat crews, the Volksturm, even the police and fire brigade lent a hand.

The plan was for 8 Brigade to force their way on the Bassum–Fahrenhorst road towards Brinkum. 185 Brigade would be on the right flank towards Leeste and then Dreye and Arsten. On the left flank were 9 Brigade with the objectives of Heiligenrode, Gross Mackenstedt and Kirchhuchting, but East Yorks of 8 Brigade would clear the first two villages.

8 Brigade Attack

On Friday 13 April 1 Suffolk led and South Lancs covered their left flank. Nordwohlde was not defended and Brinkum via Fahrenhorst was 8 miles north-east. The South Lancs were pushing towards Delmenhorst, as Joe Garner related:

> I was but a humble carrier driver at the time and my section commander was Sgt Ernie Wright. We were the vanguard, rolling along in a formation known as mutual support. My carrier was Point Carrier as usual. We were about 6 miles along the road to Delmenhorst when enemy small arms fire came our way from the right flank. The carrier section (who were battle hardened warriors) managed to take evasive action by rolling along a hedgerow on the left flank of a house with a smallholding attached. We rapidly dismounted from the carriers and rushed into the house with our weapons. In the meantime Capt Percival and Capt Lacey came forward to where we were. I was ordered upstairs to get a better view and firing position. The enemy were spotted in farm buildings about

50 yards away on the right flank. Capt Percival immediately mounted a local attack. We managed to kill and wound some of the enemy and take the remainder prisoner. Meanwhile our anti tank detachment had arrived and took a position about twenty yards away from the house.

I carried out my usual looting recce – looking for Nazi militaria – nothing worth bothering with. Going into the cellar, however, we discovered the shivering house owners sheltering therein. One of our section had gone into the hen houses and brought back a couple of dozen eggs (a luxury in those days). No. 2 cookers were ignited and we borrowed a huge frying pan. In went the eggs which were cooked sunny side up. They were dished out one on top of a hard tack biscuit.

The amusement was produced by Sgt Ernie Wright who had the enemy prisoners doubling along the road with hands above their heads and knees raised. I heard him shout, 'Now Master Race, goose step you b—s', or words similar.

Four companies, each of two hundred young SS fanatics of the Horst Wessel Battalion, held the key crossroads in Hallen-Seckenhausen (1,500 yds south-west of Brinkum), the village of Leeste, the hamlet of Erichshof and Brinkum itself.

It was a long straight road to Brinkum, lined with houses, down which marched Maj. H. Merriam's 'A' Company of the 1 Suffolk. After clearing several road blocks, with confused house-to-house fighting and under Nebelwerfer fire, the first two platoons fought their way to the crossroads.

Left to right: Lt.-Col. Dick Goodwin, CO 1 Suffolk; Tom Hardy, DAA and QMG; Tubby Butler, CO 1 South Lancs; Van der Heyden, Dutch LO.

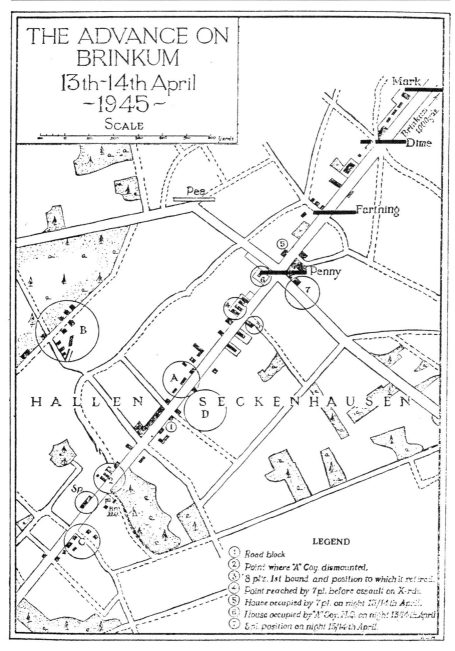

1 Suffolk attack on Brinkum.

Maj. Albert Claxton, OC 'B' Company, was killed on the left flank. The Horst Wessel SS launched several counter-attacks and in confused fighting some Suffolk were overrun. Much the same pattern continued on the next day, and on 15 April a major mixed-brigade attack was put in, with tank support from Stafford Yeo and 4/7 Dragoon Guards, backed by 7 RTR Crocodiles and barrages from five regiments of gunners. The four objectives from the vital crossroads north-east to Brinkum were called 'Penny', 'Farthing', 'Dime' and 'Mark', 400 yds apart. The Suffolk could hear drunken SS songs emanating from Brinkum! The hapless Suffolk were still pinned down, but at 2015 hrs two troops of Crocodiles squirted flame into every house. Maj. J.C. Vines of 'C' Company and Capt. Jones of 'B' were killed, and Maj. Merriman and Lt. Broadbent wounded. Mopping up continued during the night.

On the morning of the 15th 2 Warwicks would come in from the east on the right flank, capture Leeste and the village of Erichshof and so make way for 1 Norfolk to pass through and deal with Brinkum. At midday Maj. Illing led 'A' Company into the northern half of Leeste under a smoke screen, while 'B' went into the southern half, each with a troop of tanks. Finally 'C' would push up the Brinkum road to clear Erichshof. It was a brutal fight under a huge barrage. During the day 'A' Company killed 25 Germans and captured another 160, and 'B' took 70 prisoners without a casualty. By 1430 hrs Lt.-Col. Macdonald, CO 2 Warwicks, sent off 'C' to capture Erichshof, a mile to the west. A 6-pounder A/Tank gun was used to knock out snipers' nests and knock down houses. Sgt. W. Frost fought with his platoon although wounded and in great pain, killing twelve Germans and capturing fifteen more. He received an immediate MM, and Maj. Illing was awarded a bar to his MC.

1 Suffolk were still having a hard fight to hold the Leeste–Brinkum crossroads. By 0130 hrs 'A' Company had reached 'Dime', and in the three-day battle had 61 casualties, but had taken 31 POWs and killed at least 30 enemy. 'Gradually the crack of German 88 mm shells and the surprisingly soft accent of the Spandaus was overborne by the litany of the 25-pounder and the matter-of-fact Bren gun,' wrote Marcus Cunliffe, 2 Warwicks.

At 1800 hrs 1 Norfolk passed through 2 Warwicks for the final attack on Brinkum, described by Humphrey Wilson as 'a compact town roughly 1,000 yds by 800 yds. The far side ended abruptly against low ground flooded by the enemy. After clearing a bridge of two enormous bombs the battalion with a squadron of 4/7 Dragoon Guards tanks, a troop of Crocodiles from 7 RTR, MMG and 4.2" mortars of 2 Middlesex and a troop of Valentine SP 17-pounders advanced [at 1600 hrs]. It was a pretty formidable Bn Group.' Two Canloan officers were casualties. 'It was the last stand for 18 Bn SS, a battalion of great fighting record.' The fighting went on until 1700 hrs of the next day, when a company of Warwicks was needed to finish the job. 1 Norfolk killed 60 SS, took 5 officers and 203 OR prisoners for the loss of 3 killed and 12 wounded. 'Brinkum was a model

Royal Norfolk officers at Brinkum. Left to right: Maj. F.C. Atkinson, OC 'A' Coy, Lt.-Col. F.P. Barclay DSO, MC, Maj. J.D.W. Millar, OC 'B' Coy.

Royal Norfolks, 17 Platoon, 'D' Coy entering Bremen.

battle for co-operation of all arms . . . the physical effect of the Crocodiles and Wasps . . . close fire from tanks when properly controlled by the troop leader on his feet and in the platoon commander's pocket, will produce the results.'

The East Yorks attacked and captured Heiligenrode and Gross Mackenstedt on the left flank, south of Delmenhorst. Lt.-Col. Bill Renison had made a recce by Air OP of the area and the GOC had called in on the morning of the 16th to wish him and the East Yorks good luck. Despite mines and house-to-house fighting, 'A' Company crossed a wooden bridge over a stream into Heiligenrode, occupied the village, 'C' and 'D' moved through, and 'A' and 'D' continued for Gross Mackenstedt. Blown bridges and opposition from determined SS trainees did not prevent all objectives from being taken. The battalion and the brigade were then saddened by the news that the 2 i/c, Maj. 'Banger' King's carrier had been blown up on a mine. 'Early the following morning', said Lt.-Col. Renison, 'the news I had been dreading came through – "Banger" had died during the night. All of us had come to regard "Banger" as invulnerable . . . that he as a Regimental Officer should become a legend almost throughout the Army was no more than his due.' He was buried in an orchard at Fahrenhorst and the sappers named a bridge 'Banger' Bridge in his honour.

Jack Harrod, 2 Lincolns:

185 Brigade had already captured Brinkum and Kirchweyhe and 8

Lt.-Col. Bill Renison DSO (second left) with fellow officers Rutherford, Bone, Baker, Clift and Simpson of the East Yorkshires.

Brigade held a firm base for our own Bde attack on Stuhr, Moordeich, Mittelshhuchting and Kirchhuchting. At 0600 on 18 April with a squadron of Sherwood Rangers, there followed one of the best day's hunting the Bn has ever had. It was a long and gruelling day for the fighting throughout was hard. The enemy was deficient in artillery support, while we had everything we needed including Crocodiles. Each company in turn went into action and with such dash and determination that the Hun, though in no mean strength, comprising units of 18 SS, Horst Wessel Div, U-Boat and R-Boat crews, Volksturmes could do nothing but retreat before this onslaught. We took over 100 prisoners. Early the next morning 'B' Coy put in so fierce an attack that the enemy broke in complete disorder, mown down in the open ground by our artillery and MG fire.

Lt.-Col. Firbank helped them on their way with fifty rounds rapid fire from an attic window: 'It is doubtful whether the Germans noticed Bremen as they passed or stopped running before they reached Hamburg.' The Lincolns had the bit between their teeth and continued 'at 1000 on the 20th to capture Kirchhuchting and completed the Brigade task 24 hrs in advance of schedule', cut the railway from Delmenhorst to Bremen and took over 250 POWs. Indeed the brigade took over a thousand prisoners in April. 2 Lincolns lost twenty-nine casualties in the two days' fighting.

From Barrien 2 RUR moved up behind 2 Lincolns on the night of 18 April to capture the village of Moordeich, 1,400 yds north-west, the following morning. Cpl. Holt, 'B' Company, checked some burnt-out houses, already searched by the Lincolns, and 'found 15 Germans under an officer shuffling around the building and in the ditches. "D" Coy took the main crossroads of Moordeich and Major Bird sent back 50 of the 94 POW taken plus 3 20 mm flak guns and the usual host of LMGs, Bazookas, Schmeissers and Lugers captured or destroyed,' wrote Charles Graves, the Ulster Rifles' historian.

On 19 April Monty visited 2 Warwicks, 'my Regiment', inspected and addressed them. In return they presented a large Nazi standard captured in Leeste. No wonder 'Bolo' Whistler wrote in his diary:

20 April. Monty keeps a very close eye on everything. He has certainly done me jolly well and made my battle both possible and profitable. We have captured five officers and 1259 men on April 15th and another 1800 between 15–19th. We have killed about 200–300 more. Not much shelling from the Boche for which I am duly thankful. Lovely weather! Had a close look at Bremen yesterday. It appears rather undamaged in spite of Bomber Harris and his efforts.

The savage battle for Brinkum was over.

CHAPTER TWENTY-SEVEN

The Attack on Bremen

The 'Schwim-Panzers'

There were two key roads into Bremen from the south-west. The western one went from Brinkum to the village of Kattenturm, and thence into the suburbs – the Neuenlander Vorst – past an airport and into the Süder Vorst; this was 9 Brigade's route. The southern road ran parallel to the river Ochtum from Sudweyhe, over a marsh to Dreye, through the villages of Arsten and Habenhausen into the Bremen suburbs and the Stadtwerder Vorst; this was 185 Brigade's route.

Capt. J.A. Brymer, historian of 33rd Field Regiment:

On the evening of 22nd April the heavy bombing of the city could be seen. The attack looked disappointing and many bombers turned back with their bombs as the weather was not good. A counter-flack 'Applepie' was fired. At night HF was fired on those parts of the city which had been set alight by the bombers. On the 24th the heavy bombing of Bremen was still continuing and it was now receiving Victor (Corps) targets. Operation Bremen or Popeye or Test Match – a great duplication of codewords for the operations – opened at midnight 24th April by 2 RUR on the Kattenturm bridge. The area between Brinkum and the Ochtum canal was flooded and the attack was made in Buffaloes.

Jack Prior, 92 LAA: 'We conducted a ground shoot in support of 185 Brigade at Brinkum and then 36,000 rounds at Kattenturm, the barracks and the airfield south of Bremen.'

Brig. W.F.H. Kempster, 9 Brigade, wrote an account of the battle:

During the afternoon of the 24th we watched 40 medium bombers attack targets and also Typhoons (rocket projector fighters) attacked and 'brewed up' several nasty little strongpoints we'd noted from air photographs. Bremen contains 30,000 inhabitants, many factories and two airfields heavily defended by 88 mm dual purpose artillery guns. The plan was for 185 Bde to assault on the right with 9 Bde on the left. It was essential to secure the bridge over the canal at Kattenturm *intact*, so by clearing the aerodrome and Focke Wulfe Aircraft Works we could provide a first class axis for the Division early on. The bridge was known to be prepared for demolition with four 500 lb aerial bombs connected up and ready to blow. [The brigadier decided] not to advance straight down the badly cratered main road but to take the bridge area and Kattenturm village in the flank with a special RE and infantry party as 'commandos' to tackle the bridge demolition preparations.

Gen. 'Bolo's' diary for 24 April: 'We now set about Bremen. I have laid this one on very carefully but still feel the same sick tummy effect before the thing starts. I hope and trust this will be the last time I have to set my good chaps into battle.'

Capt. Harris, 4 RTR, commanded the fleet of 47 Buffaloes as 2 RUR 'em-buffed', having had an hour to drink hot tea and a tot of rum. Brig. Kempster was there to wish them 'bon voyage' over the 2,000 yds of flooded landscape. Two gentlemen of the press, one Reuters, the other Associated Press, were there as well. Zero hour was midnight and the Pepperpot started two hours before. The Ulster Rifles' historian wrote:

A hotchpotch of 4.2" mortars, MGs, Bofors saturating the defences. The voyage across went well, 'C', 'A' and 'D' Companies leading. Sergeant McAleavy and Corporal McCullum had a good start, killing or taking

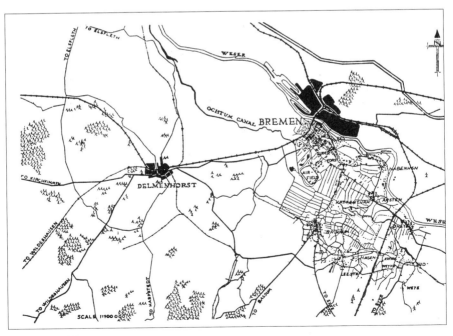

The battle of Bremen.

prisoner 23 enemy, and [they] turned two captured guns to fire against Arsten [a village to the north-west] until ammo ran out. 'A' Coy charged along the 'bund' winkling out enemy, taking panzerfausts and small arms. Lt Songest and Corporal Lambourne [he received the MM for this] captured a well-concealed 88 mm gun. Rifleman Wilkes, the Coy runner, was hit in the face by an exploding panzerfaust. L/Corporal Dalton took over as a platoon sergeant. 'A' Coy had a splendid action, took 40 POW, killing, wounding many enemy, capturing 3 Flak guns, but their casualties were 25. 'B' Coy then went through 'D' to take the vital Kattenturm bridge. Corporal Holt and Lt McCrainer helped seize the bridge before it could be blown, capturing 4 officers, 25 ORs. The sappers rendered innocuous the aerial bombs around the bridge. The German CO was goggle-eyed at the 'Schwim-Panzers'. Later disaster struck 'D' Coy. A magnetic mine destroyed a carrier with Major Bird, Lt Hancock, L/Corp McCoy, Riflemen McGlennon and Stevens.

Brig. Kempster's story continues:

Then at 0530 hours came an excited Ulster voice over the radio: 'By God, we've got it. I say again (radio procedure) bridge captured intact and demolitions disarmed, 3 officers and 80 ORs P.W now on their way back.' [Later] I've never seen a Bn so excited and thrilled as they were. I brought with me a keg of rum so they could 'splice' with speed. They'd done magnificently – the Hun had fought fiercely, our casualties in that Bn were 10 killed and 44 wounded. [Later] To continue the story 1 KOSB were passed through 2 RUR at about 0730 and fought against fairly heavy opposition and got their objectives by about 1100 after a really well fought battle. The bridge at Kattenturm was almost untenable due to it being under close fire, 2000 yards range from 88 mm and 40 mm guns, so at 0800 I committed 2 Lincolns to pass through 1 KOSB at 1200. Three hours later they had occupied the Focke Wulfe Factory and airfield, capturing two 88 mm, two 40 mm and several 20 mm multi-barrelled guns. The Lincolns and 1 KOSB between them took over 350 P.W.

Jack Harrod, 2 Lincolns: 'We went into the final battle under our 2 i/c Major L.H.B. Colvin as our CO Lt-Col Firbank had been promoted to command 71 Brigade of 53rd Welsh Division.'
Maj. Raymond Burt, 22 Dragoons:

We were to support 9 Brigade. 'B' Sqn with 2 Lincolns, 'A' Sqn with 1 KOSB. At half past eight 'A' crossed the bridge, seized by 2 RUR, in support of 1 KOSB who pushed steadily forward into the Neuenlander suburbs and into the barracks. [Later] Here if anywhere were the time and the place for the defenders of Bremen to declare themselves. The Bn

'B' Company, 2 Lincolns, Osnabrück, June 1945. (P.W. Bowes)

and our tanks swung in a long line lefthanded down a track towards the airfield, its right flank wide open. But nothing moved. Occasionally there was the whine of a sniper's bullet or the sudden chatter of a MG, or the unexplained crash of a shell explosion.

'In the chilly morning light of the 25th as the guns continued to pour shells into Bremen, one could feel that the great port was in its death-throes and that its doom was approaching,' wrote Iain Wilson, 1 KOSB, 'the approaches to the city were flooded and in the ruins we knew the SS were waiting to fight it out . . . life became more precious and desirable as the chances of death or wounds became less.' The Borderers' company pipers were playing and piping into their last action in the campaign. 1 KOSB were in action at 0915 hrs and captured their objective easily, taking fifty POWs. A little later, at 1800 hrs, they leap-frogged 2 Lincolns to capture a large built-up area extending to the main railway line. Sgt. Fred Hartle recalls:

'A' Company 1 KOSB started to search a barracks, snipers were taking pot shots. Two lads were hit, one in the head. Bullets were whizzing all over the place. More men of the platoon were hit but we could not locate the snipers. I shouted to the PIAT men to put a bomb into the nearest barrack block. The lad lying next to me was hit and rolled over. I was shouting for the stretcher-bearers when my right arm seemed to burst open. Blood poured out. I was losing a lot of blood and started to black out.

From the RAP, treated with morphia, an ambulance took him to a

Dakota. The navigator was Flt. Sgt. Billy Hill, who lived in the same street as Fred. While he was in 101 British General Hospital, Cpl. Richardson came to see him and told him that twenty-two members of the platoon had been killed or wounded in the barracks battle.

Brig. Kempster again:

> Excitement was now terrific. Here we were at only 1500 hrs on the first day of our attack going 100 per cent better than the most optimistic estimates and nearly 500 P.W in the cage. 185 Bde on our right after a very good start were slowed up and finally got going as a result of our cutting into the rear of the enemy opposing them. To keep the enemy on the run I passed 1 KOSB through 2 Lincs on to the railway station. They started this about 1630 hrs and by dark had consolidated on their objectives after severe street fighting – then the enemy broke up and started to surrender all over the place. It was most exhilarating, even the Brigade Commander took 25 P.W – quite in error I may say!

185 Brigade Attack

On the right flank 2 KSLI were to lead 185 Brigade attacking at 2300 hrs. Guy Radcliffe:

> We were to attack Dreye in the dark. Slightly after our attack had gone in the Warwicks were to attack Arsten also in the dark using 'buffaloes' for the men, the anti-tank guns and vehicles needed immediately. As soon as the road Sudweyhe–Dreye–Arsten had been cleared their other vehicles would pass through. The Norfolks were to remain in reserve ready either to move in 'buffaloes' to Arsten or by road through Dreye and then attack Habenhausen. 'Z' Coy were to attack up the railway line, 'Y' Coy to clear a factory area and 'X' to clear the village between the factory and the river floods. We had the support of 4/7 Dragoon Guards, REs with AVRE bridge and petards to deal with road blocks and Crocodile flame-throwers. The greatest RE problem was the railway bridge over the main road Dreye–Arsten.

Capt. Heatley, OC 'Y' Company, was wounded by a panzerfaust as the factory proved to be a tough proposition. Capt. Clapham from 'X' Company took over, quickly reorganised 'Y' under intense fire, took the factory, and both companies quickly cleared the village. Maj. Read, firing from the hip, led 'Z' Company in a bayonet charge on the railway line post and AA gun position. He was wounded, but used his machine carbine as a club, cheered on his men, and won a bar to his MC. Pte. Wood, Intelligence section, went ahead calling on the Germans in their own language to surrender. 2 KSLI had taken two hundred POW by this time despite a SP shelling the road and a fearsome roadblock with two enormous drums of explosive sunk into the road – which took time to deal with.

Marcus Cunliffe recalled:

At 0215 on a mild moonlit night 'A' and 'D' Coys 2 Warwicks crossed their start line each in six Buffaloes and trundled into the water. The noise of their engines drowned by the greater thunder of the artillery barrage. To the inhabitants of Bremen crouching in their shelters, it must all have sounded like the final intimation of doom. Crammed into the 'holds' of the Buffaloes the Warwicks could only see the sky overhead traversed at five minute intervals by the red trace of three Bofors shells [fired by 92 LAA] firing over the objective as a guide to direction.

Everything went like clockwork. The CO, Lt.-Col. Macdonald, described the hundred POWs captured at Arsten – without any casualties to the Warwicks – as 'a spineless lot'. Enemy SP guns, some medium guns in Bremen and a group of 88-mms now intermittently shelled the Warwicks, who linked up with 2 KSLI at 1000 hrs. By noon the causeway road through Dreye was open to traffic. So 1 Norfolk came through to take the suburb of Habenhausen, as Humphrey Wilson, 2 i/c, relates:

The preparation and softening-up had been complete and the enemy were only too glad to give up without a fight. The great might of tanks and SPs moved quietly forward. By 1800 it was all over. The village policeman was supervising the locals to fill in bomb craters. [Later] Lt A.R. Gill, the Pioneer officer, went out to prove the route for tomorrow's final advance. He caused great anxiety at Bn HQ. No sign of him by 2300. Later on he returned with 100 POW, found in a brickworks, waiting to give up!

The Surrender of Bremen – The Final Days

On 26 April Brig. Kempster, 9 Brigade, wrote: 'At first light I passed 2 RUR through 1 KOSB to capture the gasworks and a docks on the south bank of the river. By then the Hun was utterly demoralised, 2 RUR just walked on to their objectives and by 0930 I reported to Division that we'd done our job – nearly 30 hours in advance of the estimate.'

Iain Wilson, 1 KOSB: "B" and "D" Coys cleared the area completely. Some interesting spectacles resulted – the bag of prisoners included besides many SS, some weary old men and young boys, a sadistic Displaced Persons Camp Commandant and a large portion of the Bremen police force.'

2 Warwicks had some trouble. At 0530 hrs, after 2 KSLI had cleared the barracks, 'B' and 'C' Companies plus two Crocodiles came under fire from the main railway embankment. Marcus Cunliffe wrote:

The enemy proved to be stubborn. Fire from the tanks failed to dislodge them. One man in 'B' Coy was hit by a bullet and fell in the roadway. Corporal Stacey and Private Rice dashed out and picked up the wounded man. They had almost reached cover when Corporal Stacey was shot in the back and fell dead. The two flame-throwing Crocodiles were brought up and one ran straight up to the embankment, loosing its terrifying jet. Twenty-five Germans showed themselves, hands in air. For the rest of the day the 2nd Bn Warwicks hunted down and found another 20 PW among the buildings. Corporal Stacey, dying for the sake of one of his men was the Bn's last fatal casualty.

8 Brigade came up and passed through 9 Brigade at dawn. The South Lancs cleared up the area round the gasworks. They had lost twenty-three casualties in the battle for Bremen. Lt. Eddie Jones noted: 'Survival was mainly a matter of luck.' They had a new CO from 21 April, Lt.-Col. M.A.H. Butler DSO, MC, after Lt.-Col. Orgill and Maj. Hegg, 'C' Company, were blown up on a mine at Heiligenrode. 1 Suffolk went into Bremen to the Mutilenhausen area behind the South Lancs, and collected 140 POW. Then the East Yorks went into the north-west sector of Bremen–Seehausen and Hasen Buren near the river Weser. Their CO, Lt.-Col. Bill Renison, wrote in his journal:

'D' Coy came up against two young Nazi fanatics dug into the side of a dyke but they did not fancy their chances against a Crocodile. 'C' Coy sent me a message that they had 9 officers and 150 ORs as PW. Hallam had caught the control centre of the local AA defences – underground – expecting an attack from Delmenhorst in the west. 'C' Company then had a stream of prisoners – Luftwaffe, sailors and all sorts. Brigadier Goulburn was in great form armed with a 12 bore standing in the middle of the road behind the leading troops with his gun at the ready.

The next day the East Yorks were sent off north-west along the banks of the river Weser and met more opposition. Meanwhile, 52nd Lowland Division was mopping up in the old part of Bremen, and 43rd Division – the fighting Wessex Wyverns – was tackling Burgher Park, a stronghold on the eastern side of the city, capturing Lt.-Gen. Fritz Becker, the C.-in-C. Bremen defences. 9 Brigade, and a couple of days later, 185 Brigade, moved to Delmenhorst on the 26th to take over from 51st Highland Division.

Brig. Walter Kempster wrote:

Between 16–20 April 9 Brigade took 800 PW from the 18 SS Regt, composed of experienced officers and NCOs and Hitler Jugend, average age 16–17. One fine young sprig of the SS nobility, a PW of Lincolns in my presence committed suicide by picking up a bayonet and sticking it into his neck. This was applauded by his comrades. Nobody followed

Brig. Goulburn and two Dutch liaison officers.

Lt. Eddie Jones (left) and three other South Lancs officers, Detmond, May 1945.

1 KOSB, Bremen, May 1945. On the right are Ptes Henry Aldis and Jimmy Stark. Bill Robertson is at the back. (Lt.-Col. Colin Stonor)

suit. The applauding comrades were then doubled 2 miles escorted by carriers to damp their spirits. [Later] Other prisoners included the Chief ARP warden of Bremen and a city fire engine complete with crew. Several Volksturm (Home Guard) officers surrendered complete with packed suitcases.

Raymond Burt, 22nd Dragoons, whose squadron had been supporting 2 RUR, 2 Lincolns and 1 KOSB, described the last days of Bremen:

So this was how the city was falling – without fight, in rain, and betrayed by those who had brought it to its present squalor. For all their boasts and threats, the Nazi leaders had gone and the city was abandoned to a few thousand AA gunners and marines and the old men and women and children who waited our arrival in the air raid shelters. The advances into the suburbs were something of a formality. But they were carried out, block by block, with care and precision – companies and supporting tanks leapfrogging through one another along the silent and mined streets. It looked formidable enough: the road blocks were defensible. Slit-trenches and antitank ditches had been dug across street intersections: enormous land-mines had been laid and wired ready for explosion by the roadsides. The windows of the ruined houses provided the 'heroic twilight' of the Nazis of the city of Bremen. But no shot was fired.

Monty inspects 1 KOSB, Germany, 1945. (Lt.-Col. Colin Stonor)

Hitler's war was running down – it had collapsed into a dreary mopping up operation which went on because no one in authority had the desire to cry 'stop!'

The GOC wrote in his diary: 'April 26th. Even though I say it, our assault could scarcely have been more successful. It really has been a brilliant little job.' And Raymond Burt wrote: 'What was left of Bremen was formally surrendered by the Burgomaster in the evening of April 26. In disbelief we saw ourselves surrounded by acre after acre of ruin that either fire or high explosive had created. It seemed to be a signal not only of the defeat of Germany but also the death of a civilisation.'

Ray Paine, mortar platoon 1 KOSB, watched an eclipse of the sun: 'All the birds stopped singing and we stopped talking and it seemed that the world had stopped for that moment in time.' Possibly it was on 3 May when

Berlin fell to the Russian armies and Adolf Hitler was reported dead.

The next week was in many ways an anticlimax. Maj. J.K. Warner, 3 Recce, wrote: 'On 30 April we took our last two prisoners but felt the War was nearly over. It was taking rather a long time to finish and when the Field Marshal had the "Cease Fire" sounded at 0800 hrs on 5 May it came without the thrill and excitement most of us had expected.'

Padre Iain Wilson, 1 KOSB, wrote:

In Ibbenburen, came the long-expected announcement of the unconditional surrender of all German forces. The next day – 8th May – would be observed as VE Day.

So this was the end. Partly because it had come so gradually and partly through sheer mental exhaustion, the news was received without emotion. There was little inducement to wild celebrations surrounded as we were by the defeated Germans between whom and ourselves lay the barrier of silence. We were neither elated with success, nor were we filled with emotions of hatred or revenge. We were simply thankful, far below consciousness that the destruction and slaughter had ended.

From the Normandy beaches to the taking of Bremen, Monty's Iron Sides had left 2,586 young soldiers dead along the savage centre lines.

1 KOSB Pipes and Drums, Germany, 1945. (Lt.-Col. Colin Stonor)

Bibliography

Brymer, J.A., *History 33rd Field Reg. RA*, 1945
Burt, Raymond, *History XXII Dragoons 1760–1945*
Corbally, M.J.P.M., *History Royal Ulster Rifles*, 1956
Cunliffe, Marcus, *History Royal Warwickshire Reg.*, 1956
Gates, L.C., *History Tenth Foot (Lincolnshires) 1919–50*, 1953
Graves, Charles, *Royal Ulster Rifles*, 1950
Gunning, Hugh, *Borderers in Battle*, 1948
Harrod, Jack, *History 2nd Bn Lincolnshire Reg. 1944–5*, 1946
Lane, A.J., *What More Could a Soldier Ask of a War?*, 1988
Lincoln, John, *Thank God and the Infantry* (Royal Norfolks), 1994
McNish, Robin, *Iron Division 1809–1977*, 1978
Moberley, Robert B., *History 2nd Bn Middlesex Reg.*, 1946
Mullaly, B.R., *The South Lancashire Regiment*, 1952
Nicholson, W.N., *History of the Suffolk Regiment*, 1948
Nightingale, P.R., *History East Yorkshire, Duke of York's Reg.*, 1950
Radcliffe, Guy L.Y., *History 2nd Bn King's Shropshire Light Infantry*, 1947
Scarfe, Norman, *Assault Division*, 1947
Smith, Wilfred I., *Codeword Canloan*, 1992
Smyth, Sir John, *'Bolo' Whistler*, 1967
Warner, J.K., *History 3rd Reconnaissance Reg.* (Northumberland Fusiliers), 1946
Wilson, Humphrey M., *History 1st Bn Royal Norfolk Reg. 1939-45*, 1947
Wilson, Revd W.I.G., *Short History 1st Bn KOSB*, 1945

Unpublished Journals

John Eales, private journal, 2nd Bn RUR
Lt.-Col. Hugh Gillies MC, '1 KOSB in Normandy'
Lt.-Col. R.E. Goodwin DSO, 1st Bn Suffolk Reg
F.J.R. Hartle, personal reminiscences, 1 KOSB
Lt.-Col. Edward Jones MBE, 1st Bn South Lancashire Reg.
Maj. Harry G. Jones MC, 'D-Day to 9 July 1944: 2nd Bn KSLI'
Brig. W.F.H. Kempster DSO, 'Battle of Bremen'
Lt.-Col. Eric Lummis, '1 Suffolk in Normandy'
Lt.-Col. M.A. Philp, 'Worm's Eye View'
Jack Prior, notes, 92nd Reg. LAA (Loyals) Reg. RA
Lt.-Col. Bill Renison DSO, diary and journal, 2nd Bn East Yorkshire Reg.
Lionel Roebuck, 'Five Yorkshire Tykes', 2nd Bn East Yorkshire Reg.
Maj. R.R. Rylands, '"W" Coy 2nd Bn KSLI in NW Europe'
S. Perring Thomas, notes, 41st Bty, 20th A/Tank Reg. RA

The Commanders

Divisional GOC

Maj.-Gen. T.G. Rennie CB, DSO, MBE; Maj.-Gen. L.G. Whistler CB, DSO

8 Brigade

Brig. E.E. 'Copper' Cass CBE, DSO, MC; Brig. E.H. Goulburn DSO

1 SUFFOLK
Lt.-Col. R.E. Goodwin DSO; Lt.-Col. R.W. Craddock DSO, MBE;
Lt.-Col. R.E. Goodwin DSO

2 EAST YORKS
Lt.-Col. C.F. Hutchinson; Lt.-Col. Dickson DSO; Lt.-Col. Bill Renison DSO, TD

1 SOUTH LANCS
Lt.-Col. J.E.S. Stone; Lt.-Col. R.P.H. Burbury; Lt.-Col. G.A. Bolster;
Lt.-Col. J.H. Orgill; Lt.-Col. 'Swazi' Waller MC; Lt.-Col. M.A.H. Butler DSO,
MC

9 Brigade

Brig. J.C. Cunningham MC; Brig. A.D.G. Orr DSO; Brig. G.D. Browne OBE; Brig.
W.F.H. Kempster DSO, OBE

2 LINCOLNS
Lt.-Col. C.E. Welby-Everard; Lt.-Col. D. Wilson; Lt.-Col. C.L. Firbank DSO

1 KOSB
Lt.-Col. G.D. Renny; Lt.-Col. J.F.M. Macdonald OBE; Lt.-Col. W.F.R. Turner DSO

2 RUR
Lt.-Col. I.C.H. Harris; Lt.-Col. J. Drummond DSO

185 Brigade

Brig. K.P. Smith OBE; Brig. E.L. Bols CB, DSO; Brig. F.R.G. Mathews DSO

2 WARWICKS
Lt.-Col. H.O. Herdon; Lt.-Col. D.L.A. Gibbs DSO; Lt.-Col. R.C. Macdonald DSO

1 ROYAL NORFOLK
Lt.-Col. R.H. Bellamy DSO; Lt.-Col. F.P. Barclay DSO, MC

2 KSLI
Lt.-Col. F.J. Maurice DSO; Lt.-Col. C.G. Millett OBE; Lt.-Col. P.D. Daly DSO, MBE

3 RECCE REGT.
Lt.-Col. H.H. Merriman DSO, MC

2 MIDDLESEX
Lt.-Col. G.P.L. Weston DSO, OBE

7 FIELD REGT. RA
Lt.-Col. N.P.H. Tapp; Lt.-Col. H.C. Bazeley DSO

33 FIELD REGT. RA
Lt.-Col. T. Hussey; Lt.-Col. E.S. Lindsay DSO, OBE

76 FIELD REGT. RA
Lt.-Col. M.A. Foster

20 A/TANK REGT. RA
Lt.-Col. G.B. Thatcher

92 LAA REGT. RA
Lt.-Col. H.C. Bazeley DSO; Lt.-Col. P.R. Henderson DSO

Divisional Staff

CRA	Brig. G.G. Mears CBE, DSO, MC
CRE	Lt.-Col. T. Evill; Lt.-Col. R.W. Urquhart
CREME	Lt.-Col. E.H. Biggs
CRASC	Lt.-Col. A.K. Yapp OBE
RAOC	Lt.-Col. R.S. Blundell OBE
GSO 1	Lt.-Col. W.F.H. Kempster DSO, OBE
AQ	Lt.-Col. Rae; Lt.-Col. H.O. Hinton OBE

3rd British Division Casualties June 1944 to May 1945

The official summary of battle casualties at the close of hostilities gave the following figures: killed in action 1,579, wounded 8,039, and missing 1,636. Some of those wounded died of their wounds. Some of the prisoners were subsequently found to have been killed. The true losses are shown below.

8 Brigade

1 Suffolk 215
2 East Yorks 252
1 South Lancs 288

9 Brigade

2 Lincolns 254
1 KOSB 190
2 RUR 219

185 Brigade

2 Warwick 286
1 Norfolk 271
2 KSLI 204

2 Middlesex 33; 3 Recce (8th Northumberland Fusiliers) 90; 7 Field Regt. RA 36; 33 Field Regt. RA 36; 76 Field Regt. RA 27; 20 A/Tank Regt. RA 46; 92 LAA Regt. RA 18; 17 Field Coy RE 25; 246 Field Coy RE 24; 253 Field Coy RE 24; 15 Field Park Co RE 1; 3 Div. Signals 27; RAMC 10; Ordnance RAOC 1; Provost CMP 2
    Total 2,586 killed in action.

Index

Airborne armada 171

battle exhaustion 134
beach groups 24, 30
Belgians
    friendship 134–5, 157
    grateful offerings 106, 113
Beuville 67, 69, 70
bicycle transport 43
Biéville 42–4
bocage country 92, 96, 98, 100
Bremen 186–7
    attack 196–206
    suburbs 189–95
    surrender 201–6
Brinkum, battle of 190–5
Brussels, leave 134, 147

Caen
    civilians 72, 77
    destruction 77
    taking 58, 72–7
Cambes
    countryside 59–60
    first battle 50–2
    second battle 55–7, 59–61
Canloan officers 28, 32, 66, 111, 192
Carpiquet airfield 72
celebrations
    Christmas, Maas 148–9
    Minden Day 90–1
    New Year's Day 150
    Oploo 145–6
    St Patrick's Night 169
censorship 145
Channel crossing 17–21, 47–8
Churchill, Winston, Rhine visit 171
clothes, army supply of 134
'Cod' strongpoint 33–5
codenames 12, 23
communion service 93

D-Day, casualties 25–6, 32
Displaced Persons 186, 201
divisional sign 3, 133

drums, regimental 147
Dunkirk 3, 4
Dutch, friendship 134–5

embarkation 16–17
exercises
    Baron 12
    Fabius 13
    Handsup 13
    Kilbride 11
    Leapyear 11
    Millhouse 11

Flers 101–2
food
    Belgian 157
    Christmas 145, 148
    Dutch bread and ham 127
    fresh white bread 80
    fried eggs 190
    German rations 113
    German supper 103
    'liberated' eggs 114
    Normandy 104
friendly fire 83, 88, 95, 185
friendship
    Belgians 134–5, 157
    Dutch 134–5

Gadforce, RASC 107
George VI 14
German army, courage 66
glider fleet 45, 48
graves, battlefield 67
gunner support 44, 130–1
    Goodwood 80
    Lebisey 74
    Maas 145
    operation Heather 160
    operation Plunder 171–2
    Overloon 119
    Rhine battles 168, 171

Hermanville, French welcome 36, 41
'Hillman' strongpoint 36–8, 44–5

Hitler, Adolf 187, 206
Horrocks, Maj.-Gen. Brian 3
  on Arnhem 116
  Bremen 186
  operation Plunder 170
  operation Veritable 168
  praise from Gen. Whistler 167
humour
  2,000 bad women 124
  April Fool 9
  baptism of fire at La Londe 108
  Boche PW trench-digging 79
  Churchillian French 41
  democracy in action 115
  drowning by beer 66
  dugout billiard table 87
  enemy goose step 190
  French waitress 67–8
  GI innocence 93
  head down in red poppies 45
  Hollywood style 30
  'Jerries' sights up 56
  'jerry' wounding 169
  Laird's pet rabbit 105
  lunch with the Führer 173
  mud covering 69
  nearly waterproof 12
  no flowers for German 174
  pig named Monty 100
  proficiency pay 52
  songs 61
  tea on French soil 33
  'the Paddies' 56
  water-cart 'captures' Tinchebray 101
  white duck reserved 100

interpreters, Dutch 115, 139
Iron Sides, name ix

Kattenturm 197–8
Kervenheim 161–5

La Londe chateau 62–6
Landing Craft Assault (LCAs) 9, 12,
    17–18, 28–9
landing plan 23–4
Landing Ships Infantry (LSIs) 12, 17, 18,
    45
landings
  beach obstacles 34–5, 40–2, 48–9
  Sword beaches 21–39, 45
Le Bas Perrier 96
Le Landel 62–4
Le Mesnil wood 50–2, 55

leave
  Belgium and Holland 134, 138, 147
  UK 153–4
Lebisey wood, battles 43, 49, 52–4, 67, 71–4
liberations
  Belgium 106
  Caen 75
  Dutch towns 174–5
  Flers 101–2
  Helmond 115
  Weert 113–14
Lille St Hubert 110, 116
Lingen, battle of 175–82
Lion-sur-Mer 23, 24, 35, 47
loot 87, 180, 190
love stories 47, 70–1, 104
Luftwaffe
  anti-personnel mines 87
  Bénouville 70
  comeback 150
  Lebisey 73
  Lingen 176, 179
luxury, Barrien 188

Maas river 134–49
  winter 142–9
maps
  attack on Venray 126
  battle of Bremen 197
  Caen sector 79
  capture of Overloon 118
  Chateau de la Londe 63
  Dortmund–Ems canal and Lingen area
    battlefields 184
  East Yorkshire actions during Aintree 131
  from Goch to the Rhine 166
  from the Rhine to the Ems 170
  invasion beach La Brèche 28
  invasion beach Lion-sur-Mer 34
  Kervenheim and Winnekendonk 159
  plan of operation Overlord 51
  Suffolk attack on Brinkum 191
  winter on the Maas 152
memorial services 79–80, 103
Meuse–Escaut canal 110–13
minefields, Peel country 132
mines 136–7, 172
  laying 70
Molen Beek 119, 120–2, 124–7, 133
money, issue of francs 14, 17
Montgomery, Field Marshal Bernard
  on 'Bolo' Whistler 59
  Brussels investiture 169
  Cazelle 66, 90

discipline memorandum 1–2
  Goodwood 78
  human touch 4–5
  long-term plans 158
  newspaper delivery 90
  pep talks 14, 15
  presentation of awards 136, 137, 139, 146
  takes command of 3rd Division 1
  visits 'my Regiment' 195
  on winning battle of Germany 146
Montisenger 92, 93
'Morris' strongpoint 36, 37, 38
mosquitoes 78, 88

Nazi school mistresses 187
Normandy, landings 6, 8, 21–32, 35–6, 38–9,
    47–8

O'Connor, Maj.-Gen. Richard 132, 138, 142
operations
  Aintree 116–33
  Bluecoat 91
  Bremen 196–206
  Charnwood 72–7
  Goodwood 78–89
  Grouse, *see* Wallop
  Heather 158–67
  Market Garden 110–15
  Mitten 64–6
  Plunder 168–82
  Ventilate 156
  Veritable 156–8, 168
  Wallop 98–103
  Walter 98–103
Oploo, parties 145–6
Overloon
  battle of 116–19, 132
  civilian evacuation 143

patrols 87
  Cambes 59, 60, 61
  German 150–1, 156, 169
  Lebisey 67
  Maas 154, 156
  night 136–7
  Rhine 169
  Venraij area 137, 139
  winter in Holland 146
Pegasus bridge 47, 49, 80
'Pepperpots' 155, 168, 170, 173, 197
Perier ridge 38
Periers-sur-le-Dan 42–3
pipers 48, 90, 104
  Cambes 51

last action 199
  memorial service 79–80
propaganda, fired into Bremen 187

radio jargon 145
rations, drink 134, 138–9
refugees 143
reinforcements, integration
  difficulty 68
Rennie, Maj.-Gen. T.G. 10, 11, 17, 47
  death 172, 175
  Hermanville 38
  marching pace 13
  operation Heather 166
  orders 50
  wounded 58, 82
resistance movements 114, 154
rest and recreation
  Cazelle 66, 90
  Flers 103, 107
  Holland 147
  Luc-sur-Mer 78–9
Rhine crossing 171–5
  build-up 168–71
Roberts, Maj.-Gen. 'Pip' 136
rockets, V1 68
role of 2 i/c 105
Rommel, Field Marshal Irwin, Caen 58,
  78
Royal Air Force (RAF)
  bombing of Bremen 196
  bombing of Caen 72, 75
  domination 50
  Lingen 180
  'Morris' 37
  Rhine bombing 168, 171
Royal Navy
  bombardment of Caen 75
  Carpiquet 72
  combined operations 9
  invasion fleet escort 19–21, 23, 48
  support at Cambes 55

St Servatius monastery 122, 138, 143
Sannerville, destruction 87
secret agents 169
sentries 146
snipers, 'suicide boys' 88
Sourdevalle, battle 94–5
stalemate 59–61
surrender, German forces 206
Sword beaches, landings 21–39

Tinchebray 98, 101, 102

training (1940–4) 5, 6–15
trenches
 digging 61, 69, 70
 German 88–9, 120
Troarn 78, 80–3, 88, 90
 casualties 82, 83, 84
 defence by German army 84

Venraij
 battle of 116, 122, 124–33, 139
 civilian evacuation 143
Venray, *see* Venraij
verse 68, 140–1, 147, 148
Victoria Crosses 95, 162, 175
Vire 92, 102

Wanssum 144–5, 150–3
war correspondents
 Bremen 197
 McMillan, Richard 69

Marshall, Howard 155
Wilmot, Chester 136
waterproofing, vehicles 12
Whistler, Maj.-Gen. 'Bolo' 104
 attack plans 122, 173
 before Bremen 197
 Brinkum 195
 character 58–9, 108–9
 Christmas message 1944 149
 command changes 89
 operation Heather 166–7
 operation Walter 98
 out of battle 107
 praise for Iron Division 102, 107, 167
 Rhine crossing 174–5
 shooting 'bag' 142
 'Yorkshire' bridge 161
Winnekedonk 161, 165–7
winter, Maas 142–9, 154–5
wounds, description 74–5, 160